MAKING CITIZEN-SOLDIERS

MICHAEL S. NEIBERG

Making Citizen-Soldiers

ROTC and the Ideology of American Military Service

HARVARD UNIVERSITY PRESS

Cambridge, Massachusetts, and London, England

First Harvard University Press paperback edition, 2001

Library of Congress Cataloging-in-Publication Data

Neiberg, Michael.
  Making citizen-soldiers : ROTC and the ideology of American military service /
  Michael S. Neiberg.
      p. cm.
  Includes bibliographical references and index.
  ISBN 0-674-54312-2 (cloth)
  ISBN 0-674-00715-8 (pbk.)
  1. United States. Army. Reserve Officers' Training Corps.
  2. United States. Air Force ROTC.
  3. United States. Naval Reserve Officers Training Corps.
  4. United States—Armed Forces—Officers—Training of.   I. Title.

U428.5.N45 2000
355.2'232'071173—dc21   99-044354

To the memory of Ethel Neiberg and
Renee Saroff Oliner

Acknowledgments

In completing this book I have accumulated debts that I cannot hope to repay. The deepest of these debts is to my wife, Barbara, who has had to live with this project almost as long as she has had to live with me. I will be forever grateful for her patience and understanding. She also read the manuscript in its entirety. Thanks are also due to our families, Larry, Phyllis, and Elyssa Neiberg, and John, Sue, and Brian Lockley, for their support while I ran around the country.

This project began as a doctoral dissertation, and I must acknowledge the debt I owe to those who helped me at Carnegie Mellon University and elsewhere. My dissertation committee of John Modell, Peter Karsten (of the University of Pittsburgh), and Edward W. Constant III top this list. Professors Mary Lindemann, Steven Schlossman, and Peter Stearns also served as important informal advisors along the way. The more I talk to graduate students about their experiences, the more grateful I am to these professors for both their intellectual and their personal support. Other friends and colleagues at CMU, including Etan Diamond, Gail Dickey, Dan Holbrook, David Jardini, and Montserrat Martì Miller, gave help and advice (and wonderful Catalan food), for which I am grateful. John Shy at the University of Michigan got me started and helped along the way. I must also thank Walter Harrison; Robben Fleming; Richard Jessor; Elvis Stahr; Captain Michael Riordan, USN; William Snyder; Mark Grandstaff; Maggie McCaffery; and Richard Kohn for going above and beyond the call of duty.

At my new home, the United States Air Force Academy, I wish to thank Brigadier General Carl Reddel (Ret.); Colonel Mark Wells; Elliott Converse; Lieutenant Colonels Lorry Fenner and Tony Kern; Jeanne Heidler; Major Edward Maldonado, USA; Captain David Arnold (who read the entire manuscript); Jacob Abadi; and John Jennings. Dennis Showalter of Colorado College, a frequent visitor here at USAFA, was kind enough to read the manuscript on short notice, and I am grateful for his comments. I would like to thank the entire history department, but space forbids it. My colleagues there, to a person, have been helpful and supportive of both my teaching and my research efforts. I thank them.

I wish I had the space to thank all the archivists and librarians who helped me find the materials that allowed me to write this book. They were all wonderful. In the interest of brevity, let me single out Carnegie Mellon's Sue Collins, Michigan's Francis Blouin, the Air Force Historical Research Agency's Archie DiFanti, and the University of Illinois's John Straw. Pat Mazumdar of the University of Kansas and Josh Silverman and David Wolcott, both of Carnegie Mellon, provided research assistance and friendship and read part or all of the manuscript. The United States Army Center of Military History, the Mark C. Stevens Travel Fellowship at the University of Michigan Bentley Library, and the Spencer Foundation all saw enough merit in this study to fund it. Jeff Kehoe at Harvard University Press and two anonymous reviewers helped me to make this a much better book. Jeff's support of this manuscript made the final revisions a joy instead of a burden. If any errors remain, they are my own. Portions of this work have previously appeared in *New Interpretations in Naval History: Selected Papers from the Twelfth Naval History Symposium* (Annapolis, Md.: U.S. Naval Institute Press, 1997) and Elliott Converse, ed., *Forging the Sword* (Chicago: Imprint Publications, 1998).

Since I began this project I have lost two people who were very special to me. I dedicate this book to the memory of Renee Saroff Oliner and Ethel Neiberg. I wish with all my heart that I could be handing you a copy of this book instead of dedicating it to you.

Contents

Tables

MAKING CITIZEN-SOLDIERS

Introduction

We must train and classify the whole of our male citizens, and make
military instruction a regular part of collegiate education.
—Thomas Jefferson

In the summer of 1996, the University of Connecticut requested that the
army reassign the head of its ROTC unit because the colonel "allowed classes
to be run like a boot camp." At first glance, the idea of dismissing a military
officer for running a military training program like a boot camp seems para
doxical if not ludicrous. Rather than treat the issue as such, however, the
army quickly acceded to the university's request and transferred the officer.
Both parties agreed that the transfer was in the best interest of both the
army and the university, because the colonel, according to one University of
Connecticut official, "just didn't realize what a university was like, and he
tried to impose a structure on it that just didn't belong here."[1]

That same summer, Massachusetts Institute of Technology officials made
strident efforts to defend ROTC in the face of objections from student groups
who contended that ROTC, bound by the military's "don't ask, don't tell,
don't pursue" policy toward homosexuals, violated the nondiscrimination
policies of the university. MIT responded in a fashion similar to that of other
universities faced with the same controversy. It pledged to keep ROTC, in
large part because of "its contribution to the important goal of preparing 'citizen-soldiers.'" Rather than expel the program, it sought, in the words of the
MIT faculty chair, to "remake it in our own image."[2]

These cases are contemporary examples of a process of remaking military
training (and thus the military itself) in the universities' image that has been
ongoing since the inception of military training on civilian campuses in the

nineteenth century. Indeed, when seen in historical context, the controversies at Connecticut, MIT, and elsewhere have roots that reach back as far as the eighteenth century, when the fledgling American military inherited its traditions from the English army. These controversies also have more recent precedents in the visible conflicts between universities and the military seen in the 1930s and the Vietnam War era, as well as in the less visible conflicts of the 1950s and 1970s. In this study I examine those roots and the evolution of ROTC training on civilian campuses, from the creation of the Reserve Officers' Training Corps in 1916 through the solidification of the current all-volunteer force (AVF) by 1980. I argue that the creation of ROTC just before America's entry into World War I, the confrontation that characterized ROTC in the 1960s, and the reform of ROTC in the 1970s are all rooted in a deeply held and enduring American belief, shared by educators, politicians, and college students alike, in the importance of populating the military with nonprofessional officers produced outside the traditional military academies.

Civilian colleges and universities, not the armed services, led the way in creating on-campus military training programs. From the early nineteenth century to the present, the administrators of American higher education have believed firmly that the national defense requires skilled young officers, but that these young men should not be prepared exclusively by the military itself. As the universities were taking the lead in preparing young Americans for other professions, they also assumed the task of preparing military officers, sometimes without the active cooperation of the formal military establishment. The officers so produced, however, were never supposed to be mere additions to the body of junior officers being produced at the insular military academies at Annapolis and West Point.

The officers produced through on-campus training programs were designed to counterbalance, not complement, the professional officers coming out of the academies. Many Americans, including many educators and administrators of the nation's colleges and universities, viewed the elite military academies as a "bastion of aristocracy" whose graduates were increasingly "isolated from [their] civilian contemporaries." Educators also derided the "uneven" education of the academy-trained officer. Formally mandated boards of visitors described it as "so dogmatic [that the curricula] discouraged initiative."[3]

By contrast, university and college administrators believed that civilian-educated officers would bring to military service a wider and more rounded background. They would also bring to the military a value system more consistent with American society, by virtue of having lived in a civilian environment. These officers were thus close to the "citizen-soldier" tradition that Americans have idolized in the icon of the minuteman. Furthermore, cooperation with the military offered university communities a means of contributing to the nation's well-being.

At first these citizen-soldiers were trained to serve in state militias (later the National Guard), but as the United States took on global military responsibilities after 1950, it was a natural and easy next step to use thousands of ROTC graduates in the active-duty forces. Academics and educational administrators judged that these new officers should play a dual role: they should serve the interests of national security abroad by joining the armed forces, and they should protect the freedoms of American society against encroachment by the very military system they were joining. In other words, training citizen-soldiers allowed the United States to have a military large and professional enough to protect the nation from without while avoiding the dangers of heightened militarism, which, if unchecked, could destroy the nation from within.

Lawrence Cress has argued that two English intellectual traditions have dominated American thinking about the military since the colonial period.[4] The "Radical Whig" tradition "opposed professional armies as invariably dangerous to liberty and civic virtue."[5] Radical Whigs preferred a militia system composed of men whose primary livelihood did not derive from their military service, even if such a military system would be less organized and less reliable. A militia, they argued, correctly placed the responsibility for national defense in the hands of men who would fight for property and family, not for a wage. Radical Whigs argued that "military service should be the obligation of every citizen and the profession of none."[6] In their eyes, a military populated by professionals threatened to become an instrument of ministerial power in the hands of an Oliver Cromwell or a William III.

Conversely, "Moderate Whigs" argued that while the military possessed the "means for the subversion of the political order," it would not destroy republican values if proper safeguards were created. Moderate Whigs like Adam Smith and George Washington understood that the complexities of eighteenth-century warfare necessitated a division of military labor and the creation of a professional soldiery.[7] For Smith, military professionalism was nothing more than a positive expression of the complexity of contemporary European (and, increasingly, American) society. In other words, soldiering had become too complex for part-time militiamen; national security had to become the responsibility of professionals. American experiences after Bunker Hill proved this point to Moderate Whigs like Washington, who became convinced of the need for a professional American military.

Furthermore, Moderate Whigs believed that a standing military was necessary both to protect civil liberties from foreign threats and to project the state's interests abroad. They argued that the military would not threaten republicanism if legal controls existed to take the army out of the exclusive control of the executive branch. To that end, both English and American Moderate Whigs supported the right of citizens to bear arms, legislative control of the power of the purse for all military requests, and limits on gubernatorial power to appoint militia officers. They understood the power that a professional military could bring to bear in the protection and projection of civil liberties but demanded that that very power be constitutionally controlled.

While the idea of the militia remained central to republican ideals of citizenship, the Radical Whig position faded—although it never disappeared.[8] As a result, the dominant Moderate Whig ideology greatly influenced the creation of the professional American officer corps. This ideology held that standing armies were not antithetical to individual liberty so long as "proper constitutional safeguards existed."[9] As American ideas about military service evolved, Moderate Whig ideology remained dominant.

ROTC has survived and received support from military officers, educators, students, and politicians in large measure because it is consistent with an American consensus that favors an updated and modernized version of the Moderate Whig position. ROTC allows for an acceptable level of civilian control of the military through the influence of civilian colleges and universities. In this way, it plays a critical role in creating an American military firmly rooted in the Moderate Whig tradition.

College and university administrators have thus seen ROTC not as an example of the military in the university but as an example of the university in the military. ROTC's staunchest and most important critics have been in uniform, not on campus. The military has often resisted diverting resources toward programs that it has perceived as citizenship programs, not essentially military programs. Local and national politicians have often thrust upon the military the responsibility of teaching civic virtue and patriotism through programs like the Civilian Conservation Corps (CCC) of the New Deal era. Before World War II, ROTC looked more like the CCC than a realistic program for developing junior officers. Despite the military's occasional dislike for, and indifference to, ROTC, educators have believed in it stridently enough to defend it against threats from the military itself. University administrators have also challenged the services to make changes that have enabled the program to keep pace with changes in American culture, military technology, and university dynamics.[10]

This book, consistent with much recent scholarship, argues that military systems are not institutions that act according to their own dynamic by virtue of ancient traditions, sacrosanct ceremonies, and a distinct mission. Rather, they are extensions of the societies that produce them.[11] The military officer, in the words of John Keegan, is now understood to "act as a man of his time and place."[12] The traditional Western military academies at Annapolis, St. Cyr, Sandhurst, and West Point all developed monastic pedagogical styles designed to reduce as much as possible any civilian influence on prospective officers. Nevertheless, as Keegan and others have demonstrated, even officers so produced reflect the values, beliefs, and interests of their society.

Since the beginning of the Cold War, the United States has relied heavily on the active cooperation of civilian institutions of higher learning to produce the majority of its active-duty officers through the Reserve Officers' Training Corps program. ROTC is one part of a system for developing junior officers that is consistent with the localized, federal structure of American government and society. The program has evolved and changed in character since 1916, but the relatively incremental change that had characterized the program before World War II yielded to revolutionary change with the onset of the Cold War. In 1950, ROTC was primarily composed of white male students from private eastern schools and land-grant universities nationwide. These students took a curriculum of 480 contact hours that included heavy doses of drill and military ceremony. The program, mandatory for two years on most campuses for all physically fit males, served largely to populate the reserve component of each service.

I chose 1980 as an endpoint for this book because in that year, incoming President Ronald Reagan's support for the concept of the all-volunteer force made ROTC an entrenched part of the American military system. By 1980, ROTC, voluntary almost everywhere, had jettisoned its heavy military emphasis; the curriculum included as few as 180 contact hours and included courses taught by regular civilian faculty. Its students were now primarily from the South and the Midwest, and they included large numbers of women and minority students. Furthermore, ROTC had become indispensable as a means of populating the active-duty officer ranks.

These and other remarkable changes over a relatively short (thirty-year) period were the result of changes to the ROTC program itself, combined with developments in the two institutions primarily responsible for its oversight: American higher education and the military. Like those institutions, and American society more generally, ROTC became more specializd, differentiated, and open to persons of all ascriptive categories. Understanding ROTC, then, has importance beyond understanding officer procurement and training. In this book I use ROTC as a lens through which to examine the evolution of the military as well as higher education's relationship to the military.

My work complements and expands on recent scholarship on both higher education and the military. For the field of higher education, studies by Roger Geiger and Julie Reuben are helping a new history of higher education in America to develop beyond individual case studies and an antiquated narrative style.[13] Adam Garfinkle's *Telltale Hearts* and Kenneth Heineman's *Campus Wars* provide fresh examinations of the working dynamics of American universities in the tumultuous and often misunderstood 1960s.[14] These books take serious and probing looks at the goals, ideologies, and achievements of the various actors on American campuses during that decade.

Scholars concerned with the military have recently begun to focus more attention on the people that the military recruits and how they affect the function and operation of the American military system. Christian Appy's *Working-Class War* is a fine example of such scholarship for the Vietnam period.[15] My book thus represents, along with Appy's and others, an effort to examine more carefully the origins and preparation of the American officer. Most important, these studies look carefully at the beliefs and values of men and women before their entry into the military and how those values affect the military as an institution in American society.

Studying ROTC therefore presents an opportunity to examine the history of military personnel procurement, American higher education, and American beliefs about the military. Despite the potential value of this subject, ROTC has been the subject of just five book-length studies, all now at least fifteen years old and all of limited utility for the purposes just described.[16] These studies, while informative, share three important flaws. First, they all focus exclusively on the military side of ROTC, exploring the effectiveness of the program in producing and training military officers. The most influential of these studies, Gene Lyons and John Masland's *Education and Military Leadership: A Study of the ROTC,* published in 1959, explored ways to reposition ROTC to meet the challenges of the Cold War era. In doing so, however, it focused exclusively on changes to the military curricula and an argument against unification of the army, air force, and navy programs (the Marine Corps receives officers through the navy's ROTC program). It did not address the university-military relationship in any substantive detail.

Their second flaw is that their attempts to examine ROTC historically generally consist of a short chapter or two devoted to an undocumented (and rather uninteresting) narrative. None of these studies has attempted to place ROTC within the American cultural, social, and political context. Nor have they placed ROTC within the context of American military traditions. Only Victor Hirshauer's 1975 study uses primary materials to examine changes to ROTC, and his materials consist solely of army and Pentagon records.[17] Four of these studies examine only one service, further narrowing their utility. These studies make no effort to examine events within universities themselves or the interaction of military and civilian officials. As this book will show, the quality of that relationship has been a critical variable.

The first two flaws contribute to a third: all of the previous studies assume that universities have acted as units of the military services, following orders just as any other component of the military would. One study argues that ROTC was administered "virtually the same way . . . at all Air Force detachments."[18] These studies examine only the military side of ROTC, and they assume that only those issues of concern to the military were significant to ROTC's development. Therefore they contain such erroneous statements as "the method of designating officers for ROTC duty and the fact that the military curriculum was determined in Washington did not become important issues at most colleges and universities participating in the ROTC program."[19] As the following chapters will make clear, both of these issues have been hotly debated outside Washington since at least 1950. To understand ROTC, one has to understand it as it has operated in places like Ann Arbor, Urbana, Seattle, New Brunswick, and Austin.

Past studies have overemphasized top-down leadership and high-level decision making. I argue that decisions made on local levels contributed significantly to the course and direction of ROTC between 1950 and 1980, and I demonstrate that the ROTC program was necessarily dependent on both the military and higher education for its survival. Both of these institutions, in turn, rely on the support and confidence of American society.

When Americans lose or gain faith in education or the military, ROTC feels the effects, if at times indirectly.

For many people, when they think of ROTC, they think of the time in the late 1960s when radical student groups on American campuses questioned connections between the university and the military. The images of burning ROTC buildings and campus protests have remained powerful. The years between 1968 and 1972 were indeed a time of rapid, fundamental change for ROTC, but it was only one such period, and the student movement was only one cause. The introduction of curricular reforms in the late 1950s, the 1964 implementation of the ROTC Vitalization Act, and the introduction of the all-volunteer force in 1973 also brought about important changes in the program. In short, this study looks at several periods of controversy and reform.

Despite such controversy, the ROTC program has survived two world wars, the Cold War, intense scrutiny from academics, violent opposition from a small but dedicated group of students in the Vietnam War era, and the end of the draft. It has survived because it was (and is) consistent with fundamental American values and ideas about the place of the military in American society. ROTC allows Americans to support a large standing military without the fear that the military will develop a value system alien to their own.

This book covers four chronological phases of ROTC development. Chapter 1 deals with the roots of the Moderate Whig position and the evolution of civilian officer education programs before 1950. Those programs had a modest quantitative impact on the active-duty American officer corps, but they laid the groundwork for the development of a regularized ROTC program that later produced officers for the active-duty military. Chapters 2 and 3 cover the years 1950 to 1964, which I refer to as the Cold War period.[20] This period was marked by relatively slow, incremental changes within the context of global international crisis. Nevertheless, even amid a general consensus that civilian institutions had to cede latitude and power to the military, the Moderate Whig position still dominated discussions of the role of military training and the proper role of civilian authority in officer preparation.

Chapters 4 and 5 cover the years of most intense reform, between 1964 and 1972. As fears about the growth of a military-industrial complex spread, educators stressed their desire to retain their role in officer production. The war in Vietnam did not lead most administrators, faculty, or even students to argue that ROTC should be expelled from the campus. Rather, the academic community reached a consensus that ROTC, properly reformed, could reinforce civilian influence over the military and that in this way, the worst excesses of the Vietnam experience might be avoided in the future.

Chapters 6 and 7 cover the years 1972 to 1980, when no conscription legislation existed to coerce men into military service. With the elimination of conscription (for the first time since the Cold War began), many Americans believed that the nation might return to the citizen-soldier concept, which had been lost when the draft took a disproportionate share of the nation's soldiers from those at the bottom of the society's social and economic scales. For both ROTC and the all-volunteer force to survive, the very definitions of citizenship and soldiering had to be changed. Throughout all of these changes, the Moderate Whig argument, rooted in fears of excessive military influence in civilian affairs, held considerable sway over the course of ROTC's evolution.

National-level changes, such as the end of the draft and the growing technological sophistication of military officers, affected all ROTC units. The ROTC program itself, however, evolved from school to school with variations to account for university traditions, the desires of local faculty and administrators, and the particular strengths of a given institution. I have therefore relied heavily not only on military archives but also on the archives of ten different schools. I chose these universities both for the availability of records in their archives and for the range of schools that they represent. The Universities of Colorado, Illinois, Michigan, Pittsburgh, Texas, and Washington, and Georgia Tech, Kansas State, Kent State, and Rutgers, are all large, public universities, but they offer a variety of geographical settings and relationships to ROTC.[21] This sample includes five land-grant universities, six charter Army ROTC (AROTC) units, two charter Naval ROTC (NROTC) units, and five universities that had significant student movements in the 1960s.

No clear distinction emerged between land-grant and other public universities in their treatment of ROTC issues. Rather, I found that public universities of all kinds reacted similarly. In all ten cases, the university communities under study demonstrated a willingness to work out problems relating to ROTC in order to be assured that the program would continue to serve as one of the "safeguards" that Cress argued were critical to Moderate Whig ideology.

Of course, ROTC exists in a much larger variety of settings, including private schools and military academies like Virginia Military Institute (VMI), Norwich, and the Citadel. However, my approach—focusing on public universities—provides three distinct advantages: first, public school administrators understood that their taxpayer-supported institutions had a distinct responsibility to deal seriously with ROTC; second, these schools have a remarkable ability to preserve and document their own history, and to make that documentation available (many private schools close their archival records for as long as fifty years); and third, faculty and administrators from such institutions served on national organizing bodies and advisory committees.

Several umbrella organizations also paid careful attention to ROTC, including the National Association of State Universities and Land-Grant Colleges (NASULGC), whose papers I examined at the University of Illinois, and three joint civilian-military advisory boards. Because of its prominence and its long history of hosting military training programs, the NASULGC served not only as a representative of its own interests but also as a conduit for the interests of schools outside the land-grant system. The Air Force Historical Research Agency at Maxwell Air Force Base (AFB) in Montgomery, Alabama, the United States Army Center of Military History in Washington, and the Suitland Federal Records Center in Suitland, Maryland, were invaluable resources for understanding the military side of ROTC.

This study uses ROTC to gain insight into the nature of American attitudes toward the military, reforms within the military itself, and the nature of the American public university's commitment to service. Antiwar protest has often been simplistically interpreted as a rejection by university communities of all things military. Such an analysis reduces to black and white a picture that is full of color. It certainly was possible for an individual to hate the war in Vietnam, hate the military, and, at the same time, be a firm supporter of ROTC. This position was entirely consistent with eighteenth-century beliefs that "the condemnation of the army as an agent of ministerial influences did not include an outright denunciation of military professionalism."[22] Dominant Moderate Whig ideology demands civilian controls on the military, not a sharp delineation of military and civilian spheres.

I would like to reiterate what this study does *not* do. I did not undertake an exhaustive study of private institutions or of state military schools like the Citadel and VMI. Public universities, whether involved in the land-grant system or not, act under a different dynamic than private ones. Like Kenneth Heineman in his book *Campus Wars,* I have chosen to limit my analysis to those schools that rely heavily on public funding and have to answer to publicly elected state legislatures and, in some cases, publicly elected trustees. Of course, such a choice of schools does not limit the importance of private universities to the overall story.

Furthermore, I have not attempted to deal with the issue of class dynamics in ROTC. It is surely possible that the services have used ROTC to gain access to men and women from less privileged socioeconomic backgrounds than their academy counterparts. It is also possible that ROTC students, generally less privileged than their non-ROTC peers at the same school, have used their military scholarships as a way to gain entrance into schools otherwise out of their financial reach. ROTC's role in "bluing" both the officer corps (witness Colin Powell) and the student body is fascinating, but beyond the purview of this study.

Although the service academies produce more senior leaders and generally attract more attention than does ROTC, the accomplishments of the Reserve Officers' Training Corps ought not to be ignored. ROTC permitted the first large-scale introduction of college-educated men into the officer corps. It also was the first significant means of entrance into the officer corps for women and African Americans.

This book covers a period when both higher education and the military became increasingly important to American society in a wide variety of overlapping realms. The interactions of the two institutions at the time of their growing centrality to the American identity deserves careful attention. As these two very different institutions have evolved along occasionally congruent paths, they have often tried to use each other for their own improvement and that of the nation. Part of this process has been the quest to find a middle ground between the academic world and the military.

CHAPTER 1

ROTC and the American Military Tradition

> They come to us at the supercilious and sophomoric stage of their development and seriously need restraint and guidance such as the Army is so well equipped to render.
>
> —Dean of Men Fraser Metzger, Rutgers University, March 15, 1944

The buildup of the large, peacetime military force that began in earnest in 1950 is an exception to the rule in American history. Traditionally, American beliefs about the military from all points along the ideological spectrum have been characterized by suspicion, charges of elitism, and vigorous efforts to place limits on both the size and the power of the professional military. The pressures of war and internal security in the twentieth century have led to a general consensus in favor of an increased standing military, but not to an increased desire to turn that military over to a professional elite.

Even in the Cold War era, when the American military's prestige and influence were at a historical peak, questions arose regarding the wisdom of placing the military in the hands of a small, careerist clique. Scandals involving the encroachment of career military officers on civilian authority include West Point graduate Douglas MacArthur's challenge to President Truman's authority during the Korean War and Annapolis graduate Oliver North's subversion of congressional intent during the Iran-Contra affair. Both of these men had a vocal public following, but, notably, neither was able to use his military career to propel him into a successful political career.[1] In the words of Professor Samuel Huntington, "While the American people like their political candidates to be military heroes, they want their military experience to be an interlude in, or a sideline to, an otherwise civilian career."[2]

The American polity has consistently rejected professional officers who cross a firm, if not always visible or definable, line separating proper conduct from improper conduct.

The American dilemma, then, has been to support a military strong enough to achieve the nation's political and economic goals without being so strong as to threaten the civil liberties and civilian oversight consistently valued by the Moderate Whig tradition that Lawrence Cress argues characterizes American military attitudes.[3] Over the course of the twentieth century, ROTC came to encompass a large share of the solution to achieving that delicate balance. ROTC offered the means to produce nonprofessional officers sufficiently civilian to assuage the fears of Moderate Whigs. At the same time, however, these officers could be professional and competent enough to fill the company grades of the officer hierarchy, with a relatively small percentage of such officers moving on to field grade and general grade.[4]

To understand ROTC, one must understand the nature of America's distrust of standing armies as well as the role that universities and colleges played in shaping the military before the onset of the Cold War. These two traditions created historical forces that operated on the decision-making process involving ROTC in the Cold War era and beyond. Campus protesters, university presidents, and secretaries of defense alike were operating in an environment whose roots had been established centuries earlier. While the actors in the ROTC debate were rarely cognizant of the context within which they were operating, that context nevertheless set the terms of debate and made some courses of action, such as the abolition of ROTC, impossible. ROTC played a critical role in fulfilling a powerful American belief: that the military must be subservient to civilian interests for it to truly represent and defend the interests of the society it serves.

Newburgh and the Anti–Standing Military Tradition

The American dilemma of relying for national defense on a military populated by large numbers of nonprofessionals was inherited from a similar British dilemma. Virtually all of the men who shaped early American military beliefs were trained in the British system. In the eighteenth century, Britain's military shared with other European systems an emphasis on fighting low-intensity wars for limited political goals. Unlike many of its European counterparts, however, the English system firmly emphasized civilian control over the military, even at the tactical and strategic levels; only civilian leaders decided what political goals were worth fighting for and how much force to use in trying to achieve those goals. Consequently,

> an eighteenth-century British or American general might admire a Caesar or a Frederick. But he knew that he would never have the kind of military and political power that such men possessed. He knew that he could not alone decide how to wage war—that his government would determine not only when to go to war but also what kind of war the people could and would support. An Anglo-American general would have to receive instructions from or at least discuss his plans with his government before embarking on any campaign.[5]

Despite the triumph of the American army in the War for Independence and the popularity of its commander, General George Washington, the end of hostilities did not produce a desire to elevate the place of the military in the new American state. Rather, it yielded a desire to return to a "traditionally antimilitary" society that treated its returning veterans poorly and remained suspicious of professional soldiers.[6]

American fears of a military takeover seemed entirely justified in 1783. A group of senior officer veterans of the Revolution led by General Horatio Gates opposed what they saw as an excessively moderate government under Washington and the alleged indifference of that government to their own financial problems. They envisioned a more centralized and aristocratic social and political system. Their plan to wrest control of the government from civilians was, according to Richard Kohn, "the closest that an American army has ever come to revolt or coup d'état." General Washington had to intervene personally at a meeting in Newburgh, New York, to prevent the officers from, in Washington's words, "sowing seeds of discord and separation" between the military and its properly constituted civilian overseers.[7]

Public awareness of the details of the Newburgh conspiracy reinforced Americans' "real fear" of a revolt from the professional standing army.[8] It convinced many civilians, Thomas Jefferson among them, that a large standing military was the greatest threat to the personal freedoms so recently won. It also "positively reaffirmed Anglo-American tradition: the first national army in American history explicitly rejected military . . . independence from civilian control."[9] That civilian control, many came to believe, was all that stood between American liberty and totalitarianism.

Constitutional controls over the military, traditionally favored by Moderate Whigs, appeared in the Articles of Confederation and in all state constitutions as well as in the U.S. Constitution. All thirteen governors served as commander-in-chief of their state's militia, while state legislatures retained the power of the purse and the power to mobilize. The Constitution maintained firm civilian control over all aspects of the national military as well. The president had ultimate authority as commander-in-chief, Congress held the power to declare war and controlled all military funding (the Constitution forbids Congress to provide military funding for more than a two-year term), and a civilian secretary of the navy and secretary of war headed up the military departments themselves. While the new United States made conscious efforts to break away from English traditions in some realms, the tradition of firm civilian control over military activities not only did not substantially change but, as a result of the Newburgh conspiracy, probably intensified.

After 1783 Congress pared the United States Army down to a single regiment. Because civilian fears of a standing military "remained strong in all regions of the country," Congress preferred to rely on "distance and foreign forbearance alone" to protect the nation from overseas enemies. Similarly, Congress did not judge any internal enemies to be sufficiently strong to merit the risks of creating a professional military. Native Americans on the frontiers were left to "the sheer weight of an advancing population" and whatever actions local and state military forces deemed just.[10]

One of the proposals that emerged in the wake of Newburgh foreshadowed later solutions by proposing cooperation with civilian colleges to ameliorate the excesses of a professional military. In 1783, New York governor George Clinton proposed that one civilian college in each state in the union offer military training to selected male students. Graduates of these programs would then serve brief stints as officers in the national army.[11] Clinton hoped that his plan, which Congress chose not to fund, would staff the professional military with men who were not professional soldiers. As civilians, well-schooled in the need to protect and preserve American freedoms, they would work against the tyrannical and aristocratic elements believed to exist among military professionals.

James Madison shared Clinton's fears of a standing military. Such a force, he argued, could be "dangerous," even "fatal," to the liberties of a free people. A strong federal union, Madison contended, had the virtue of making a standing military unnecessary. "The distance of the United States from the powerful nations of the world gives them the same happy security," he said, that Great Britain enjoyed by virtue of its "insular situation." The British monarchy had "never been able, by real or artificial dangers, to cheat the public into an extensive peace establishment." A strong federal union, combined with America's distance from Europe's internecine warfare, would eliminate quarrels between the states and therefore obviate the need for a standing military.[12]

Americans from most political perspectives preferred local militias as the solution to the problem of how best to defend the nation. Under this scenario, Americans could avoid the threats to civil liberties inherent in a standing army by localizing national defense and relying on individual state militias to complete the tasks expected of a national military. The Constitution guaranteed the rights of states to operate and staff local militias, and these units assumed much of the constabulary role that otherwise would have fallen to the national army. Acquiescing in the development of state militias also permitted Congress to reduce the funding for an army it did not trust. According to Harry Coles, "leaders in both parties had reason to suspect that money spent on the army was soapsuds down a rat hole."[13]

Strong local authority had the additional benefit of taking a large federal army out of the hands of potentially despotic civilians. Colonial politicians argued that a strong federal army in the hands of a civilian such as George III was every bit as dangerous as an army whose officers planned a coup d'état. The only reasonable course of action that these men saw involved reducing the power and authority of a central, professional armed force in favor of citizen-soldiers. The minuteman who beat his plowshares into swords became the model of the future American soldier.

In 1784 Congress explicitly stated that "standing armies in time of peace are inconsistent with the principles of republican government, dangerous to the liberties of a free people, and generally converted into destructive engines for establishing despotism."[14] The congressional plan in the event of foreign invasion, then, was for a small professional navy and army to delay the arrival of an invading force just long enough for latter-day Paul Reveres to rouse latter-day minutemen into action. By 1785 the Congress had further weakened the professional military by selling almost all its naval vessels (the navy had one combat-ready frigate to fight the "quasi-war" with France in 1798) and by directing that regular officers be assigned only to West Point and Fort Pitt (at the site of present-day Pittsburgh, then still considered the frontier).

Furthermore, Congress was willing to permit the states to develop militias or not, according to local wishes. Without professional leadership or direction, these militias rarely developed into respectable fighting forces and were often beaten badly in combat with Native American nations. Federalists such as Washington and Alexander Hamilton argued that in the absence of a reliable militia system, the professional army needed to be strengthened, but Congress did not agree to create a military academy at West Point until 1802, and then it was limited to a cadet class of ten engineers and run by a superintendent with no military background. West Point was fifty-six years old before it created a Department of Tactics.[15]

The ideal of a small standing military served the nation well in peacetime, but in times of war the weaknesses of a disorganized and unprofessional military became glaringly evident. During the War of 1812, a small fraction of the British army (most of which was busy fighting Napoleon on the Iberian Peninsula) moved at will, burning most of the public buildings in Washington, D.C., forcing the president to flee into the countryside, and threatening Baltimore and New Orleans. Some New England states refused to allow their militias to leave their state. These units drew the scorn of professionals for their amateur leadership; officers tended to be businessmen and politicians who had achieved their position based on their popularity back home. The hero of the war was, of course, Andrew Jackson, a nonprofessional who owed his fame to the commonly held perception that his Tennessee volunteers (also nonprofessionals) were primarily responsible for the American victory over the British near New Orleans. Despite its evident disfunctionality, the volunteer/militia system continued to capture the imagination of the American people.

The strength of the militia system lay not in its mastery of tactics and operations but in its ability to mobilize men for war and keep them highly motivated. The system received much of the credit for the isolated military successes of the war (such as New Orleans). Americans continued to prefer that their military units be constituted of local men and officers, not part of a federal army. The military failures of the War of 1812 did nothing to diminish Moderate Whig fears of a large federal force, and the immediate postwar years did not produce an enduring movement to strengthen the national army and navy.[16] After a brief period of attention to military matters, traditional anxieties returned. An economic slump in 1819 and the general indifference that Congress showed toward the army in the absence of a foreign threat resulted in a reassertion of traditional antimilitarism. In 1821 Congress cut the army in half, from 12,000 officers and men to 6,000 officers and men, and ordered that only one major general (then the highest rank) be retained.[17]

In typical American fashion, the problems and tensions that resulted from the humiliation of 1812 produced a desire to provide better training and preparation for the militia officers before it produced enduring efforts to improve the preparation of professional officers. Recalling George Clinton's plan, these efforts focused on civilian institutions of higher learning. Before the war only the University of Georgia had offered military training, but after the war other schools soon developed ideas for military training programs independent of West Point.

In 1819 the American Literary, Scientific, and Military Academy (now called Norwich University) began military training to produce, in the words of the school's founder, Alden Partridge, officers "identified in views, in feelings, [and] in interests with the great body of the community."[18] Partridge resigned his army commission after serving as West Point's third superintendent in order to create a new academy that would help to build "a balance between the militia and the Regular Army, a balance that would bring the popular support and allegiances of the militia system into harmony with the training and discipline of an efficient army."[19] This solution, Partridge hoped, could walk the tightrope inherent in American military attitudes. With civilians trained in the skills needed of military officers, the nation could avoid another disaster like 1812 as well as another threat to civil liberties like the one so narrowly averted at Newburgh.

Other schools developed similar programs in the years between 1815 and the Civil War. In 1820 Thomas Jefferson directed that the University of Virginia require military training for all students, in the hope of creating officers for a national militia and, perhaps, making military science an academic field of study. By 1840 the University of Tennessee and Indiana University were also requiring military training.[20]

The programs at civilian colleges also helped to counterbalance changes occurring at West Point. During the 1820s, John Calhoun led a determined effort to reform West Point and make it the principle source of entry into the officer corps. Part of the reformation involved guaranteeing that the cadets came from a narrowly defined social background. As a result, West Point "increasingly restricted access to the officer corps to established old-stock families."[21] In an era of Jacksonian egalitarianism, the military became one institution to which access could be restricted by virtue of its relatively small size and the aristocratic traditions it had inherited from Europe.

While the reform of West Point gave it, and the army, more respect and prestige, it also led to increasing charges of elitism. The socialization process at the Military Academy produced "a distinct military subculture . . . subtly apart from the expansive individualism which permeated contemporary civilian society." The army responded to antimilitary attacks by developing antipathetic attitudes toward the civilian world and by creating an increasingly separate "band of brothers." Officers often married daughters or sisters of other officers, and loyalty to the army grew more intense.[22]

A resulting tension emerged regarding the militia and the citizen-soldier. As the professional military grew more insular and more protective of its role, its members came to feel "notorious contempt" for nonprofessionals.[23] Similarly, as they derived more identity from their status as officers, they grew more suspicious and distrustful of the enlisted men. As William Skelton noted, "Increasingly, the officer corps consisted of long-term, West Point–trained careerists who identified strongly with the army, especially their particular branches, and who viewed the civilian world with suspicion."[24]

The formation of the United States Naval Academy at Annapolis in 1845 intensified these patterns. Naval officers had even more elite backgrounds than their army contemporaries. Annapolis midshipmen came disproportionately from affluent manufacturing, commercial, and professional backgrounds. The naval officer corps quickly became, in the words of Peter Karsten, a "naval aristocracy" that socialized, married, and interacted with other navy families.[25]

Before the Civil War, then, two trends dominated decisions regarding American military personnel. The first was a perceived functional need, consistent with the prevailing social structure, for a small, highly professionalized officer corps drawn from an increasingly small group at or near the top of the American social structure. The second, contradictory, trend was a cultural preference for citizen-soldiers, ill-prepared and unprofessional though they were, to act as a counterbalance to the antidemocratic tendencies Americans feared in their own officer corps. Relying on local forces also allayed antifederal fears that another Cromwell or George III would use his civilian authority to command a large army for the purpose of removing democratic freedoms. The crisis of the Civil War and its aftermath brought these two ideas together and eventually produced the modern antecedent to the twentieth-century ROTC program.

The Morrill Act

In 1861 the Union army estimated that it would need about 20,000 officers to lead its units in the initial phase of the war against the South. Loyal West Point cadets and Norwich graduates could provide at best only 1,500 officers.[26] Faced with such a tremendous shortage of officers, leadership of the Union army fell to civilian officers in charge of local units. Many of these men lacked any formal training in military matters and relied on their familiarity and authority at home to command. Some, like Robert Gould Shaw and Joshua Chamberlain, performed their tasks very well, but on the whole, the nonprofessional officers were often overwhelmed by the responsibilities of command.[27]

The professionals did not perform much better. Throughout the war, West Pointers drew a great deal more scorn than praise. Few career officers had had any sustained experience in commanding large units, and many quickly found their academy training in the teachings of Baron Antoine-Henri de Jomini outdated in an era of rifled weapons, telegraphs, and railroads.[28] The Union army went through a series of military commanders, such as George McClellan, Joseph Hooker, and Ambrose Burnside, who failed to achieve victory and were frequently humiliated in battle by smaller Confederate units. The two most popular Union generals were the distinctly unaristocratic Ulysses Grant, who wore a private's coat instead of a general's uniform, and William Sherman. Both were West Point graduates, but they were of a different breed and were comfortable with civilian dominion; notably, both had experienced problems fitting in with their Military Academy colleagues.

The initial inability of American officers, however trained, to provide leadership on any level impelled considerations of reforming the military system. Few people considered expanding the military academies, both because of their aristocratic reputation and because the performance of West Point graduates in the Union army did little to inspire awe or confidence. Instead, within a year of the outbreak of the war, Americans had already begun to look to the nation's civilian colleges as the solution, just as they had after the War of 1812.

In the Jacksonian period, Whigs and Democrats had debated the federal funding of state universities and colleges. Whigs had consistently favored the use of funds from the sale of government-owned lands to create public academies to teach Latin, Greek, mathematics, and other subjects. Democrats had either opposed the idea as elitist or favored the creation of these schools as institutions to teach what they contended were more practical subjects, such as farming and mechanics. Before the Civil War, comprehensive action on either plan had failed to come to fruition.

The formation of the Republican Party, which picked up the Whig banner on the issue, and the departure to the Confederacy of several key southern opponents of the Whig plan opened the way for the public funding of colleges to be considered anew. Vermont Representative Justin Morrill led the fight to get the public colleges created. Morrill was a friend and neighbor of Norwich founder Alden Partridge and was particularly impressed with the level of preparation and competence of Norwich graduates serving in the Union army. Morrill's bill proposed that 30,000 acres of public land be sold in each state to generate funds to create public colleges. These colleges could teach any other subjects they wished, but they had to offer courses in agriculture, mechanical arts, and military tactics.[29] Congress approved the Morrill Act in July 1862.

Morrill had envisioned that his plan would produce more men trained in the Norwich model, men who had military knowledge but were not military professionals. "Like Partridge, [Morrill] offered the alternative of military training in civilian educational institutions as a means by which a democratic people could gain a competent officer corps . . . without endangering their basic liberties."[30] Men trained at these land-grant colleges were to be citizens first and soldiers second. Furthermore, the Morrill Act left decisions on the amount, intensity, and regularity of military training to the discretion of local officials at the new schools.

The Morrill Act was consistent with many traditional American beliefs about the proper way to commission officers for the army: it localized training and offered a civilian alternative to West Point graduates, yet it did not compel individuals actually to serve in the military if they chose not to do so. The Morrill system attracted significant support in Congress after the war, and supplementary acts quickly followed. Between 1866 and 1890, Congress passed acts authorizing the War Department to dispatch a total of 20 (later 100) officers to teach military classes, to supply small arms and equipment for training purposes, and to provide on request both men and material to schools outside the land-grant system (as well as to "separate but equal" black schools created by the land-grant system).

By 1900, forty-two colleges and universities had military training programs in operation that received support from the War Department. Several other programs received support from the hosting institution, usually in the form of finding Civil War veterans to conduct drill sessions. The army's own support of on-campus military training was "lukewarm" between 1870 and 1910, while the army's leadership focused its energies on wars against the American Indian nations of the West. The army was often reluctant to assign officers higher in rank than lieutenant to college campuses; in one noteworthy case, it assigned an eighty-year-old major to North Dakota Agricultural College.[31] Between 1898 and 1902 it assigned no one to Kansas State; the unit was commanded by a cadet selected by the school's board of regents.[32]

Like militia units in the era between the Civil War and World War I, campus military training programs had no standard uniforms (indeed, Kansas State cadets did not even have uniforms until 1885) and no systematic access to modern equipment, and they did little except teach men how to march in straight lines. Nevertheless, the militia system's main supporter, the National Guard Association, secured a doubling of federal funds in 1887 and kept up the pressure on Congress to make the National Guard and local militia units the primary means of guaranteeing national security from within and without. Localism and nonprofessionalism remained powerful.

Thus, until World War I military programs on campuses remained quite informal and inefficient. These programs had no connection to the system of appointing and commissioning officers for either the active-duty forces or the National Guard. However, the groundwork for such a system had been laid. A loose connection between the War Department and civilian institutions of higher learning had been established, and a preference for nonprofessional officers had become a consistent feature of American culture. These factors formed the background for the creation of the ROTC program in a form that is still recognizable today.

The Birth of a Formal ROTC Program

The preparedness movement that preceded World War I argued for a more formal connection between officer training programs and the larger military system, which was itself under review. Progressive emphasis on efficiency and rationality had already created a "virtual revolution" in the army and the navy between 1890 and 1910.[33] The reborn military had more modern weapons, a streamlined promotion system, a General Staff to centralize decision making, and war colleges to study the problems of wars past, present, and future.

This movement also led to the passage of the 1916 National Defense Act (NDA), which created the three components of the American military system still in use today: the active-duty forces, the organized reserves, and the National Guard. The active-duty forces are composed of men in uniform and under the direct control of the army, the navy, the marines, and, after 1947, the air force. The reserves, also under the direct control and supervision of federal authority, were intended to be composed largely of veterans of tours of duty with the active forces, supplemented by men recruited with bounties and other incentives. As the name implies, it is a force "in reserve," subject to periodic rudimentary training and, if need be, emergency call-up to active duty.

The reformed National Guard was the result of a compromise between local officials who wanted a militia organizationally distinct from the federal government and national military officials who saw the state militias as little more than militarily inept social clubs, unreliable should the United States be drawn into war. The former group fits Cress's "Radical Whig" position: they wanted the militias to remain structurally and functionally independent of the regular army so that they might stand guard against the tyrannical potential inherent in a professional, federally controlled army. Regular army officers, however, had long been suspicious of the National Guard and militia units for their lack of formal training, their election of officers, and the familiarity between those officers and the enlisted men they led.

Despite its inefficiencies, eliminating the National Guard altogether or absorbing it into the army reserves would have been impossible. The 1898 Spanish-American War, the "splendid little war," had been largely fought by local units, commanded by locally elected officers who often allowed their men to address them on a first-name basis. The units had had "few hours given to serious training, almost none to long marches," but had made significant contributions to victory.[34] The national hero of the war, Theodore Roosevelt, was a nonprofessional whose soldiers, the Rough Riders, were also nonprofessionals.[35] This evident success, fresh in the minds of Americans, produced wide support for keeping the militia system basically intact.

As a result, the NDA dictated that the new National Guard units were to grow in size from 100,000 men to 400,000 and remain under the control of the states in which they served. They were, however, to be subject to mandatory training periods directed by regular military officers and to federalization in the event of a national emergency. Discipline, quality of leadership, mission, and supply were to be roughly the same across the three components of the reconfigured military, although in reality, patronage and local popularity continued for many years to dominate the process of awarding National Guard officer commissions.[36]

To professionalize the officer corps of the reserves and National Guard, the NDA also called for the creation of a Reserve Officers' Training Corps to absorb and build on military training programs already in existence at land-grant schools and many other large universities. The army's General Staff saw the creation of ROTC as the "only foreseeable option . . . to a greatly expanded military academy." Such an expansion would have been prohibitively expensive, and the staff knew that it would have required a massive effort to convince a majority of congressmen to vote for an increase at any cost.[37]

ROTC served as an effective compromise that offered something to all interested parties. The program allowed the War Department to standardize curriculum and equipment, thereby regularizing the type of military training young men received. Standardization also pleased military educators, who had been lobbying since 1913 for the army to institute minimum standards so that military training would do more than teach men how to march.[38] The ROTC plan also pleased proponents of the National Guard, because the graduates would be primarily available to them, not the regular army. Since the vast majority of students, especially those in the land-grant system, attended colleges close to home, ROTC reinforced the localized nature of the National Guard system and remained consistent with traditional beliefs in the value of the militia.

The initial number of ROTC units was limited, due to the relatively meager funds the War Department made available for the new program; therefore intense competition developed among schools that wished to acquire a unit. Professors Lyons and Masland argued that patriotism and a sense of public responsibility were the primary motivations for university officials seeking a unit for their campus.[39] Students seemed to share these sentiments. At many private eastern colleges, for example, students demanded that their school be included in the ROTC system along with the land-grant schools, so that the latter would not have a monopoly on patriotism. Students at Bowdoin, Williams, Harvard, Princeton, Yale, and Dartmouth all circulated petitions asking to have an ROTC unit; all were approved.[40]

In 1916 at the University of Pittsburgh, administrators and students, like their peers nationwide, began military training to prepare for American participation in the Great War. The Pittsburgh trustees authorized such training, without support from the War Department, in May. At the same meeting, they authorized the chancellor to apply for one of the new ROTC units.[41] Pittsburgh officials told the army that they were "extremely anxious" to get a unit and offered to pay as much as $80 per month of an active-duty officer's salary, if one could be assigned to conduct training programs.[42] Chancellor S. B. McCormick then sent one of the university's deans to Washington, D.C., to solicit the help of Pennsylvania's two senators, "in order that we may not only get ROTC, but that we may get it in a short time."[43] Georgia Tech's president and the chairman of the board of trustees made a similar trip to Washington to make a personal appeal for an ROTC unit at Tech.[44]

Collegiate administrators and faculty believed in the university's responsibility to serve society, and they "volunteered to help in whatever ways they could during World War I."[45] Working with the army provided universities with several benefits. Princeton's Edward Corwin argued that working with the army gave university professors "self respect by giving us some useful work to do while drawing our salaries."[46] Such work also protected one from undue suspicion. In 1917 the American Association of University Professors (AAUP) Committee on Academic Freedom in Wartime stated that faculty could legitimately be fired because of their "attitude or conduct" related to the war.[47]

Support for the war and ROTC thus imparted patriotism and shielded one from allegations that could lead to dismissal. With enthusiastic support from trustees, administrators, and faculty, the land-grant system alone provided 28,000 officers (including 43 generals) and 51,000 enlisted men to the army, navy, and marines during World War I.[48] Schools outside the land-grant system contributed as well. The University of Washington opened special programs to train navy and marine officers and ran the Student Army Training Corps program for the army.[49] Washington produced more naval officers for the war than any other school except Annapolis.

These experiences demonstrate the desires of students, faculty, and administrators to participate formally in military training programs. To the university communities, such participation represented a visible demonstration of patriotism and national service, even given the army's great difficulty in meeting the universities' demand for equipment, instructors, and guidance. In 1918 the army suspended the entire ROTC program for the duration of the war in favor of the Student Army Training Corps, which prepared men for enlisted service. After the war, however, enthusiasm for ROTC remained high. A 1919 student report at the University of Pittsburgh argued that ROTC "promises much for the future of higher education in America."[50] The *Kansas State Collegian* said in the same year that ROTC "gives promise of being a great thing for college men."[51]

One hundred thirty-five institutions had been granted ROTC units by the end of 1919. These institutions all agreed to offer a two-year basic course, mandatory at many schools, of at least three hours per week, and a voluntary two-year advanced course of at least five hours per week. Students who completed the latter could receive a reserve or National Guard commission. The War Department agreed to pay the salaries of the instructional staff, the cost of books, and the stipends of advanced cadets. In return, the host schools agreed to provide classrooms and office space and to give senior officers the title of professor of military science and tactics and junior officers the title of assistant professor of military science and tactics. By January 1922, 57,419 students were enrolled in 131 units.[52]

Administrators devoted considerable resources to their quest for ROTC units. University of Washington president Henry Suzzallo donated ninety-eight acres of the campus in the hope of attracting a navy ROTC program to train navy and marine reserve officers "exactly as the university is now training army reserve officers." Suzzallo was the first official to suggest such a program, but he would have to wait until the 1926 creation of the Naval Reserve Officers' Training Corps for his suggestion to become a reality.[53] Georgia Tech's president was no less enthusiastic. He credited ROTC with raising the athletic standards and "manly bearing" of students at Tech; in 1919, 90 percent of Tech's male students were enrolled in the program.[54]

While World War I provided the immediate impetus for these campus communities to seek an ROTC unit, other, more subtle, processes had been at work for decades. Julie Reuben has recently argued that the period from 1915 to 1930 in American higher education represented an "extracurricular" phase that followed religious and scientific phases. In the late nineteenth century, conflict between the traditional religious orientation of American colleges and universities and a more secular, Darwinian approach revealed "religion's intellectual marginality" to a generation of university reformers at prominent schools like Harvard, Johns Hopkins, and Michigan. By 1910, the reformers' scientific approach had won out. That approach, however, failed to give the campus the emotional and moral organization that religion had formerly provided. As a result, reformers "began . . . to emphasize secular sources for moral development."[55]

Reuben was primarily concerned with an intellectual history of the notions of truth and science, not with a study of moral guidance in the curriculum. Carrying her argument a small step further, however, one can easily see how the military came to be one of the institutions to which the universities turned for much of the secular guidance that the reformers believed had fallen away. The army, with its focus on discipline, patriotism, and the building of "men," fit in almost perfectly. The military thus stepped into a sort of moral guidance vacuum on the nation's campuses.

In this vein, the president of Rutgers University welcomed ROTC because he believed that it "was good physical and moral training for the student."[56] Devotion to country, symbolized by the availability (in many places the requirement) of military training, came to serve as a substitute for devotion to God and "the unity of truth," symbolized by chapel attendance and theology courses that had earlier been mandatory at some of the same schools that required ROTC. ROTC was not, of course, the only such program (intramural athletics, begun at the University of Michigan in 1912, offered another sort of structure), but it did provide the secular moral guidance that reformers sought while simultaneously fulfilling the desires of educators to provide service to the nation.

In response to military needs and the requests of educators, the army standardized the ROTC curriculum and mandated that military instructors teach map reading, military history, military law, basic tactics, camp sanitation, drill, and marksmanship. It did not take long, however, for serious problem areas to develop. Since the program produced Reserve, not active-duty, officers, "a sense of urgency and immediacy was often absent." As budgets tightened, the War Department resisted assigning high-quality officers to campuses. It also assigned fewer and fewer instructors, until by the mid-1920s, officer-to-cadet ratios in the basic course often fell as low as 1 to 100.[57] Furthermore, the General Staff quickly realized that patriotism alone would not provide the numbers of advanced cadets that they had hoped to attract. An early proposal by the General Staff to provide scholarship authorizations for selected students failed to get congressional approval, but the proposal itself acknowledged that financial incentives would be necessary for the program to have the quantitative impact it was designed to have. Moreover, differences between the military's subject matter and civilian aims for higher education created friction. In the interwar years "there developed a good deal of antagonism between military men and educators on the problem of accepting the ROTC courses as legitimate educational programs . . . Basically, the ROTC courses had two lessons to teach, the techniques of soldiering and the obligations of citizenship and neither was academically appealing."[58] These problems all intensified as a result of the overlapping system that managed ROTC problems. No single agency in the War Department had direct oversight for ROTC matters, and as a result no single office existed to regularize policy or even to meet with educators who came to Washington to discuss ROTC.

This friction was symptomatic of the secondary importance of ROTC to the active-duty forces in the immediate postwar years. The program primarily existed to provide officers for the Reserves or, in some cases, the National Guard. The addition of a Navy ROTC program in 1926 (inaugural units were established at Harvard, Yale, Georgia Tech, Northwestern, Washington, and California) made the nation's civilian colleges an indispensable source of reserve officers for all arms of the military. A limited number of ROTC graduates received active-duty commissions, but the American officer corps of the 1920s and 1930s remained small enough for it to be trained by the service academies; therefore, the best jobs went to the graduates of Annapolis and West Point. In 1935, fifty-two of the army's sixty-four generals and sixty of the navy's sixty-one admirals had graduated from the academies. Only five of the generals and none of the admirals had graduated from civilian colleges or universities.[59] The sole interwar attempt to open pathways for ROTC officers, the 1935 Thomason Act, made available 1,000 one-year active-duty appointments. However, no more than fifty of those men would receive permanent commissions at year's end. Even future U.S. Air Force chief of staff Curtis LeMay was unable to obtain an active-duty commission, because there "just weren't any vacancies" when he finished ROTC training at Ohio State in 1928.[60] This policy remained in effect until World War II.

It is unlikely that these advancement restrictions caused too much consternation among cadets. Most men who joined the advanced ROTC course did not desire an active-duty military commission.[61] Rather, they saw ROTC as a means to prepare themselves as citizen-officers for future emergencies. ROTC was designed to produce men who would go on to serve their country in myriad civilian occupations, from lawyer to farmer to architect. Their skilled presence in the organized reserves or the National Guard would allow the active-duty military forces to be kept at appropriately small levels.

ROTC's early years thus established it in good stead on the nation's campuses. Both the army and the navy supported it as an appropriate means to train young men for military service outside the traditional academies and such less formal arrangements as the prewar Plattsburg training camps and locally run National Guard training programs. By 1940 ROTC had become responsible for producing 80 percent of the organized reserves' officer corps and had commissioned more than 100,000 men.[62]

For the campuses, ROTC demonstrated patriotism in a bold and evident manner. Within twenty-four years of its creation, 220 colleges and universities had successfully acquired a unit, and many more sat anxiously on waiting lists.[63] The young men who took the classes were often ROTC's biggest supporters, creating military honor societies and campus traditions like military balls. For some of the large number of students who did not desire military training, however, mandatory ROTC classes became a symbol of the potentially perilous influence that the military could wield over civilian institutions. For most of those who shunned or ignored it, ROTC was just another campus inanity.

ROTC in an Era of Isolationism

The most important pre–World War II challenges to ROTC occurred in the environment of isolationism in the 1920s and 1930s. In the wake of reconsiderations about the wisdom of the U.S. involvement in World War I came concerns over the influence of military ethics and manners on civilian life. Traditional American fears of a standing military reawoke and helped to kill a postwar conscription plan proposed by the army. Pacifist groups on American campuses sought to change university policies regarding the military as a step toward removing militaristic elements from American society generally.

The two-year compulsory nature of ROTC at land-grant colleges, called for in the 1916 National Defense Act, attracted the most attention on campus. Representatives of the American Friends Service Committee, the Young Men's Christian Association (YMCA), the Women's International League for Peace and Freedom, and other secular and religious groups formed the Committee on Militarism in Education in 1925 to eliminate the compulsory military training required of students at land-grant colleges. Requiring military training of young men, they argued, developed a habit of warfare that was not instinctual but learned. "If the habit were broken, humanity would make some other response besides violence when the causes of conflict appeared."[64]

The University of Wisconsin was the first land-grant college to challenge compulsory training in 1923. The Wisconsin state legislature interpreted the Morrill Act as calling for schools only to offer military instruction to interested students and voted to make all military instruction elective.[65] Private schools were not mandated by the Morrill Act to offer military instruction, and therefore they had more latitude to change their policies. Most of these schools had initially chosen to adopt the compulsory two-year program in existence at land-grant schools, but by the mid-1920s several were reconsidering. By 1927 ROTC had been made voluntary at such schools as Johns Hopkins, the University of Pennsylvania, and Princeton.[66] In 1930 the U.S. attorney general voiced his support for Wisconsin's move, and in 1934 the Supreme Court ruled in favor of a voluntary ROTC.[67] By the mid-1930s, twenty-one schools had made the program voluntary, including another land-grant school, the University of Minnesota.[68]

The anticompulsory forces never focused their efforts on removing ROTC itself; their primary goal remained the elimination of ROTC as a graduation requirement. They objected to the imposition of military training, not its existence for students who desired it. The navy and the war departments held conflicting views on the issue. Higher officials opposed the change, arguing that removing compulsory ROTC might serve as a first step toward eliminating the program altogether. ROTC instructors themselves, however, often argued that the army could gain by acquiescing. Requiring men to participate in ROTC was unpopular, but ROTC itself was not. Requiring the program, then, served only to give ROTC a bad reputation and to bring thousands of disgruntled and unmotivated men into the units.

The army was uninterested in managing the character-building aspects of ROTC thrust upon it by Congress and college administrators. Congress had also put the army in charge of a high school version of ROTC and the Civilian Conservation Corps, neither of which served any direct military role. Congress put an unwilling army in control of both programs, because of the military's perceived ability to turn boys into men. To the extent that the collegiate ROTC program could provide officers, it had the army's support. But the army consistently tried to separate that role from what it argued was the discrete role of instilling patriotism in college men. Mandatory ROTC was, of course, also uneconomical. In a typical year, the army had to train, equip, and outfit 150,000 young men to produce just 3,500 reserve officers.[69]

The 1930s' controversy over compulsory training resulted in the first wave of required programs that elected to go voluntary. A second wave, discussed in Chapter 2, would play out along almost identical lines in the early 1960s. In both debates, the vast majority of educators and students either supported the ROTC *status quo* or supported it as an elective course of study. Indeed, the universities supported ROTC much more intensely than the army did. By 1936, as international tensions were increasing, educators warned the army that it needed to begin to prepare ROTC for the role it would have to assume should the United States get drawn into war. The Land-Grant Association told the army that "no . . . explanations or alibis can persuade anyone that the Army is not indifferent toward ROTC . . . [W]ith the all-time high appropriations in peacetime, there is no evidence of sincere and vigorous effort to provide for ROTC."[70]

The compulsory debate, then, should be read not as evidence of academic unwillingness to participate in military training but as evidence of an unwillingness to continue those programs as a requirement for graduation. Nor were all universities interested in abandoning compulsory ROTC. No anti-ROTC movement developed at schools where the program was voluntary. Kansas State won a 1935 lawsuit brought against the college by a student who refused to participate in military training activities.[71] Seventeen schools switched to voluntary programs in the 1930s, but a national bill to make ROTC programs entirely voluntary failed in 1936. The failure of the bill, combined with the rise to power of Nazi Germany, effectively ended the movement.

Most educators and students in the 1930s believed in the program enough to support it and keep it operating in the face of challenges from isolationists and pacifists, but few campus officials showed the enthusiasm for it that they had shown in the years after World War I. Moreover, rearmament programs under President Franklin Roosevelt focused primarily on technology and materiel, not personnel. As a result, ROTC's purpose was ill-defined. Most men completed their required training and quickly tried to distance themselves from the program. Robert McNamara recalled his ROTC training at the University of California, Berkeley: "What I learned was that nobody took the military seriously. My classmates and I saw [ROTC] as a pointless ritual, irrelevant to our world. On the day of our final parade, when we had to march before the president of the university, we threw our rifles down as soon as we were done—the hell with it!"[72]

The School of the Soldier

World War II was as a watershed in American attitudes toward the military and the military model of social organization. Prewar isolationism and anti-militarism disappeared almost overnight. After the war, hundreds of thousands of men and women returned from military service to direct corporations, run universities, and use their GI Bill benefits to attend college. Many brought with them a belief that some, if not all, of what they had learned in the military could be profitably incorporated into their civilian lives.

They also learned that "the army as a whole is a vast school."[73] To convert civilians into soldiers, sailors, marines, and airmen, the military ran a wide array of schools and programs, including the navy's V-12 program and the army's Advanced Student Training Program, which built on the infrastructure of prewar ROTC programs. As they had done during World War I, the services suspended ROTC for the duration of the war in favor of faster, more specialized training programs. The University of Colorado hosted a V-12 unit and navy language-training programs in Japanese, Malaysian, Russian, and Chinese.[74] A shared consensus that the World War II experience had been a "school for the soldier" helped legitimize the military's reconstruction of ROTC on college campuses beginning in 1946. "Just as school colors the war," noted Paul Fussell, "the war colors school."[75]

Military leaders credited ROTC, rudimentary though it sometimes was, with having played a critical role in the early days of mobilization following Pearl Harbor. More than 100,000 ROTC-trained men served as officers in the wartime army and navy. The power of nonprofessionalism remained strong; American soldiers in Europe derived great satisfaction from the fact that a "bunch of soda jerks and grocery clerks" were beating the best professional soldiers in Germany and Japan.[76] These men were, by most measures, qualitatively inferior to academy-trained officers, but they provided a reservoir of nonprofessional men with at least some military knowledge at a time when few Americans had any serious or sustained experience with the military. General George Marshall was particularly impressed: "Just what we would have done in the first phases of our mobilization without [ROTC graduates] I do not know. I do know that our plans would have had to be greatly curtailed and the cessation of hostilities on the European front would have been delayed accordingly."[77]

The propaganda value of Marshall's observation notwithstanding, the high regard that respected military men like Dwight Eisenhower, Chester Nimitz (himself a former NROTC instructor), and Marshall had for the wartime contributions of the ROTC program helped to legitimize its reemergence after the war. Moreover, many university presidents pointed with pride to the contributions of their alumni in the war effort. More than 100 members of the University of Colorado faculty in 1950 (including a future CU president) had served in the navy during the war.[78] Georgia Tech provided more naval officers than any school except the Naval Academy and provided more ordnance officers to the army than West Point.[79]

Furthermore, the universities' largely favorable experience with the military during the war inclined them toward participation in the years that immediately followed. Wartime training programs of all sorts "brought succor" in the form of higher enrollments to institutions of higher education that had been crippled by the Great Depression. Educators' fears that the end of the war would mean the return of lean times proved unfounded, in large measure because of the one million veterans who attended colleges and universities on the GI Bill.[80] To many academics, then, the military experience in World War II had meant a return of good times and a chance to contribute to a common cause. These experiences greatly aided the process of reestablishing ROTC.

The military, too, was satisfied with its World War II experience with the nation's colleges and universities and hoped to continue that association in the years to come. The 1948 Gray Committee recommended to the army that ROTC be renamed the Army Officer Training Corps and that it become the primary source of active-duty army officers. ROTC, in the opinion of the committee, was "the best available means of producing enough officers of the right type to lead America's Cold War Army. The need for a college-educated leader capable of understanding and employing increasingly sophisticated military technology, *the predilection for an officer corps reared in the citizen-soldier tradition* and the pressure to keep the costs of officer production as low as possible all played a part in creating this sentiment."[81] The Gray Committee's report assured not only that ROTC would remain a fixed institution on American campuses, but also that its roles and functions would become more central to the overall national defense structure than had been true before the war.

The creation of ROTC in 1916 and its full implementation after World War I marked the fruition of at least a century of informal military training on civilian college campuses. Although enthusiasm for such programs waxed and waned throughout the interwar years, enough support for the idea of civilian training programs existed to keep them operating through the isolationist era of the 1930s. Indeed, educators supported the idea of ROTC much more stridently than did the War and Navy Departments. To educators, these programs represented an opportunity to have a critical *civilian* impact on the operation and staffing of the professional military.

Thus from 1819 to 1949 military training on civilian college campuses came quite a long way: it became a regularized way to expose men to the rudiments of military instruction for the navy, the marines and the army; it became a recognized and respected institution in all regions of the country; and it evolved a semistandardized and semicentralized structure—a remarkable achievement in itself, considering the intensely diverse and decentralized structure of American higher education. These changes prepared ROTC to earn a national reputation among many military officers and civilian educators during World War II. That success, in turn, validated the re-creation and expansion of ROTC on civilian campuses in the years immediately following the war.

CHAPTER 2

A Favored Position on Campus: The Military and Higher Education in the Cold War Era, 1950–1964

> Let it not be thought that objectives of communism and the Soviet Union are new, mysterious, exotic, and omniscient. Present Soviet actions are former Russian expansionism writ large—only a historic continuum of the expansionism of Peter the Great, Empress Catherine, and the ancient principalities of Kiev and Moscow from whence began the conquest of lands now idealized as "Mother Russia."
>
> —1953 Air Force ROTC textbook

Because they had been dismantled during World War II in favor of faster training programs, ROTC units had to be created anew on college campuses after the war. By 1950, as this process was completed, Americans faced a new global environment of Cold War in Europe, hot war in Asia, and atomic war in the American psyche.[1] The role of ROTC in producing large numbers of reserve and, eventually, active-duty officers became significantly more important than it had been before World War II. As ROTC units became more central to the American military system, they also became more of a factor in campus life. As Americans were adjusting to the new role of the military in American social, political, cultural, and economic life, Americans on college campuses were searching for ways to adjust to an increased role for military training programs. The belief that associations with the military during World War II had brought colleges much more good than ill greatly facilitated this adjustment.

The ROTC programs of the 1950s had two components: a basic course for freshmen and sophomores and an advanced course for juniors and seniors. The former carried with it no after-graduation military obligations, but participants obtained no benefits other than completion of the prerequisite for the advanced course and exemption from conscription. The 1916 National Defense Act, which created ROTC, required men seeking commissions to have enrolled in the program for all four of their undergraduate years (see Chapter 1). Therefore, student decisions about ROTC had to be made early on. The decision to enroll in the advanced course was more serious, since it entailed military service after graduation. Most men who entered the advanced program, which was mandatory only at military colleges, did so to further defer their draft obligations or, if the student desired military service, for the chance to serve with the prestige and higher income of an officer.

By 1955 the Reserve Officers' Training Corps program existed on 313 campuses in all 50 states, the District of Columbia, and Puerto Rico. Thirty-two schools, mostly large state universities, hosted air force, army, and navy programs; most schools hosted just one. Virtually all of the land-grant schools hosted ROTC units, but the ROTC program was not limited to public schools; many prestigious private schools, including all of the members of the Ivy League, Johns Hopkins, Stanford, and Georgetown, also had ROTC units.

The army, navy, and air force (and, through the navy, the marines), by virtue of a 1949 agreement, ran organizationally separate but quite similar programs, with the important exception of the navy's Holloway Plan, which provided scholarship support to selected NROTC students.[2] The army and air force had no scholarship authorization and no plans to pursue such authorization. Instead, they counted on congressional passage of universal military training (UMT) legislation or some other conscription policy to entice men into ROTC.

For the most part, ROTC units were popular and often eagerly sought by administrators, faculty, and students for many of the same reasons that they had been popular after World War I. Many academics argued against UMT on the grounds that "traditional higher education had more to offer toward [national security] than did military training."[3] ROTC allowed both to exist; students could participate in military training while pursuing their civilian education. Former Harvard University president Nathan Pusey recalled the consensus of his fellow educators in the 1950s: "ROTC provided an acceptable way of attracting college men with leadership potential into the military services . . . Furthermore, these units gave the students who joined an opportunity to discharge their military obligation without interrupting their education. It is not surprising, therefore, that they were sought often by many institutions, and where awarded, were welcomed by administrators and students alike."⁴ Nevertheless, ROTC would have remained marginal to the development of active-duty officers had the United States not opted for a massive expansion of the military in the 1950s. This expansion involved both men and machines. Ultimately, the army mobilized 2,834,000 men to fight in Korea and to guard against the possibility that the Soviets would use the cover of America's preoccupation with Korea to strike at Western Europe.⁵ Indeed, the events of the early Cold War convinced American military and political planners of the need for a much larger standing military than had been planned in the years immediately following the end of World War II. This new military would need men who could handle the ever more complex tasks of the military officer in the atomic age.

The services wanted high-quality men with diverse skills and abilities. The nation's colleges and universities, where a system for training officers, albeit mainly reserve officers, already existed, were the logical places for the military to find and train these men. The other two officer production methods were inadequate for this task. A sufficiently large expansion of the service academies would have been prohibitively expensive and consequently was never seriously considered. The World War II–era Officer Candidate Schools had been valuable for turning out large numbers of immediately employable candidates, but not always high-quality officers. The services in the 1950s sought not only swift training, but also officers with a diverse body of general military knowledge. ROTC offered access to university-trained men at virtually all of the best schools in America and therefore became the primary means of producing large numbers of active-duty officers in the years following the outbreak of hostilities in Korea.

From the universities' perspective, civilian participation in military training programs reinforced two traditional and generally agreed-upon principles that had also influenced ROTC in the prewar years. The first was that civilian participation would serve as a critical check on the growth of a professional military. This position was consistent with academic opposition to UMT on the grounds that the best way to prepare the citizen-soldier was first to ensure that he had a firm grounding in the demands and nature of his citizenship. Here, of course, the universities believed that they could play a great role.

Second, and perhaps more important, the universities took great pride in preparing young men for all walks of life. Why, they asked, should the military be an exception? As American interests became increasingly international in scope and as the military became a more important profession in America—in many respects, becoming like any other profession—why shouldn't the universities take an active role in the preparation of junior officers? The military fit in nicely with how Nathan Pusey understood the mission of universities in the 1950s:

> It was our national policy in the postwar years to endeavor to ensure peace through the creation of a world order built on cooperation in many fields of activity and on enlarged international understanding. The nation's colleges and universities had a role of fundamental importance to play in this, for only they could prepare the highly trained people, specialists and laymen . . . needed in the public and the private sector, in government and in business, for the implementation of the policy.[6]

Few administrators could find logical reasons to exclude the military profession from this policy. Instead they welcomed the chance to participate in the education of military officers in much the same way that they welcomed the chance to influence the development of doctors, engineers, and bankers.

ROTC thus represented a joint partnership between the military and higher education to train officers for the national defense needs of the postwar era. As such, its character would necessarily be dependent on changes in the nature of the two institutions themselves and changes in the nature of the relationship between academe and the military. Neither of these institutions, of course, existed in a vacuum; as national and international contexts changed, so did the quality and character of the academic-military relationship.

ROTC is a rather lackluster case of the increasing scale of military-academic relationships in postwar America when compared with the development of organized scientific research for the military; the latter involved more money, more faculty, and more university energy than the officer training programs. Despite differences of scale, however, national-level economic, political, social, and cultural changes affected organized research and ROTC in similar ways. In both cases, the military understood that each university was different and that some flexibility had to be introduced to account for institutional variance. Just as the Office of Strategic Research and Development and the Office of Naval Research were willing to operate under decentralization, so too did ROTC evolve with variation from school to school.[7] Such a pattern fit in nicely with the traditional authority structure of the military, especially the navy, where Vincent Davis has described a "commitment to decentralization."[8] As with captains on a ship at sea, NROTC unit heads had a great deal of latitude with which to command their units.

For all the similarities, however, the financial arrangements of ROTC were much less lucrative for the schools involved than were those of the organized military research system. While the universities profited immensely from organized research, ROTC was, if anything, a losing financial proposition for the university communities of the 1950s and early 1960s. All three services paid a twenty-seven-dollar monthly stipend to cadets in their junior and senior years, but as noted above, only the navy (the smallest program, existing on only fifty-two campuses) paid scholarship money to selected students. As had been true before the war, the services paid the salaries and benefits of the uniformed staff, but the universities were responsible for providing classroom and office facilities, maintenance of those facilities, and secretarial support. Additionally, some universities paid the full cost of new facilities to house ROTC classes and offices. In 1955 the University of Texas paid all of the $1 million needed to construct a new ROTC armory, for example.[9] Although academics found plenty of reasons to support the existence of ROTC, direct financial benefit was not one of them.[10]

A Quest for Harmony

Differences between the military and university culture, values, and mission manifested themselves often in the debates over the goals and character of ROTC. The military preferred an officer preparation program that emphasized *training*, teaching the practical knowledge a man needed to have to become a junior officer the day after his graduation from college. The obvious person to conduct such training was, of course, a uniformed officer. University administrators, while conceding that some training was necessary, came to argue for *education* as the model of officer preparation. By education they meant the teaching, by civilian faculty, of courses such as psychology, history, engineering, and other fields relevant to the military profession. The two institutions also disagreed on issues of university oversight and the exact place of ROTC on the campus.

Still, while acknowledging these differences, leaders in the military and higher education firmly agreed on the importance of ROTC to the nation and the campus. Both institutions considered ROTC sufficiently important to devote considerable resources to monitoring the progress of officer training and keeping an eye toward reform and improvement. For the military, support for ROTC was a function of several factors:

1. A belief that the military needed a place on campus if it was to compete successfully with industry for talented men.
2. A more subtle desire to maintain good relations with higher education—the locus of critical military research.
3. A belief (especially prevalent in the army) that ROTC instilled civic awareness and patriotism;
4. The great cost-effectiveness of ROTC, especially in comparison to the service academies.
5. A desire to please members of Congress, most of whom were firm supporters of an on-campus military instruction program.

University administrators and faculty had their own reasons to support, or at least tolerate, ROTC:

1. A firm belief, especially among the highest officers of universities (themselves often ardent supporters of the Cold War), that American higher education had an obligation to assist in the prosecution of the Cold War as a service to society.
2. A desire to keep the military happy in an era in which, at several large research universities, government contracts were worth many millions of dollars. Total Department of Defense (DOD) outlays to universities for basic research alone equaled $105.7 million in 1958, and they continued to climb into the late 1960s.[11]
3. A fear that any negative statement about the military could be construed as "un-American" and lead to marginalization or dismissal.
4. A belief that ROTC contributed to good order on the campus and good citizenship in the undergraduate population.
5. A belief that training officers via ROTC would "civilianize" the military by infusing it with ideas from the universities. Concurrently, ROTC would prevent the creation of a military caste composed of officers trained at the service academies.
6. A desire to please groups with influence over the university, such as alumni, trustees, and state legislators, most of whom were staunch supporters of ROTC.

These reasons were sufficiently compelling to overshadow many areas of concern and disagreement. ROTC was important enough to attract the personal attention of university presidents, who attended ROTC honor ceremonies and balls, wrote letters to incoming freshmen encouraging their participation in ROTC, and corresponded with the admirals and generals in charge of the military administration of ROTC.[12] The program enjoyed strong support from those in charge of its welfare and rarely had to deal with vocal or sustained opposition. When asked in 1954 to communicate the most serious problem university administrators had with ROTC, Russell Thackrey of the American Association of State Universities and Land-Grant Colleges (AASULGC) stated that it was the "lowering of morale among students" because the end of the Korean War (and the subsequent reduction in the need for officers) would delay their entry into the active-duty armed forces.[13]

The quest for harmony meant that areas of dissonance, especially during the height of the Cold War, were muted. The universities and the services worked out problems through an informal process of congenial reform and compromise that allowed each side to defend its position on the patriotic grounds of better preparing the American officer. Dissent rarely made it into the public discourse because of a shared understanding that the health of the overall program and public perception of military-academic unity was more important than disagreement over any single issue.

The Cold War Background: "The Supreme Contest of Our Times"

A 1960 Army ROTC pamphlet made a case for ROTC:

> The educational systems of the Iron Curtain countries train their men as soldiers of the state first, and then as scientists, technicians, even painters and poets, as part of their over-all plans for world domination. From the privileged sanctuary of our campus quadrangles, laboratories and study halls, dare we forget for whom the bell tolls? It tolls not for the murdered students of Prague, Riga, and Warsaw, but for those now bent to the task of the extinguishment of man's hopes. It tolls for those who "don't have the time," for those who cynically ask "what's in it for me?" It tolls for all who fail to realize the nature of this supreme contest of our times.

Publications like these argued for the importance of ROTC to national and international security. Against the backdrop of global struggle, this pamphlet and others challenged students and administrators alike to place a heavy emphasis on the importance of ROTC: "It is inconsistent to admit an obliga-

tion to country in principle and to deny it in practice on the grounds of interference with academic freedom or competing demands for the student's
time. The Communist threat calls for realistic thinking in terms of survival,
or there can be no freedom, academic or otherwise, only time for re-
morse."[14] Such tough talk was intended to remind those connected with
ROTC of the critical need for unity and cooperation against the perceived
monolithic Communist threat.

These publications reflected much more than military propaganda. The
Cold War was a war of ideology; many Americans, civilian and military, believed that "the moral and democratic traditions" of America were under assault from without and within.[15] The only way to assure victory, many believed, was to teach American youth good civic virtue and moral values. The
schools and the military were the obvious places to inculcate such values,
and many believed that the latter was better positioned to do so. As Michigan State University president John Hannah said, "Teaching such fundamentals should be done at home and in school but it is not being done, and
the services provide the 'last chance' for society to do the job . . . [Without
such training] there is no assurance that our country will come out right in
the end."[16] Beliefs such as these implied that the universities needed to give
the military sufficient latitude to conduct training programs whose importance was central to national security and survival.

ROTC was particularly well suited to do the training that Hannah advocated, since it was both educational and military and it allowed military
training to take place within a civilian environment. The civilian environment was a special concern of many Americans as the nation moved from
the immediate postwar years (when most Americans looked forward to
rapid, large-scale demobilization of the armed forces) to the early years of
the Cold War (when a large standing army looked increasingly necessary). A
1950 presidential committee warned that to avoid military dominance of
American society, it was critical "to preserve within the military as much of
[the soldier's] civilian life as possible."[17] ROTC training, conducted as it was
at civilian colleges and universities, fit the bill quite well.

The Cold War environment of the 1950s thus buttressed ROTC's position
on campus by giving supporters a patriotic justification for their position and
opponents an incentive to remain quiescent. The years before World War II
had been marked by considerable controversy over the place of the military
on such college campuses as Johns Hopkins, Princeton, Wisconsin, and California. No such controversy existed in the 1950s, when supporters could

more easily defend their support for ROTC as being in the national interest than they could in the isolationist 1930s.

Furthermore, the military argued that modern weapons systems, such as long-range bombers and intercontinental ballistic missiles, necessitated increased attention to national preparedness. "We've got to be ready when the bell rings," said Air Force ROTC (AFROTC) commandant Brigadier General M. R. Deichelmann, "There will be no time to train pilots after the enemy strikes." Many university administrators agreed. Note the juxtapositions in Wheaton College registrar Enock Dyrness's 1954 address to a meeting of the Association of Higher Education: "[ROTC] is a recognized and respected part of the curriculum on each campus where it operates. The world situation makes it imperative that the United States maintain an adequate active military force backed by a strong body of reserves in all branches, adequately trained and prepared to meet any emergency which might arise. Because of modern weapons, the ROTC program has taken on new significance."[18] This environment of cooperation and agreement on the national security justifications for ROTC represented a significant departure from the environment of the 1930s.

As important as the changed national and international contexts were, McCarthyite fears inspired a loyalty oath at Berkeley and the investigation of more than one hundred professors by the House Committee on Un-American Activities. Thirty-one University of California faculty members lost their jobs in 1950 for refusing to sign the oath, and the University of Michigan fired two professors for alleged anti-American activities, despite the recommendations of a special faculty committee that they not be dismissed. Loyalty oaths were the result of a movement by "American Legionnaires, frightened parents, and many other narrowly patriotic citizen groups" to "censor textbooks and curricula in schools and colleges, and, where they did not already exist, to pass laws requiring loyalty oaths of all teachers." Nathan Pusey described this era as an "agitated and difficult time" in which accusations were leveled at teachers on all levels "as a special class" because of their influence on the young.[19]

As important as the forced signing of oaths and the actual purging of professors with views critical (or believed to be critical) of American military and foreign policy were "the incalculable effects of intimidation, which encouraged acceptance of the status quo and avoidance of politics."[20] Those faculty unconvinced by the merits of arguments in favor of ROTC therefore had reason to keep their objections to themselves. All faculty could make a visible demonstration of their patriotism by supporting ROTC, even if they had their own privately held convictions. The worst excesses of McCarthyism were over by 1954, but uncertainties over the possibility of its return and memories of the purges worked on people's minds and actions for years afterward. Moreover, issues of patriotism reemerged periodically; in 1958, for example, the National Defense Education Act required that all federal grant winners sign an oath of allegiance to the United States.

For administrators, the Cold War environment meant that decisions about ROTC had to be made on patriotic as well as curricular grounds. The comments of Harvard College dean John Monro are representative:

> An abstract case could be mounted—out of ignorance, to be sure—that military training has no place in the college and that such training should be moved out to summer cruises and camps, or post-graduate OCS [Officer Candidate School] . . . The powerful reason why the ROTC should stay in the colleges is that our national defense requires it . . . We may, indeed we must, argue about what subjects our military officers teach our students, about how much of our students' time they are to have, and how much credit we will finally allow for their training effort. But no responsible college administrator of my acquaintance argues that we should deprive the armed services of their most-favored recruiting position on our campuses.[21]

Similarly, most military and higher-education officials believed that college-educated men, privileged as they were by virtue of their education, had a responsibility to serve their nation through military service as an officer. In June 1951, the army, with the support of President Truman, took advantage of the crisis in Korea to assure passage, finally, of the Universal Military Training and Service Act. Several prominent Americans, including the president of Columbia University, Dwight Eisenhower, testified before Congress as early as 1948 to argue for universal military training for all physically fit males. As we have seen, many academics had reservations about UMT, but Truman's proposal received wide support in the end, despite loopholes that offered deferment from active-duty military service to more than two million men, including 333,000 in ROTC or the reserves.[22] Indeed, since it contained a proposal to allow local draft boards to grant students deferments, the Truman plan held out the potential to dramatically increase college enrollment.

While the act hardly lived up to its name by making military service universal, it reasserted the principle that every man owed his nation military service. It also encouraged men to join ROTC so that they might have more power over when and where they entered military service. For example, if one wanted to avoid conscription into the army (the navy and the air force relied exclusively on volunteers) one could sign up for Naval or Air Force ROTC, thus assuring that if military service was likely or desirable, it would at least be on one's own terms. Enlisting could also help a man get the kind of military training or overseas assignment he desired. The Universal Military Training and Service Act therefore served to boost ROTC enrollments by providing cadets immediate deferments and more pleasant military service in the officer corps.

Service as an officer may not have been a young man's first career choice, but national and international contexts forced him to think seriously about it. The 1950s were a time of Cold War, but they were also, as Vincent Davis, Elaine Tyler May, and others have noted, an extended period of normalcy. Thus the Cold War held a peculiar place within the traditional American pattern of pacifism in peace and bellicosity in war. While the perception of a Soviet threat drove some men into ROTC so that they might be prepared should war arise, for many others the lure of good jobs in a growing economy loomed large. For these men, military life seemed "uncongenial." Though he may have been "suspicious of . . . professional military men," conscription nonetheless forced the typical college student to rethink his relationship to the military. [23]

The draft held an important place in the minds of young American men at a time when the logic of universal military participation was at its height; the air force directed internal studies in the early 1950s that concluded, to its great dismay, that UMT, not the chance to fly, was the primary reason men signed up for AFROTC.[24] The conscription of celebrities like Elvis Presley and Willie Mays made universality visible.[25] If the lives of these public icons could be disrupted, there was little reason for a college student to hope to be able automatically to avoid service. "They'll get us anyway," said one Georgia Tech student in 1951. "I'd rather be in the Air Force than the infantry."[26] The power that selective service had over college men is evident in the words of one student-poet:

> Today in college
> To gain more knowledge
> More and more I strive.
> A student deferment

Is my preferment
'Til I reach thirty-five.
But Selective Service
Has me nervous
They grant but one degree.
Despite my plea
For a Ph.D.
They offer me P.F.C.[27]

In this vein, the army executive staff argued that "it would be a waste of [the college-educated man's] knowledge and leadership potential to serve in an enlisted capacity even though that enlisted service might be in the field of his academic major."[28] In other words, it was more important for educated men to be officers and leaders than to be in a position suited to their technical talents, in part because having educated men in the officer corps demonstrated that the "best" sectors of American society were doing their part. After all, as the army argued, "It cannot be repeated too often that Man, Communist or Free, is the ultimate weapon. It behooves us to make certain that he is given the best leaders possible."[29]

The military's Cold War policy of insisting on the accession of college graduates as junior officers is consistent with the shifts described by sociologist Morris Janowitz in *The Professional Soldier.* Janowitz argued that the growing complexity of military technology and the ever-expanding links between the military and the civilian worlds necessitated by technological change greatly accelerated the military's movement away from arbitrary discipline and toward group consensus. Because of this growing technological and logistical complexity, fewer men were serving in the combat arms (the military's "tooth") and more were serving in highly specialized support roles (the "tail"). Thus the junior officer ceased out of necessity to be "the raspy-voiced cavalry officer" and became more like "the junior executive" found in civilian industries. The latter role called for more "competence and technical ability" to manage the specialized information of the new military "without resort to arbitrary and ultimate sanctions."[30]

In other words, the military now needed to recruit large numbers of experts in such diverse fields as public relations, engineering, and financial administration, in both the enlisted and officer ranks. Such men were no longer the typical laborer or foot soldier "assumed to be ignorant." They needed, in the words of a 1961 University of Washington committee, "academic skills not even dreamed of by their predecessors."[31] Having college-educated men in the officer corps, it was assumed, would create a corps of leaders familiar with a diverse body of knowledge and technical skills.

"Leadership" to the military planners of the 1950s meant something more akin to management based on psychology and group dynamics than what Janowitz called the hero model of the past. With this shift in leadership definitions came a concurrent shift away from authoritarianism as a means of structuring the military; instead, military leaders were expected to invoke a sense of "solidarity" among the men they led. Successful manager-officers therefore needed to be more sophisticated than the old "hero" types. The universities were the obvious training ground for the sort of well-rounded, educated men the military believed it needed to manage the increasingly complex and technical men and machines of the Cold War military.

The focus on education had relatively little to do with soldiering, flying, or sailing; many fine military officers lacked traditional degrees. Rather, education would help the military attain legitimacy and prestige by countering "the image of the military as something apart from and alien to civilian society."[32] In the words of Vance Mitchell:

> While academic education offered no guarantee of either intelligence or competence, it, along with experience, provided the foundation for the future growth of the individual. Experience and education constituted personal potential that, with maturation and the proper stimulation, could translate into achievement. High academic achievement also indicated individual ambition, a will to overcome obstacles, a capacity to solve problems, a capacity to deal with adversity, and the ability to get along with people. Further, college-educated officers would likely have better perspectives on and insights into the complex issues of civil-military relations, leadership, management, and America's role in the post-war world.[33]

The military was not alone in its drive to increase its legitimacy through formal education. In 1951 fewer than half of America's lawyers had college degrees.[34]

The Cold War also changed the focus of ROTC production from the reserves to active-duty forces. Prior to the Korean War, the *R* in ROTC correctly denoted its central function as producing officers for the reserves. Very few "distinguished graduates" became eligible for regular commissions in the immediate postwar years; the majority of officers produced through ROTC before 1952 entered the reserve component of their commissioning service. With the national defense buildup that accompanied the outbreak of hostilities in Korea, however, ROTC began increasingly to provide and retain officers for the active-duty forces. The American military needed more officers on active duty; one solution to this problem was simply to assign ROTC graduates directly to active duty instead of to the reserves.

In this vein, in November 1952 the assistant secretary of defense (manpower and personnel) directed that "the Reserve Officers' Training Corps program will be based upon the needs of the active-duty Armed Forces and upon a policy that all graduates will be called to active duty for a minimum of twenty-four months."[35] The percentage of AFROTC graduates assigned to active duty rose from 34 percent in 1951 to 79 percent in 1953 and peaked at 91 percent the following year. The policy of assigning ROTC cadets to active duty survived the Korean War intact; throughout the 1950s the services assigned 80 percent or more of their ROTC graduating classes to active duty, denoting the central place ROTC had assumed in the military's plans for active duty officers.[36]

The place of ROTC became even more central as academy graduates began to leave the services in increasing numbers. In 1958 *Look* magazine described what it called a "military manpower scandal" wherein unusually high numbers of academy graduates were completing their required tours of duty and then leaving. These men were resigning in larger numbers due to the strong job prospects available to them in private industry and the stress that military life placed on their families. As a result, *Look* noted, ROTC officers were becoming even more critical to staffing the American officer corps.[37]

This shift from reserve to active duty production meant fundamental changes. Previously, men could leave ROTC secure in the knowledge that, since they were entering the reserves, they could concurrently begin their civilian career. Now men completing their ROTC courses faced the real prospect of immediate active-duty service and time away from their chosen profession. In the 1920s and 1930s, ROTC had allowed a man to train for military service as a complement to his mostly civilian career. After Korea, ROTC represented a conflict between one's civilian pursuits and one's military obligations.

Sources of Tension

Despite a consensus on the importance of ROTC to the nation, fundamental philosophical differences between the military and university communities created disagreements. Despite occasional tensions, the quest for harmony was never abandoned; disagreements never produced a desire to remove ROTC from the campus or even to introduce significant structural reform. Nevertheless, four issues were argued nationwide: the place of ROTC on the campus; the appropriate level of communication between the services and the host schools; the importance of ROTC to national and campus life; and the compulsory nature of ROTC training at many colleges and universities.

The Place of ROTC on the Campus

Unlike instructors in most civilian college programs, ROTC faculty did not possess Ph.D.s, seek tenure, nominate candidates for degrees, or serve on university-wide committees. ROTC instructors rarely remained at a single school for longer than a three-year tour of duty.[38] Nevertheless, ROTC programs were set up as full academic departments to make military instruction more respectable in the eyes of students and to encourage civilian faculty to treat the uniformed officers as peers rather than interlopers. Furthermore, ROTC officers owed their first allegiance to an outside agency that paid their salary and with whom they had taken an oath of service. All of these characteristics distinguished ROTC from other academic departments, yet the universities rarely challenged the elevated stature of ROTC during the height of the Cold War.

As McCarthyism faded in the late 1950s, academics became more assertive in addressing these distinctions. The anomaly of departmental status was one concern, because it pointed out the need to clearly define the relationship between the services and the universities. Russell Thackrey, executive secretary of the AALGCSU, like virtually all administrators of this period, firmly believed that the universities, especially the public universities his organization represented, had an unwavering responsibility to the nation to cooperate with the services in producing officers. He was dismayed, however, by what he saw as an increasingly separate military program with very few intellectual links to the remainder of the university community. In writing to University of Illinois president David Henry, he said, "I doubt if we can any longer say with conviction, as we once could say, that the ROTC is wholly an integral part of the academic program of the institution, run on the basis of full cooperation and joint participation by the institution and the Armed Services. There are an increasing number—not large as yet but growing—of requirements that are non-academic and related wholly to the military, not the university." Among the strictly military issues of concern to

Thackrey was the military's policy of running security checks on advanced ROTC cadets, a policy created within the context of McCarthyite Cold War anxieties and consistent with drives at many schools, including many ROTC hosts, to require loyalty oaths from faculty.[39]

David Henry, for his part, agreed with both of Thackrey's propositions: that the universities, especially the land-grant schools required by the Morrill Act to offer military instruction, had a responsibility to assist in the national defense, and that universities "should classify the ROTC program, not as an academic program completely integrated with the university [read: department], but as a cooperative program for which we have limited responsibility."[40] These men envisioned a place for ROTC units analogous to that occupied by postwar research institutes like the University of Michigan's Institute for Social Research and MIT's Lincoln Labs. Such facilities received support exclusively from outside funds, had faculty who did not teach classes in the general university, "had extra academic origins and were products to some extent of federal interest." Like ROTC, these institutes were not frontally academic in nature and therefore "presented new problems to university administrators."[41]

A move to institute status for ROTC would separate it from the larger educational mission of the university and amount to a declaration that ROTC was not an educational program. As Thackrey and Henry must have known they would, the services viewed the proposal as a denigration of ROTC and rejected the idea. During this period, no university administrator tried to remove, or even challenge, ROTC's status as a department, but the notion that the universities should formally acknowledge the differing missions of ROTC and the academic departments had been advanced and would return.

Communication between Service and School

The universities and the services also debated the appropriate level of communication between service and university. The services designed and managed the training of their massive World War II and Korean War OCS programs and the curricula of the three service academies without interference from civilian educators. They assumed that they could operate ROTC programs in much the same manner. Indeed, for much of the 1950s administrators seemed willing to acquiesce to allowing the services to train officers as they saw fit. By the end of the decade, however, the universities were asserting their desire to have a voice in the running of ROTC.

University presidents like Michigan State's John Hannah were especially disturbed that the services were imposing changes without consulting the schools affected. In 1957, as a representative of the AALGCSU, whose schools then accounted for 55 percent of all ROTC graduates, he told an Armed Forces Policy Board how "seriously concerned" he and his colleagues were about the worsening relationship between the services and higher education.[42] Harvard's John Monro observed three years later, "I know of no program of comparable size and importance where regular communication could be so valuable, and is in fact so poor."[43] Serious problem areas were beginning to develop, and with relatively few open channels of communication, those problems did not receive the attention they deserved.

The comments of Thackrey, Henry, and Hannah reveal that some educators, while not questioning the value of ROTC, nevertheless desired to see military control of the program somewhat diminished. They wanted more input on key decisions and a voice in directing a program that was, they argued, populated by students for whom they had ultimate responsibility. They were willing to acknowledge and accept "limited" responsibility, not to yield all responsibility.

The Importance of ROTC to Campus and National Life

During the years of the Cold War, university presidents and the service ROTC staffs developed different understandings of the importance of ROTC. The presidents, conditioned by their early compromises with the military and their own Cold War ideology, saw ROTC as crucial to national security and, closer to home, as a vital instrument for maintaining civic virtue and order on campus. The University of Texas, for example, permitted students to count one semester of ROTC training as a substitute for the university's American government requirement, on the assumption that ROTC served as a kind of laboratory in American civics.[44]

The services, however, saw ROTC as an extension of the military, subject to fundamental change without consultation of the hosts if national and international events necessitated. An incident from the early 1960s demonstrates this difference in definition. The army, faced with chronic ROTC budget shortfalls, decided to save money by asking all host units to reduce AROTC enrollments to 85 percent of their previous year's freshman enrollments. To Major General Frederick Warren, the highest ranking army officer with direct oversight of ROTC, the plan seemed sensible enough, but university presidents and chancellors sent a barrage of sharp and angry letters to the army in protest both of the substance and the execution of the order. This incident is important because of how it exposed the poor channels of communication between those responsible for ROTC and for its demonstration of the high level of support ROTC enjoyed among university presidents.

Warren had erroneously assumed that Army ROTC units were detachments of the larger army and could therefore be ordered to comply with changes in army policy. In fact, he had created a policy that stood in direct conflict with university policies and, in some cases, state laws that university administrators saw as superseding any directives from the army. Furthermore, the universities interpreted his order as weakening ROTC and thus also the national defense. Campus officials saw themselves as defending the integrity of national security against the erosion proposed, ironically enough, by the United States Army.

Those institutions that required men to take ROTC to qualify for graduation opposed the army's order because, in the words of University of Kentucky president Frank Dickey, "By imposing a ceiling on the number of freshmen who can enroll in the Army ROTC you are, in effect, abrogating this college requirement."[45] Furthermore, such states as Illinois, Kansas, Maine, and West Virginia had laws requiring male underclassmen at land-grant colleges to take ROTC. The Morrill Act of 1862 that created the land-grant colleges required them to offer military instruction, and the state legislatures had interpreted the act as requiring all male students to take ROTC. In his letter to Warren, West Virginia University president Paul Miller told him flatly, "We will not be in a position to effect the modifications delineated in your letter" because they would violate the laws of West Virginia.[46]

To exempt men from military service in order to save money seemed foolish to many administrators. The Right Reverend Wilfrid Nash, president of Gannon College in Erie, Pennsylvania, wrote to Warren: "The future of the United States depends, in great part, on the caliber of men who select the Army as their career. As soon as Military Science becomes limited I fear that many qualified boys will not have the opportunity to learn from experience the value of the Army . . . I fear that the cut-back will greatly lower the standards of the ROTC in the years ahead."[47] R. H. Woods, president of Murray State College in Kentucky also felt that Warren was proposing a diminution of national defense. "I feel that Military Science is important in college life and important to our national well-being and the program needs to be stable," he wrote. "If this [reduction] is done, the result may be very harmful to the future of the ROTC program."[48]

In the midst of this debate, a Duquesne University student wrote an editorial in the student newspaper questioning the "wisdom, not the right" of the university to impose compulsory ROTC.[49] Duquesne University president Henry McAnulty responded with a personal letter to the author: "This administration feels that the required basic ROTC course for all non-veteran, male students is, at this time, to the best interests of the nation and Duquesne University . . . Perhaps you might be happier at another school more in conformity with your personal philosophy of education and life."[50] University officials had their own views of the contributions ROTC made to national defense, the development of civic responsibility, and the quality of campus life. These views were not necessarily in conflict with those of the military, but neither did they overlap perfectly. Their differences would manifest themselves again in the debate over the value of compulsory ROTC in the nation's universities (see below).

Warren's attempt to order the universities into compliance with a policy decision made without their consultation failed. Within two weeks of the first responses to Warren's letter, Secretary of Defense Robert McNamara approved additional funding so that 106,000 freshmen could be enrolled, as opposed to the 84,500 Warren had originally envisioned.[51] Warren again wrote to the presidents, to tell them that his order was rescinded "because of great concern evidenced by institutions in this matter."[52] University administrators felt strongly that ROTC was critical to the security of the nation and the quality of campus life, and they were willing to fight a two-star general to prove it.

This debate reveals the differing goals and directions that the military and officers in higher education had for ROTC. For the former, ROTC represented a cheap, reliable method for meeting annual officer production requirements. For the latter, ROTC represented a training program for both military and civilian pursuits. Most academic administrators believed that ROTC taught civic responsibility, discipline, and morality. For all these reasons, then, they hoped for continuance of what they understood as an implied agreement by the military to pay for mandatory ROTC. They thus angrily read Warren's order as being "in direct violation of a pledge [by the DOD] to maintain required ROTC at institutions desiring it."[53] In fact, the military was trying to move away from required ROTC, setting up another debate over the meaning and rationale for supporting officer education programs on civilian campuses.

Compulsory ROTC: A Military Necessity?

The furor caused by Warren's letter occurred in the midst of a debate over the national security justifications of compulsory ROTC. University administrators, as we have seen, objected to Warren's order on the grounds that it abrogated university and state requirements that all male freshmen and sophomores take ROTC and that it had the potential to undermine the national security contributions of on-campus military instruction. Even as they made the argument, however, virtually all compulsory programs were reconsidering the issue of compulsory ROTC in light of discussions with DOD and service officials that indicated, paradoxically, that those in the defense establishment saw no military reason for compulsory ROTC and, indeed, many were strongly opposed to it. Ironically, the university administrators, not the military, were the champions of compulsory ROTC.

ROTC was compulsory throughout the 1950s on more than half of the campuses hosting the program and at more than two in three land-grant colleges. As noted earlier, some of these schools had experienced controversy over the issue of compulsory military training in the 1920s and 1930s, in debates rooted in post–World War I pacifism and isolationism, but most schools had held to their compulsory programs. By the mid-1950s, few people were arguing for the abolition of compulsory ROTC on isolationist grounds; instead, the dominant arguments held that compulsory ROTC was too costly and too burdensome on the schedule of the contemporary college undergraduate. As college curricula became more demanding and student time more precious, the issue of compulsory ROTC became visible on enough campuses to compel the National Association of State Universities and Land Grant Colleges to address it.[54]

In 1957 Troy Middleton, president of Louisiana State University and chairman of the NASULGC Committee on National Defense, wrote to Secretary of Defense Charles Wilson to get clarification on the legal basis for compulsory basic ROTC programs. Most administrators were firm supporters of compulsory ROTC and expected the DOD to return an unequivocal statement of support that they could use as ammunition against the minority among them pushing for reform. They felt surprised and betrayed by the responses from the DOD. The army reported that it could find no federal authority requiring ROTC and no army policy in the history of the program to justify support of compulsory military education.[55] The secretary of the army's general counsel found that "the Army Staff has stated that ever since the establishment of ROTC in 1916, the Department of the Army has consistently held that the question of whether basic ROTC shall be compulsory or elective is purely a matter of individual institutional prerogative."[56]

If no law or policy could be found that required or compelled compulsory ROTC, the institutions next asked if the services believed that the mandatory military education of male underclassmen contributed to the defense of the nation. The air force and navy returned a quick "no." The navy, which offered the most scholarship aid to its ROTC students and therefore ran the most expensive ROTC program per capita, used the scholarship application process as a primary recruitment and selection base; therefore it did not need to select advanced midshipmen from a large population of basic midshipmen. The heart of the air force's program, flight training, was simply too expensive for the air force to expend resources on instruction and uniforms for thousands of students taking ROTC only because they were forced to do so.[57] An internal air force study conducted in 1959 showed that AFROTC taught twenty cadets for every officer produced.[58] Senior air force officials argued that dropping required basic ROTC would have no appreciable impact on advanced enrollment and, therefore, on officer production, because the cadets who were "lost" to the program were unmotivated to begin with.[59] In other words, the air force saw no value in paying the costs to educate, clothe, equip, and train men who did not want to become officers. As a professor of aerospace studies at Rutgers University noted, "There is no place in the cockpit for a man who is not a volunteer."[60]

The army, however, always concerned with numbers, argued that it needed the compulsory basic course to attract enough students to sign up for the advanced course.[61] The army also contended, in accord with the arguments of educators, that ROTC training should be compulsory because of what it did for those who did not seek a commission:

> A vital secondary mission of the Army ROTC program is to impart valuable citizenship training, develop leadership potential, stimulate and motivate the student for future service in behalf of the nation, his community, and his fellow man. This training is upheld by the Army as valuable beyond calculation in the development of healthy, public spirited citizens, aware of their responsibilities of American citizenship, willing through self-sacrifice

to assume the responsibilities of American citizenship in whatever professional pursuit the college student may elect to pursue.[62]

The army wanted its ROTC policy to be consistent with its support of the draft, partly on the basis of its ability to promote "moral welfare" and "character guidance."[63]

Officials in all services agreed, however, that compulsory ROTC had several drawbacks: it was expensive, unpopular with most students, and inefficient. Several student newspapers had opposed mandatory ROTC for years; the *Targum* at Rutgers had been arguing for a voluntary ROTC program since 1949. Like most campus newspapers, the *Targum* did not oppose mandatory ROTC on philosophical or moral grounds, but because it "imposed an unnecessary academic burden on freshmen."[64] It also acted to create a group of "cynical upperclassmen who can effectively recite drill field traumas and classroom incidents."[65]

For all of these reasons, the air force favored making all units elective. The official Air Force ROTC history for 1964 reads:

> Corollary to changing the public image of AFROTC, we pressed for elimination of mandatory attendance in basic ROTC . . . Such a requirement, while imposed by the institution, was generally believed by the student to be a service imposed requirement and for those not initially motivated for AFROTC, the requirement simply generated discontent that spread throughout the class and school, further impairing the desired image of AFROTC and the desirability of a career as an Air Force officer.[66]

The DOD emphatically agreed: "Compulsory basic ROTC is not needed to meet quality standards nor is it needed to produce the number of officers required. Surveys of the academic standings of ROTC officers in the Service Schools following commissioning do not furnish conclusive evidence as to whether elective or compulsory programs produce the higher quality officers."[67]

These responses frustrated university administrators who believed in the value of compulsory military education. John Hannah, president of Michigan State, complained, "We are now seriously concerned because of the repeated and continuing evidence that the Armed Services and the Defense Department no longer regard the ROTC programs as worthy of vigorous support by them."[68] Russell Thackrey, the NASULGC's executive secretary, wrote, "As to required ROTC: I think it fair to say that most of our Presidents feel it is a lost cause . . . With few exceptions, [university administrators] still believe that the elimination of required ROTC would be a costly mistake from the standpoint of the Department of Defense, but that it is not up to them to fight this battle."[69] Given the DOD's inability to identify a military need for compulsory basic ROTC, the administrators began to rethink fundamental assumptions. Thackrey told a reporter from the *New York Times* that the land-grant schools were now willing to consider a change. "College Trustees, faced with meeting rapidly rising enrollments and increasing costs, naturally are inclined to re-examine their responsibility for requiring a program which the Department of Defense itself does not consider of real importance to national security."[70] In 1960 the NASULGC decided on a policy of indifference toward whether its members required basic ROTC for graduation. The former policy of strong preference for compulsory basic ROTC "was chiefly predicated on the theory that the Department of Defense considered the requirement of Basic ROTC as a distinct contribution to the national defense program." Such a theory no longer being defensible, a policy of indifference now seemed appropriate.[71] The army held to an official policy of support for compulsory basic ROTC, but Warren's 1962 debacle over the 85 percent enrollment order undermined that policy's legitimacy by demonstrating that the army believed that it could operate optimally with significantly less than 100 percent enrollment.

Without a strong statement of support from the DOD and with civilian curricula becoming more demanding, many universities abandoned compulsory basic ROTC. Even at the University of Illinois, where the program had been compulsory since the school's opening in 1868 and had produced more senior army officers than any school except West Point, a 1960 poll of University of Illinois students found 71 percent against continuing the program on a compulsory basis. Later that year a faculty committee recommended changing to voluntary ROTC because of the absence of a national need for the required program.[72] In 1961 Illinois president David Henry informed the DOD that he expected university enrollment in the coming years to increase by 50 percent and that he could not ask the state to pay for facilities for the military training of all of the males if the DOD could not defend that training as necessary for national defense.[73]

Most administrators were displeased with the change. University of Arizona president Richard Harvill told Major General Warren that he believed compulsory basic ROTC to be vital to creating a large pool of men from which the services could choose their officers, but that "it is very clear that the efforts of those of us who have believed strongly in compulsory basic ROTC and have opposed relaxation of this requirement have been fighting a losing battle and did not have the support of top-level military officials in this country."[74] Those military officials were more interested in keeping ROTC inexpensive than in using it as a citizenship-training program.

The Illinois state legislature removed the law requiring basic ROTC for graduation from the University of Illinois in time for it to open the 1963–64 academic year with a voluntary ROTC program for the first time.[75] Other schools converting to voluntary programs in this era included Ohio State, Washington, Michigan State, Kansas State, Missouri, Connecticut, Rutgers, Colorado State, Texas A & M, Nebraska, Iowa, Iowa State, Oregon, Florida State, Maine, and Idaho. Between 1961 and 1965, sixty Army ROTC units and fifty-nine Air Force ROTC units switched from compulsory to voluntary. Thirty-nine of the army units and thirty-two of the air force units were at land-grant schools or their satellites.[76] Even as early as 1963 the air force had benefited from the switch to voluntary training by saving fifty-seven officer positions and $572,375 in uniform costs.[77] For the first time since its creation in 1916, compulsory basic ROTC had become the exception, not the rule.

Students across the nation rejoiced. The Rutgers student newspaper ran an extra edition to celebrate "a day that should become memorable in the history of Rutgers."[78] As expected, ROTC enrollments quickly fell at many schools (though, ironically, not at Rutgers). Enrollment in the basic AROTC program at the University of Illinois fell from 2,195 in the final mandatory year, 1963, to just 350 in the first voluntary year, 1964—a drop of 84 percent. Advanced enrollments there fell as well, though not as sharply, from 243 to 206.[79] Of greater concern to the services, predictions that the production of commissioned officers would not suffer proved to be inaccurate (see Chapter 3). Certainly much of this drop was to be expected, and some of it was welcomed in the interests of economy, but the shock of the drop and concern over where it might bottom out led to further changes to make the program "salable," to attract men freely into the program.

The ROTC of the 1950s was not the same ROTC that had existed in the 1930s. ROTC changed to meet the needs of the Cold War–era American military. It took on renewed importance because it produced active-duty officers instead of the reserve officers it had produced before the Korean War. The Cold War provided a national context of urgency—and for many, fear—that permitted the military to take almost sole control of the program until the very end of the 1950s. University administrators shared the national sense of urgency and acceded to military control, in large part because they believed it to be the best way to prepare the American officer for the tasks he would face. Tensions, however, existed over the value of ROTC and the exact character that it should assume. Throughout this period, educators and officers agreed on the value of ROTC but disagreed significantly on how it should look, act, and operate.

CHAPTER 3

The Origins of Postwar Dissatisfaction

It is important that ROTC units should be more adequately integrated into the life of the university than they are at present. Certain
aspects of the curricula, the preparation of teachers, appointments,
and promotions are items on which we do not at the present time
have common practices.

—Dean of Arts and Sciences W. F. Dyde, University of Colorado, 1956

The Cold War forced the ROTC program into the new and uncharted territory of preparing large numbers of active-duty officers for an increasingly
complex and diffuse military. The very definition of ROTC was in flux, as
was the relationship of the military to American society. In many realms, including education, the military's influence far exceeded what it had been in
the years immediately before World War II. The re-formation and re-creation of ROTC on campus, then, led to a ten- to fifteen-year period of debate
about what kind of program ROTC ought to be to prepare junior officers for
the Cold War world. These questions had a direct impact on the relationship
between universities and the military and, of course, on the daily life of the
officer candidates themselves.

Because the services assumed that "in an age of atomic weapons, the next
attack would be fast, a surprise, and would strike the homeland," the life of
the ROTC cadet in the 1950s and early 1960s revolved around training in
strictly military subjects designed to prepare him to be immediately useful
to the armed services.[1] The services were primarily concerned with using
ROTC to produce men who could step directly from their college graduation
into a junior officer position. That responsibility notwithstanding, the Cold
War represented an era of what Samuel Huntington has called "fusion" between civilian and military expertise that demanded that "military leaders

incorporate political, economic, and social factors into their thinking."[2] The Cold War thus represented a tension between the need for immediate availability (which implied a narrow training focus for officer candidates) and fusion (which implied a broader, more general education).

At the same time, American higher education was beginning to adopt a much more international focus. Universities developed several new courses and concentrations in area studies, humanities, and social sciences that were designed to better inform American undergraduates about the world to which the United States now found itself inexorably tied. Ironically, the tight professional curriculum of ROTC programs meant that military training programs stood apart from these changes. Academic thinking and fusionist ideals were thus moving in the same direction, toward a more well-rounded collegiate education for ROTC candidates. As a result, by the end of the 1950s many academics came to argue for an increased presence of civilian courses in the ROTC curriculum in order to include cadets in the new areas of instruction.

Furthermore, the ROTC curriculum became a point of contention with academics who disliked the increasing presence of vocationally based courses in American universities. ROTC, they argued, was not only vocational but also exclusively geared to producing workers for a single employer. To defenders of a more classic liberal arts model of higher education, ROTC represented one manifestation of a growing and disturbing trend. Notably, the strongest calls for reform came from academics in liberal arts colleges, while those in professional programs, such as engineering schools, were more satisfied with the status quo.

While academics were willing to cede to the military some latitude, in acknowledgment of the severity of the military and political crisis of the Cold War, they were not willing to be silent partners. In keeping with their traditional desire to be active participants in the process of educating military officers, they lobbied the military to include courses from civilian offerings that were relevant, they argued, to the military profession. Throughout the Cold War, Moderate Whig beliefs remained powerful, resulting in a push for a "civilianization" of the ROTC curriculum and closer links between the professional military curriculum and the regular civilian curriculum.

ROTC and the Campus: The Wright Stuff

In 1950 the army introduced an illustrative comic book–style recruitment ad that followed the college career of a character named Ted Wright, a freshman at "State" who lacked "what it takes to step up and introduce himself."[3] Ted, on the recommendation of his faculty advisor (an ROTC grad himself), joins ROTC, and we follow him through his classes and collegiate adventures. Ted's activities are limited to strictly military events, like parades and planning the military ball. The advantages of ROTC are clearly spelled out: "ROTC men looked mighty sharp in the officer type uniform that's issued to them! Free of charge, too!"; "This training, with it's [sic] emphasis on teamwork and coordination was a help in football and other sports"; "Squeezing the trigger on the rifle range trains the eye and steadies the nerves"; and ROTC provides "self-confidence and leadership."

"Ted found that ROTC paid off in other ways, too," when a coed asked, "Ted, you're getting so many decorations, are you a General or something?"[4] Throughout the ad, there is an unmistakable message that ROTC cadets had access to the campus's most respected women, who existed as trophies for the successful cadets. In recalling his experiences as a cadet, Ted's faculty advisor remembers a woman telling him, "You remind me of the song 'There is something about a soldier.'" Ted finds the same rewards. At the annual military ball, his date says, "I wouldn't have missed this for anything." "Yes you would if you weren't going steady with an ROTC man," he replies. A 1960 booklet, *You and the Army ROTC,* told prospective students that "at most colleges and universities, the Annual Military Ball is one of the outstanding campus social events of the year—one the girl you're dating won't want to miss."[5] ROTC thus took on a peculiarly masculine air, deriving a share of the rationale for its existence from its presumed ability to make men out of boys.

The military had long played a role in "making men" in American society, including via the army's management of the Civilian Conservation Corps in the 1930s. But ROTC did not assume a large role in carrying out the military's new policy of racial integration. In a telling example of the power of localism in ROTC management, the program focused almost exclusively on fostering white manhood, despite its traditional presence on some historically black campuses. Although de jure integration of the armed forces occurred in 1948 and de facto integration began during the Korean War, ROTC still operated in keeping with the campus's segregated local environment.[6] Formal desegregation of the armed services brought little change to ROTC units, especially in the South. Because ROTC existed as a partnership between the military and higher education, it had elements of both institutions. While the military was quite clearly still dominated by whites, it had received a formal mandate to become more inclusive. Higher education, especially in the South, had no such mandate.

Academia, like the military, could be said to have some generally unified interests, but neither institution could be said to be monolithic. The interests of northern and southern universities were sometimes at odds, especially on the touchy issue of integration. In 1961, the Presidential Civil Rights Commission, headed by Michigan State University president John Hannah, called upon President John Kennedy to complete the integration of the national defense establishment by ending the enduring segregation of National Guard and ROTC units in place in "most Southern states."[7] The problem of segregation was a serious one for many educators, including Hannah. The Air Force ROTC Advisory Panel of 1963 noted that sixteen AFROTC units, including such large units as those at Auburn, Louisiana State, Louisiana Tech, Mississippi State, Baylor, and Southern Methodist, practiced segregation.[8]

Acknowledging the existence of segregation did not necessarily imply swift action, however. The air force noted that those segregated schools produced 297 officers in 1962, about one in eleven of that year's AFROTC graduates. The air force argued that it could ill afford to lose these graduates, nor did it wish "to change institutional policy that is based on state or local laws or is fixed by institutional governing bodies."[9] Several key members of Congress, most significantly House Democrat F. Edward Hébert of Louisiana, opposed the integration of ROTC. As a result, the desegregation of these units was not a high priority for either civilian or military officials until American society and law were transformed by passage of the Civil Rights Act of 1964. Substantial integration of ROTC did not begin until the 1970s (see Chapter 5).

ROTC was most popular among white male students, and it carried some distinct advantages, such as visibly demonstrating one's patriotism. A 1950 survey of 1,503 students from twenty-six schools across the nation showed that even among the half of the survey population not enrolled in ROTC, more than 90 percent believed that ROTC should be offered, though only one in three thought that training should be compulsory. Three in four of the students who were enrolled in basic ROTC courses reported that they planned to continue on to advanced ROTC, although a somewhat smaller proportion actually did so.[10] The ROTC students surveyed noted that the program conveyed prestige and the possibility for career advancement.[11] The popularity of ROTC also derived from a shared sense among college students that ROTC was "a worthy and valuable institution, vitally necessary to the defense of our country."[12]

Students joined ROTC for various reasons, but in the Cold War era many joined because the military had become a highly respected American institution and an attractive (if, for most, temporary) employer, particularly when compared to the military job environment in the years before World War II. Mark Grandstaff argues that between 1945 and 1955 the military conducted a successful public relations campaign to convince middle-class Americans that a "modern military career was similar to other middle-class careers" and that it "offered youth a respected occupation that placed self-sacrifice above profit and was rewarded with educational and promotion opportunities, good pay, fringe benefits, and retirement pensions."[13] Whether due to this public relations campaign or not, the military enjoyed a great deal of prestige in the 1950s. In a 1955 survey, male teenagers listed "officer in the armed services" as their fifth most highly esteemed occupation, above even "minister or priest."[14]

The improvements in American attitudes toward the military were combined with real improvements in the nature of the military job environment. The Officer Personnel Act (OPA) of 1947 rationalized and streamlined officer promotions, more systematically basing them on merit rather than seniority. In fact, the OPA probably increased the control that academy graduates had over the field grades, but it made the system of military promotion appear more equitable. Two years later, Congress approved an 18.8 percent military pay raise (another large pay raise would come in 1958) and introduced a twenty-year retirement plan that was, in Grandstaff's words, "more lucrative than many companies' retirement plans."[15] In 1956 Congress approved the extension of medical benefits to dependents. In short, as the military became a more attractive military career, ROTC became a more attractive—and popular—college activity.

Still, careerism remained rare among ROTC graduates. Given the importance of the draft in student decision making, it is not surprising that few ROTC cadets expressed a great desire to make the military their life's work. In 1958 only 39 percent of AFROTC graduates stated that they had an interest in making the service their career.[16] Most ROTC graduates "looked toward a more lucrative civilian job market for their (long term) career choices."[17] Table 3.1 demonstrates the lack of commitment of ROTC officers, especially in comparison to academy graduates and graduates from the army's Officer Candidate School and the air force's Officer Training School (OTS).

The figures in Table 3.1 were borne out in reenlistment rates. In the late 1950s, 70 percent of all air force officers contracted to serve beyond their obligation, but only 28 percent of AFROTC-trained officers did so.[18] Samuel Huntington summed up the military's officer accession dilemma nicely when he wrote: "Academy graduates have education and commitment but not numbers; ROTC men have numbers and education but not commitment; OCS men have numbers and commitment but not education."[19] The services showed their desire for education over commitment by consistently preferring ROTC graduates to OCS graduates and by sharing President Eisenhower's mandate that all officers needed "a background of general knowledge similar to that possessed by graduates of our leading universities."[20] With ROTC, Eisenhower's mandate was fulfilled to the letter.

Lack of career commitment notwithstanding, the large population of students on which ROTC could draw meant that the overall quality of cadets was high. Entrance into the advanced program was dependent on a formal application process and the approval of the instructional staff of the unit. The very worst students could therefore easily be kept out of the advanced portion of ROTC. A 1952 air force survey found that 46 percent of senior cadets and 40 percent of junior cadets were in the top third of their academic class. Only 4 percent of the ROTC juniors and seniors were in the lowest third.[21]

Educators and military officers understood ROTC cadet quality to be vital. "Think of the fighter-bomber pilot with a megaton weapon," the air force chief of staff observed at a 1959 meeting with educators. "The responsibility of a second lieutenant has never been exceeded in history."[22] The preparation of that second lieutenant, then, became paramount to military officials. They argued that modern military technology had greatly increased the responsibilities of junior officers, necessitating increased attention to their

Table 3.1 Percentage of officers stating "high career commitment," by commissioning source, 1961

Commission source	Army	Air Force
Service academy	62%	65%
OCS/OTS	78%	78%
ROTC	31%	37%

Source: Samuel Huntington, "Power, Expertise, and the Military Profession," *Daedalus* 92 (Fall 1963): 792.

training and their roles in the contemporary military. According to one study, ROTC cadets underwent a total of 1,128 hours of training (and all that *before* military service actually began), compared with the 1,050 hours of training received by draftees.[23]

According to Morris Janowitz, the daily life of the junior officer was characterized by progressively less discipline after World War II. Such does not appear to have been the case for the training of the junior officer, however. ROTC classes were well known for strict, sometimes arbitrary discipline. The University of Pittsburgh's *Standard Operating Procedure for Cadets* outlined typical infractions that could provoke demerits (earning 25 demerits led to dishonorable dismissal). Some of these are listed below.

Unauthorized absence: 5
Failure to carry out specific instruction: 5 (first offense)
Failure to carry out specific instruction: 10 (second offense)
Failure to carry out specific instruction: 25 (third offense)
Failure to wear uniform: 3
Drill infraction: 1
Uniform discrepancies: 1–2
Needing haircut badly: 2
Wearing disreputable, unclean attire: 1–3
Failure to salute on campus: 3

Rules regarding the wearing of the uniform read as follows: "No civilian decorations, watch chains, pencils, fountain pens, or other jewelry will be exposed on the uniform."[24]

One cadet handbook from 1956 told ROTC students that "discipline is considered an essential part of successful military service as it is in any ordered and civilized life" and outlined the behavior expected of ROTC cadets:

Cadets will come to attention when any member of the staff enters a classroom . . . *Members of the section will remain until dismissed by a member of the department staff. When on duty as such, cadet officers are required to correct breaches of discipline, and, if circumstances warrant it, report these infractions to the Military Department.* Cadet officers are directed to observe members of the Corps and to correct any mistakes noted. It is only by doing so that a high standard may be maintained in the Corps and self-confidence and firmness of character, so necessary to a leader, may be developed in the cadet officer."[25]

Several university deans, presidents, and chancellors across the nation supported the implementation of this regimen as beneficial to the development of good character and order on the campus. Military officials, for their part, saw it as preparation for the regimented climate of the military. To assure a firm grounding in the basics of such regimentation, ROTC detachments spent considerable time on such subjects as "personal appearance, wearing the uniform, military courtesy, military discipline, leadership, drill, and customs and courtesies of the service."[26] Success in mastering these subjects largely determined one's success and advancement in the ROTC program. University of Texas Army ROTC cadets received their grades based on the following criteria:

(a) *Appearance.* Neatness, clean and properly fit clothing, shave and haircut, military bearing, standing and sitting erect, cleanliness.

(b) *Demeanor.* Calm, poise, confidence, and enthusiasm.

(c) *Courtesy* and *cooperation.*

(d) *Aggressiveness.* Voluntary, constructive participation.

(e) *Grammar.* Ability to phrase questions and answers clearly, concisely, and to the point.

(f) *Voice.* Volume, clearness, and pronunciation.

(g) *Honesty.* In answering questions. Bluffing will be penalized.[27]

Drill (also known by the euphemistic name Leadership Laboratory) served as the quintessential example of military regimentation and discipline on the campus and was usually conducted in a visible public space like a quadrangle or an open athletic field. Proponents of drill contended that it was the only way to turn individuals into a true corps—a body of men acting in concert toward the same goal. Opponents of drill, most often those men subjected to too much of it, have seen it differently. Drill would surely fall under the definition of what Paul Fussell called "chickenshit," which he defined as "behavior that makes military life worse than it need be: petty harassment of the weak by the strong; open scrimmage for power and authority and prestige; sadism thinly disguised as necessary discipline; a constant 'paying off of old scores'; and insistence on the letter rather than the spirit of ordinances."[28]

ROTC cadets sometimes spent as much time drilling and being drilled as they spent in the classroom. In 1956, University of Texas ROTC cadets described a typical day thus: "Up at 6:15. Weekly shave. Name tag, collar stay. 7:00 Drill. Breakfast. Go to Eng. 601a [Freshman Composition]. Go to [Air Science] 403a— '. . . so while I was in Bangkok, never forget that night, I'd flown in a P-38 and . . .' 12:00 Drill. 'Your OTHER left foot, mister!' Lunch. Class—7:00 Lecture: 'The Geo-Politics of Southeastern Manitoba.' Hang uniform reverently in closet. Study. Sack time."[29] At the University of Texas and elsewhere, all demerits a student had accumulated from infractions like those listed above had to be worked off by the end of a semester by participating in still more drill. Furthermore, all Texas cadets were required to join an ROTC cadet organization "to enhance the prestige of the Army ROTC and make it an organization in which every cadet can take pride." Several of these organizations were precision drill teams, necessitating further training in drill.[30]

Despite its obvious differences from other educational methods, drill encountered little opposition in the Cold War era. For most passersby it was more likely to arouse patriotic feelings than cause unease. To civilian administrators, it symbolized discipline, maturation, and good order, all values they hoped to nurture in young men. To the cadets, it was either another requirement to be borne with the best face possible or an activity that they believed instilled useful values. In a 1963 survey, 84 percent of recent AFROTC graduates said that leadership lab "served a good purpose" at their school.[31] Of course it is impossible to estimate the number of people who felt unease but did not express it out of a fear of being labeled unpatriotic.

ROTC was, then, a preprofessional program of an unusual sort. While engineering, nursing, and fine arts programs could also be called preprofessional, they prepared students for a field, not for one exclusive employer.[32] Here was yet another difference between ROTC and other university programs. Since ROTC training was geared for one employer, the training was not only preprofessional but also specifically geared to the needs of the service (and sometimes to the specific branch of that service) with which the student had contracted. In the 1950s this training included indoctrination into the customs of the military profession: discipline, courtesy, and care of the uniform. It also meant a technical curriculum designed around strictly military courses, to meet the needs of the services.

From Specialized to General Military Training

In the Cold War era the military updated the ROTC curriculum to fit the rapidly changing and increasingly complex responsibilities of the junior officer. The same conditions that argued for a professional curriculum argued also for preparing officers to fill a wider variety of roles and giving them a wider understanding of the military. As a result, the first post–World War II changes to the military curriculum sought to make military training less specific to individual branch skills than it had been before the war.

Educators largely agreed with the military's stated goals but saw the problem slightly differently. They argued that the junior officer needed a wider range of civilian courses to complement the military courses and expose officer candidates to new fields in the humanities and social sciences as well as traditional civilian courses relevant to the military. Curricular changes in the civilian world, they argued, should be a part of total educational and professional preparation of officer candidates. By the late 1950s, as the specter of McCarthyism faded and as academics reached rough consensus on their ideas for the inclusion of civilian courses, civilian faculty and administrators began to lobby the services for the inclusion of civilian courses relevant to the military in the ROTC curriculum.

The first step in postwar curricular reform aimed at separating military training from the specific functions of the branches. Army ROTC training had, since World War I, been tied to the twelve branches of that service: Armor; Army Security; Artillery; Cavalry; Chemical; Engineering; Infantry; Military Police; Ordnance; Quartermaster; Signal Corps; and Transportation. The air force, sprung from its army parents in 1949, also began its training of ROTC cadets with a branch-based system that offered preparation in eight air force areas analogous to the army's branches: Administration and Supply; Comptroller; Armament; Aircraft Maintenance Engineering; Air Installations; Communications; General Technical; and Flight Operations. The branch system was a product of World War I, when weapons and logistics had grown sufficiently complex to merit formal specialization. Branch-oriented ROTC curricula in the Cold War era had the advantage of producing immediately employable junior officers who possessed knowledge of a particular branch. As noted in Chapter 2 and earlier in this chapter, the military assumed that if the Cold War turned hot, mobilization would need to take place much more quickly than it had in 1917 or 1941.[33] The specialized training system, many believed, made the assignment and use of recently activated reserve officers more rational.[34]

To many army, air force, and DOD officials, such a system of training officers was antiquated and irrational for several reasons. First, it hampered recruitment. Schools like the University of Colorado, which offered ROTC only for the Engineering branch of the service, effectively disqualified all of its nonengineering students from serving. Second, some branches were less appealing than others, the University of Missouri, which offered only artillery training, thereby "lost" students who might have wanted to join the army but not as an artillerist. Third, it made the assignment of instructors difficult, because the army and air force needed to staff ROTC units with officers who possessed the specialized training taught at that unit. Fourth, the branch system created shortages in some areas and too many officers in others and, to make matters worse, produced officers incapable of working outside their branch. The imbalances created were therefore difficult both to predict and to correct.[35]

Finally, many senior uniformed officers and two important civilian analysts believed that the training was too specialized. The mobilization exercises for the Korean War had demonstrated that technical knowledge was either not mastered or had quickly become obsolete in the "complicated and intricate" world of the modern military.[36] The army and air force needed a system that taught men how to be military leaders and well-rounded officers, not just branch specialists who knew how to operate equipment that was often replaced within a short time, rendering training that irrelevant.[37] According to a 1959 study of recent trends in ROTC by Gene Lyons and John Masland, the post-war military officer needed "a rich store of general knowledge as well as specialized knowledge of military affairs."[38] In the words of the branch system's most important uniformed critic, Major General Hugh Milton, "It is more essential to develop leadership qualities in these students and provide them with a broad base of military knowledge than to give them predominately branch specialized training."[39]

This was not, of course, to argue that a military officer did not have need of specific knowledge for his occupational specialty. Rather, it was an argument for keeping on-campus training general enough to give the officer sufficient knowledge of the rest of his service and to prepare him for specialized training once he was in service at one of the various professional military facilities, such as Ft. Benning for Infantry and Ft. Hood for Armor. Lyons, Masland, Milton, and others were, in effect, making the case that the military officer needed more than just the specialized knowledge taught under the branch curriculum and, further, that on-campus time was too valuable to spend on matters that could be easily taught to men in uniform who possessed a good general military education. Men were therefore asked to develop, as cadets and as junior officers, a knowledge of *both* their specialty and the more general world of the military.

General Milton played a large role in devising a new system, the army's General Military Science curriculum, or GMS. The army designed GMS without significant input from civilian higher education, and it had strictly military goals. The military was able to eschew significant civilian advice on GMS due to its sole intellectual ownership of the ROTC curriculum during the height of the Cold War. The GMS curriculum had three main goals: to reduce the production fluctuations of the branch system; to permit the assignment of a wider field of officers to ROTC duty; and to broaden the recruitment base by accepting students from all majors.[40] It reflected a change in the emphasis of the military environment more generally from the more heroic (to paraphrase Janowitz) military of years past to the more managerial and technologically complex world of the contemporary military.

The GMS curriculum and a concurrent air force equivalent, the General Military Course, aimed to make military training less technical and specialized, representing an important shift in the understanding of what an officer needed to know. These new curricula implicitly acknowledged that regular university courses such as psychology, political science, and communications had relevance for the junior officer. As such, they opened the door to changes that occurred in the late 1950s (see below). They did not, however, make any attempt to upgrade the academic quality of conventional ROTC courses. The motivations of the GMS curriculum were strictly and explicitly military. ROTC cadets, whether trained under a branch or a general system, continued to take courses understood by civilians to be of marginal academic value, taught by men without traditional academic qualifications.

The general absence of civilian input into ROTC curricula meant that the courses ROTC students took, whether at summer camps and cruises or on campus, were strictly military in their subject matter and quite squarely professional in their application. In the early 1960s the army described the goals of the national ROTC curriculum model thus: "the ROTC curriculum is not designed to educate the student, but to train him in the basic skills required of a second lieutenant."[41] NROTC students at the University of Colorado in 1953 described their classes thus: Naval History and Orientation; the Uniform Code of Military Justice; "a maze of ordnance and navigation"; "customs of the Navy"; the "innermost workings of the Navy's ordnance equipment"; "the art of pin-point navigation"; and "sea stories."[42]

This view, of course, stood in opposition to traditional modes of instruction in higher education, especially in colleges of liberal arts. So long as the Cold War seemed sufficiently threatening to national security, however, higher education officials by and large accepted the military's argument that cadets and midshipmen needed to use on-campus time to learn the nuts and bolts of military service in order to be immediately useful upon commission. Over time, however, the dissonance between pedagogical goals resulted in conflict.

Whenever possible, the services worked within the diversity of American higher education. They gave the senior unit officers (known as professor of military, air, or naval science) tremendous latitude and discretion in shaping the ROTC program to meet, within reason, the demands of local officials. In the air force only three officers, the chief of staff, the deputy commandant, and the commandant, could sign a letter denying a request by a professor of air science (PAS).[43] ROTC staff officers created a standard national curriculum that allowed local officers to make changes, but few officers strayed very far, out of the fear that their graduates would fare poorly in postcommissioning tests, which were designed to assess officer mastery of the material in the standard ROTC curricula.

The national army curriculum model, which predated the introduction of GMS in 1953 and had been virtually unchanged since World War II, required 480 hours of "academic" contact over four years and 264 hours of contact in two summer camps before the junior and senior years. Although the army sold part of the curriculum as academic, it was more technical and less reflective than the curricula of most liberal arts colleges and many engineering colleges as well. The official list of ROTC courses is shown in Table 3.2.

These courses did not follow a liberal arts pattern of reflection and analysis and often taught very different material than civilian classes, even in analogous subjects. The army course in military history stressed "the history of the Army and leadership as inspirational and integrating factors."[44] Summer camp courses were even more martial in orientation. In the first camp, after the student's sophomore year, courses included: Drill, Military Customs and Organization of the Army; Bayonet and Hand-to-Hand Combat; Field Sanitation and Inspections; Weapons and Marksmanship; and Basic Tactics. After the junior year, courses included: Drills, Parades, and Ceremonies; First Aid; and Field Problems.

Ted Wright, the hero of the comic book discussed earlier, first learned how to shine his shoes ("only an officer and a gentleman shines the heels"), then he learned hygiene, first aid, drill, and the use of crew-served weapons. Once in the advanced program, he learned how to set a road block, fire the new 57mm recoilless rifle, conduct a court martial, and, as we have seen, deal with women.[45] These, then, were the subjects the army saw as most vital: weapons training, drill, and how to dress and act like an officer.

Real ROTC students took courses similar to Ted Wright's. Army ROTC cadets at Kent State in 1952 took courses titled Military Organization, First

Table 3.2   Standard army curriculum, 1950s

Year	Courses	Contact hours
Military Science I (freshmen)	Introduction	5
	Weapons and Marksmanship	25
	Leadership Lab (drill)	30
	Military History	30
Military Science II (sophomores)	Role of the Army	10
	Map and Aerial Photo Reading	20
	Crew-Served Weapons	30
	Leadership Lab	30
Military Science III (juniors)	Leadership Lab	30
	Branches of the Army	30
	Tactics and Communications	55
	Leadership	10
	Military Principles	20
	Pre-Camp	5
Military Science IV (seniors)	Operations	50
	Logistics	20
	Leadership Lab	30
	Administration and Military Justice	30
	Service Orientation	20

Source: Gene Lyons and John Masland, *Education and Military Leadership* (Princeton N.J.: Princeton University Press, 1959), p. 182.

Aid, Drill, and Marksmanship. In their junior year they took Infantry Tactics, Field Fortifications, Gunnery, and (again) Drill. Their air force peers took such ambiguously titled courses as Applied Air Power (which taught desert, jungle, and arctic survival), Military Publications, and Flight Operations, along with the ubiquitous Drill.[46] Eight years later at the University of Pittsburgh, Weapons and Marksmanship, Leadership Laboratory, Operations and Tactics, Branches of the Army, Service Orientation, and Tactics formed the core of the ROTC curriculum.[47]

The description of the Kent State Air Force ROTC course Military Publications indicates the courses' strictly professional content:

Military Publications: The course provides a basic knowledge of military publications, their indices, filing, and use. The ingenuity of the instructor is relied upon to some extent in that he must present specific questions, which will require the students to be familiar with the procedures to be followed in using military publications in order to determine the answers. Publications covered will include Air Force Regulations, Air Force Letters, Manuals, Technical Orders, M & S Directives, T/O & Es, TMs, and TBs.[48]

While not questioning the national need for ROTC, or the university's obligation to sponsor ROTC classes, these courses seemed to many higher education officials to be out of step with the goals of higher education in general and liberal education in particular. ROTC, with its squarely professional classes based on repetition and memorization (symbolized by the automatonic drill) did not fit in with a careful reading of goals like those of the University of Pittsburgh's College of Liberal Arts:

> The School believes that liberal education is a life-time process of intellectual and aesthetic development and that, while it cannot and should not be a professional training program, it does provide the best foundation for one's future professional interests. The dynamic balance of observation and participation, of reflection and action, of free minds and a free society, is the essence of life itself and, in turn, of liberal education.[49]

If ROTC had a place in the curriculum, and few doubted that it did, it was surely not the same place as English, philosophy, or chemistry. University of Texas officials noted that ROTC "is not to be viewed as a scholarship program" but as a specifically military program.[50] It is illustrative, then, that at many schools, including the University of Pittsburgh, ROTC had the same curricular standing as physical education. Students could complete four semesters of either one to fulfill a graduation requirement.[51]

A tension therefore existed between the steadfastly acknowledged national need for officer training programs on civilian campuses and the awareness that the courses offered were tangential to the mission of many colleges and universities. The general support among those in higher education for the ROTC curriculum began to be undermined in the late 1950s by the desire of some faculty members to make the ROTC curriculum more compatible with civilian curricula. For the most part, however, top-level administrators preferred not to interfere too deeply with the military's decisions about what a junior officer should learn. Indeed, the universities formally approved the courses by awarding academic credit. At Kent State, army and air force ROTC cadets received two hours per quarter for the basic course and three hours per quarter for the advanced course.[52] Texas allowed ROTC courses to count for as many as 24 of the 120 hours needed for graduation.[53] The University of Pittsburgh's colleges of liberal arts and engineering permitted students to count 8 ROTC credit towards the 124 and 144 credits needed, respectively, for graduation.[54]

A Green Pasture

As with the content of ROTC courses, the universities by and large permitted the services to determine the qualifications of ROTC instructors. Although the qualifications of military faculty were quite different from those of civilian faculty, throughout the 1950s this variance produced little formal opposition. Cadre officers, despite the customary title of professor for senior officers and assistant professor or associate professor for junior officers, very rarely held or even sought an advanced degree; indeed, the military did not believe that such a degree was necessary to teach the professional subject matter of the ROTC curriculum. Nor was the need for such qualifications obvious to some university officials. When queried by the air force about its preferences for officers assigned, the University of Illinois replied in 1957 that "academic major, degrees beyond the baccalaureate, section of the country in which raised, and type of school from which graduated are not matters of importance in carrying out the responsibilities of the PAS."[55]

ROTC duty developed a reputation as a "pre-retirement sinecure" for officers who failed to qualify for promotion.[56] ROTC duty was often a terminal assignment, understood as signaling the end of the productive years of one's career. As early as 1950, the Association of NROTC Colleges complained to the navy that it had been "several years" since a professor of naval science had been promoted to rear admiral. The association noted that of the fifty-two professors on duty, only fifteen even had the qualifications to be considered for such a promotion.[57]

Many others saw an ROTC assignment as a reward after a long overseas tour of duty. One observer described ROTC duty as "a 'green pasture' where officers about to be retired took it easy."[58] Indeed, ROTC positions were understood to be among the safest posts in the military, they allowed an officer to establish a home, and the work was not particularly difficult. The services did not require the officers to have teaching experience, nor did they offer training programs to help them learn how to teach.

Although civilian faculty sometimes lacked teaching experience as well, their professional qualifications (measured by degrees earned) served as indicators to fellow academics that they had sufficient expertise to merit inclusion in the faculty. Few people argued that an officer needed a master's degree to teach logistics, but to many academics, giving faculty titles to men who had neither professional qualifications nor teaching expertise seemed irresponsible and a breach of academic protocol.

In theory, the universities had the right to reject candidates nominated by the services, and they did exercise that prerogative on occasion. More often than not, however, candidates recommended by the services and endorsed by the cadre were quickly approved. Since the officers applying for ROTC teaching positions rarely had publications or other standard academic materials to evaluate, there was little on which administrators could base a decision. In many cases, it was impossible for the cadre or university officials to interview or even meet the candidate, because he was assigned to an overseas post. As a result, personnel decisions were made on the basis of service records or some arbitrary criterion, such as the "neat military appearance," in one case, of an air force major who came to the University of Illinois for an interview in 1960.[59]

Sometimes the schools even accepted instructors with no college degree at all. In 1958 an air force captain with no college education and "little formal class room instructing" was nevertheless found to be "quite acceptable" to University of Illinois associate provost Royen Dangerfeld.[60] Of the seventy-eight officers assigned to ROTC duty at Duquesne and the Universities of Illinois, Pittsburgh, and Texas between 1957 and 1963 whose education could be determined, only twelve had a degree beyond the bachelor's; seven had no degree at all at their time of appointment. Further instruction from men without degrees came from cadets themselves, who were often called upon to teach freshmen classes, especially drill, as part of their training in leadership.

Attempts to rectify this situation faced several obstacles. In 1962 only 12.6 percent of all air force officers had an advanced degree, and nearly one in five lacked even a bachelor's degree.[61] Given these limitations, air force reforms were aimed at eliminating non–degree holders from ROTC duty and, somewhat ironically, lowering the age of the instructor. Between 1961 and 1964, the number of non–degree holders on the ROTC staff dropped from fifty-four to just four. Oddly enough, however, in the same period the number of full colonels on staff fell by fifty percent, illustrating a determined effort by the air force to put more young officers, particularly lieutenant colonels and majors, on campus. "These efforts have placed younger, more adaptable and ambitious Air Force representatives on campus, men with academic backgrounds compatible with those of other faculty members with whom they associate. All these measures have served to improve both the stature of the AFROTC on the campus and the rapport between its representatives and the college community."[62]

Surely the air force was being sanguine in expecting that eliminating non–degree holders would make the cadre's "academic backgrounds compatible with those of other faculty members with whom they associate." Nevertheless, the new requirement of the completion of some college education pleased educators. The universities were willing to accept somewhat lower qualifications for military instructors than for civilian instructors, provided that a minimum standard could be maintained.

Still, some administrators tried to address ROTC's reputation for poor instruction more systematically, and such attempts usually centered around standard academic indicators like advanced degrees. Demanding an advanced degree for all ROTC instructors would have been folly, since there were simply not enough officers with master's degrees. The University of Minnesota nevertheless tried to set higher minimum standards than the air force had done, as evidenced by this letter from President O. Meredith Wilson to Secretary of the Army (and future Indiana University president) Elvis Stahr: "We have had many fine officers here, but in some cases, the officers assigned have not met those standards which we attempt to meet for the remainder of the faculty. We therefore have decided that our minimum academic requirement for those officers nominated for duty in the ROTC units shall be that they be fully qualified for entrance into our Graduate School . . . We, of course, would prefer officers who already have graduate degrees, but we know that this is not now practicable."[63]

The debate over instructor qualifications indicated another area of dissonance that, throughout the 1950s and early 1960s, was acknowledged but, in the quest for harmony, not hotly contested. Once again, the perceived needs of national security took precedence over addressing ROTC's anomalous place in the university.

Substitution: The Coming Order of the Day

By the late 1950s, when the bipolarity of the early years of the Cold War was replaced by a more complicated understanding that included the Third

World, educators developed several ideas to integrate more fully the military and civilian instructional programs. Furthermore, the 1957 Soviet launch of the first *Sputnik* satellite reawakened an interest in officer education, just as it reinvigorated interest in American education more generally. Such an environment proved fertile for the development of civilian suggestions for changes in the ROTC curriculum.

Various ideas for the larger incorporation of civilian faculty into ROTC programs developed independently at several institutions nationwide. One such plan, developed in 1957 by the Association of Naval ROTC Colleges and Universities (ANROTCCU), a group constituted of the presidents and provosts of those schools hosting NROTC units, involved using civilian faculty as guest lecturers to broaden and supplement the instruction provided by uniformed personnel.[64] The use of civilian lecturers, the ANROTCCU argued, could upgrade the academic quality of instruction while playing on one of the traditional strengths of ROTC. Part of the value of officers from civilian colleges was in their exposure to civilian ideas. It made sense, then, to take advantage of civilian faculty who taught subjects relevant to the general education of the junior military officer. Rutgers University introduced guest lecturing on a broad scale in 1958 with "excellent" results.[65]

The most important military objection to such a plan, and to subsequent similar plans, was that, if carried out on too grand a scale, it would reduce the number of contact hours between officer and cadet or midshipman. Such contact was vital, some argued, for the officers to be able to determine the leadership potential of their students, as that potential is not easily measurable through papers and exams. Any reform that took time away from direct officer-student contact therefore met with resistance from many officers. Still, the idea of using civilian instructors was logical and consistent with the recent switch from branch training to GMS. If the goal was a broader general education, then an understanding of history, political science, geography, mathematics, and languages could only help to produce the better-educated officers desired by proponents of GMS.

Some universities were even developing plans to use civilian faculty to teach entire ROTC classes, not just selected lectures. At the same time that the ANROTCCU plan was developed, the Ohio State University AFROTC detachment began to work out a plan to have civilian instructors teach "such courses as International Tensions and Security Organizations, Fundamentals of Global Geography, Military Aspects of World Political Geography, Communicating in the Air Force, Problem Solving and Leadership Management."[66] In this pilot program, civilian Ohio State faculty taught courses that were military in their orientation but more reflective and academic than those courses taught by uniformed officers.

The Ohio State plan had the support of the air force, which also introduced the idea of asking universities to develop specific courses to be taught by civilian professors according to air force requirements. These courses would be offered as a joint military-civilian enterprise and open to any student.[67] Ohio State, for its part, was anxious to have other schools try what was becoming known as "substitution," the replacement of vocational, military courses by academic ones. Civilian faculties strongly resisted the idea of the joint courses because of the fear of outside influence on course design. They received the idea of substitution more favorably, as it involved the use of existing academic offerings. By 1960, 48 of the air force's 176 host schools used some variant of substitution.[68] To be sure, 128 schools still used strictly military curricula, but a strong alternative was emerging.

The localized nature of the ROTC curriculum meant that experimentation in the use of civilian faculty could be carried out at any school whose faculty and administration showed an interest. The University of Pittsburgh showed such interest early on and developed its own plan for substitution without significant input from Ohio State officials. A 1959 faculty senate committee's review of the Army and Air Force ROTC programs at Pittsburgh had found that what was known as the "academic" portion of the ROTC curriculum did not merit the credit awarded and that "the academic courses might profitably be replaced by courses already existing in our regular department offerings." The committee recommended that "the University should request the ROTC to consider a change in their curriculum which would recognize the suitability of regular departmental courses for credit toward military commissions . . . These courses would be taught by regular non-military university faculty" in the departments of political science and geography.[69]

The air force proved receptive to Pittsburgh's suggestions and responded with quick and enthusiastic approval. For the spring trimester of the academic year 1959–60 the air force authorized Pittsburgh to substitute two courses, International Relations and Political Geography, for air science courses. University of Pittsburgh military affairs coordinator Alan Rankin told the faculty senate that the changes in the air force curriculum, and discussions with the army for changes in its curriculum, had improved the academic legitimacy of ROTC:

Colonel Hills (the Professor of Air Science) and Colonel Wolff (the Professor of Military Science) join me in expressing appreciation to the Chancellor and the Senate for their interest in developing ROTC Programs which will enrich the educational experiences of the students and at the same time recognize the requirements of the Departments of the Air Force and the Army . . . In undertaking the study of the steps necessary to implement the Senate Committee's recommendations, we have found the Departments of the Air Force and the Army favorably disposed to change . . . The Army is hoping to give purely academic courses a greater emphasis, to reduce on-campus instruction in purely military subjects and to allow ROTC credit for courses in psychology, mathematics, and physics.[70]

A reduction in the teaching of military subjects on campus would be necessary to make time for the new substituted courses. Under most proposals considered for national implementation, those military subjects would be moved to the summer camps.

The same motivations that produced substitution produced coincident changes at the three service academies aimed at broadening the educational background of academy-trained officers. In 1957 the Air Force Academy became the first service academy to allow elective courses, thereby jettisoning the "straitjacket" curriculum formerly required of all cadets; West Point and Annapolis followed suit within two years. All three academies, arguing, in the words of the Naval Academy's superintendent, that "the time has passed . . . when it was simply enough to teach cadets and midshipmen how to shoot guns and run ships," sharply reduced time spent on "purely military training."[71] All three academies increased time spent in humanities and social science classes, "junking . . . hardware courses . . . in favor of studies of a fundamental nature which will not soon go out of date."[72]

Substitution in the ROTC curriculum succeeded both because it was consistent with similar changes at the academies and because it easily overlapped the interests of military and civilian officials. Substitution met the services' desire for more broadly educated students and higher education's desire to raise the academic standard for ROTC course instruction in the absence of highly qualified military teachers. The University of Pittsburgh's Alan Rankin attended a 1959 AFROTC conference and noted with pleasure the participants' warm reception of substitution:

The most interesting feature of the conference was the unmistakable sentiment on the part of both institutional representatives and the Air Force officials to liberalize the AFROTC program in exactly the same direction as the University of Pittsburgh is moving. Our regular academic courses taught by our regular faculty members is the coming order of the day, and I would anticipate little difficulty in getting approval from the Air Force headquarters for whatever modifications in our curriculum we might want to undertake.[73]

The following year, Pittsburgh introduced eighteen more hours of substitution for AFROTC. Freshmen took speech and one class in math, natural science, social science, language, or the humanities. Juniors took social psychology and either Technical or Expository Writing. Cadets still took a core primarily composed of military subjects, but these were now complemented by cognate civilian courses.

The army, too, moved quickly to substitute academic courses for purely military subjects, but it gave substitution less emphatic support than had the air force, out of a desire to maintain a high number of contact hours between cadre and cadet. Along these lines, the Army in 1960 rejected a proposal by the Army ROTC Advisory Panel to substitute 135 of the curriculum's 480 hours, but it did agree to reduce the amount of time spent on weapons and marksmanship by 45 hours.[74] The time freed up could be used to substitute civilian-taught classes in science, psychology, communications, and political science.[75] The army made it clear to schools that they were free to reject the idea of substitution. Not surprisingly, Pittsburgh chose to take the army's offer and introduced courses in four general groupings: effective communication; science comprehension; general psychology; and political institutions.[76]

The navy's ROTC program had, since 1946, used a scholarship program designed to produce officers "capable of going to sea" right after graduation. The navy therefore was hesitant to take any time away from its rigid curriculum for nonprofessional courses that might reduce its ability to turn a college senior into an immediately employable ensign. Nevertheless, by 1960 the navy had, at the insistence of its host schools, authorized substitution of two courses, General Psychology and Naval Engineering, across the curriculum. The navy also turned over the NROTC course on the history of sea power, which accounted for 60 of the first year's 120 contact hours, to civilian instructors at appropriate institutions. Naval officers in charge of NROTC stood firm, however, in saying that they would not authorize any substitution beyond those three courses, because "we just cannot see how it is possible to relinquish more time" to nonmilitary instructors.[77]

Substitution had the added virtue of making it easier for students to fit

ROTC into their increasingly demanding schedules. The services had long recognized time constraints as an important detriment to advanced ROTC enrollment. A 1950 study noted that students gave "too time consuming" as their most frequent complaint.[78] In 1961 the Army ROTC Advisory Panel noted in its report that "some educators are exerting pressure to further reduce on-campus military instruction. They consider that reduction is necessary in order to integrate student academic requirements and to reduce the impact of the pressure of time on the students."[79] An ROTC curriculum conference sponsored by Ohio State advocated the substitution policy by praising its ability to "reduce the overload on advanced students."[80] Basic-level cadets were under time constraints as well; at Georgia Tech the AFROTC program reduced classroom time for freshmen and sophomores from eighteen hours a week to six "in order that each student may have more time for academic activities."[81]

Substitution thus had many virtues: it made the program more appealing to a large minority of military officials, primarily in the army and air force, who wanted ROTC to move in the direction of education, not training; it pleased educators by injecting academic material from a wide variety of disciplines into the vocational curriculum; it pleased undergraduates by allowing them effectively to count some classes twice—once as credits for their diploma and once as requirements for their commission. This last advantage partly explains why the services were so quick to adapt substitution to their curricula. The army felt compelled to respond to air force plans that made it easier for students to enroll in and complete AFROTC training—especially on those campuses where both programs existed—lest it should lose potential cadets to the other service. Substitution was not widespread enough to allow the services to save money by assigning fewer officers to the ROTC programs, but it did bring all of the above advantages without any additional costs. Therefore the new programs steadily spread, making at least a portion of the ROTC student's curriculum more academic in nature and demonstrating the benefit of close working relationships between the two agents in charge of ROTC.

For all of substitution's virtues, the debate over the policy did point out that the military and academia had different, if sometimes compatible, goals for ROTC. Representatives of the military, especially those in the navy, wanted to focus on-campus time on strictly military (and less reflective) subjects, such as drill, courtesy, and the wearing of the uniform. The universities pushed to add required cognate areas to the curriculum, such as psychology, political science, and communications. While substitution proved to be an effective compromise, the military remained suspicious of ceding too much time to civilians at the risk of reducing its ability to judge leadership capabilities in their cadets. Meanwhile, university officials continued to contend that on-campus time was more properly spent learning group-dynamics theories than the rudiments of crew-served weapons.

Because virtually all of the civilian and military agents in charge of ROTC saw the program as an inexpensive, efficient means of expanding the talents and numbers of the officer corps without resorting to a larger academy-trained military elite, ROTC came to possess a highly elevated status on American campuses. It thus occupied a peculiar position in the university: it received the status of a department despite not sharing important qualities with civilian academic departments, its courses were accredited despite faculty reviews that found them substandard in content, and its instructors received the title of "professor" despite their having backgrounds very different from those of civilian faculty.

In spite of these anomalies, little sustained opposition to ROTC emerged. The period from 1950 to 1964, while witnessing some changes, was one of great continuity for ROTC. The quest for civilian-military harmony born of the Cold War led to a great deal of university acquiescence which in turn buttressed the elevated stature of the program. Beginning in 1964, however, ROTC began to experience rapid reform, first as a result of new legislation and then, more fundamentally, as the nation's shared sense of purpose during the Cold War gave way to the uncertainties and doubts of a new era that brought into question the role of the university in America's prosecution of the war in Southeast Asia.

CHAPTER **4**

The ROTC Vitalization Act, 1964–1968

> These symbolic practices when viewed outside their context may appear unnecessary, and civilians sometimes express impatience or irritation with them . . . [but] ceremonies involving drill are practices in the [military], and the student will have to acquire some skill in performing these activities if he is to participate in them on active duty.
>
> —*ROTC Curriculum Handbook, 1968*

By the late 1950s and early 1960s, critics as diverse as radical sociologist C. Wright Mills and President Dwight Eisenhower began to argue that the military, and the industrial system to which it had become tightly connected, had gained too strong a hold on American society. With McCarthyism in remission and with the replacement of early Cold War hysteria with a more complex view of global affairs, critics could more confidently express their concerns about the militarization of American society. Mills decried the "military ascendancy" and the new role that the services had taken in many fields traditionally dominated by civilians, including education. "Some universities," Mills argued, "are financial branches of the military establishment, receiving three or four times as much money from the military as from all other sources combined."[1] He identified ROTC as one manifestation of this influence, noting that, while "prestigeful," ROTC linked the "pursuit of knowledge" in the American university to "the training of men to enact special roles."[2]

President Eisenhower sounded a less radical but no less concerned tone in his 1961 farewell address. The preeminent military hero sounded like the model Moderate Whig:

In the councils of government, we must guard against the acquisition of unwarranted influence, whether sought or unsought, by the military-industrial complex. The potential for the disastrous rise of misplaced power exists and will persist. We must never let the weight of this combination endanger our liberties or democratic processes. We should take nothing for granted. Only an alert and knowledgeable citizenry can compel the proper meshing of the huge industrial and military machinery of defense with our peaceful methods and goals, so that security and liberty may prosper together.

Eisenhower also warned against the unprecedented growth of the military into American higher education. "The prospect of domination of the nation's scholars by Federal employment, project allocations, and the power of money is ever present—and is gravely to be regarded."[3] Sentiments such as Eisenhower's and Mills's reflected a reemergence of Moderate Whig fears all along the American ideological spectrum after a period of notably more yielding attitudes toward the military at the height of the Cold War era.

Emerging concerns such as these may have sowed the seeds of later opposition to the influence of the military on campus, but to judge from the correspondence and policy decisions of educators and the military, they had little immediate impact on ROTC in the early and mid-1960s. Military officials and educators alike were more concerned that the ROTC program was not well constructed to meet the future. Both the military and academia had experienced significant recent change. Furthermore, the universities were expected to expand dramatically to accommodate the large numbers of American baby boomers that would be reaching college age. ROTC, many argued, had outlived its 1916 enabling legislation.

In 1964, as a response to declining ROTC enrollments (in an era of rapidly expanding collegiate enrollments more generally) and the increased demands that American higher education was beginning to place on its students, Congress passed the ROTC Vitalization Act to update the program and to prepare it for its future as the nation's primary source for active-duty officer procurement. The debate over the bill provides insight into ROTC's value to those agents responsible for its oversight—ROTC staff officers, the universities, service headquarters officers at the Pentagon, and Congress—and set the precedent for later negotiations. The debate also reveals what Congress and the services sought to gain from ROTC and what they thought the program could achieve.

Even as the Vitalization Act was being implemented, faculty and students at several universities nationwide, with Mills as an intellectual ancestor, were beginning to question American involvement in the widening war in Southeast Asia. The creation of Students for a Democratic Society (SDS) in 1962, itself not initially an antiwar organization, provided a national infrastructure on which opponents of the war would eventually build a significant and compelling movement.[4] While real, sustained opposition on the campuses did not arise until 1968, nascent student and faculty hostility to the Vietnam War affected ROTC, if only indirectly at first, as early as the 1965 teach-ins at the University of Michigan and subsequent teach-ins across the nation. Just as the Vitalization Act set the framework for later negotiations between the schools and the services, so were precedents set for how ROTC units would respond to campus disorder during the Vietnam era.

This period was also one of tremendous expansion for higher education as America strove to make college attainable for a larger percentage of the population (see Table 4.1). The 1960s were dynamic times for American universities, with the government, and the DOD specifically, funding much of that dynamism. The faculty and students of the 1950s had not expressed great concern about how such government influence could distort the mission of a university.[5] Many people in the 1960s, however, believed that the university would have to curb government influence if it was to remain objective and able to pursue truth. All of these dynamic changes of the 1960s would eventually play a role in the reform of ROTC.

Table 4.1   Growth of American higher education, 1960–1964

Factor	Growth
Number of faculty	30%
Undergraduate enrollment	38%
Expenditures	64%
Federal support	133%
Revenue from student fees	64%

Source: Bureau of the Census, *Historical Statistics of the United States, Colonial Times to 1970, Part 2* (Washington, D.C.: Government Printing Office, 1975), pp. 382–386.

The Genesis of the ROTC Vitalization Act

The 1916 National Defense Act, which initially authorized ROTC, had assumed that ROTC's role would be to provide officers for the reserve components of the armed forces. The Cold War, however, had forced a reexamination of that role as ROTC became the primary source of active-duty officers. Now the air force, for example, expected that one of every two active-duty officers commissioned in 1964 would come from ROTC; the army expected that figure to be three in four.[6] ROTC had therefore taken on a new role, but it still operated under legislation designed to help it fulfill an antediluvian one.

As early as 1960 the air force had called for new legislation to replace the "outmoded" 1916 law.[7] Colonel (later Brigadier General) William Lindley took personal charge of developing new legislation to bring AFROTC into line with the needs of the services for high-quality, active-duty junior officers. His goal was to produce a program that would be available to more male undergraduates, take up less of the student's time than the five hours per week mandated by the NDA, and shift the focus of ROTC training from drill and military ceremony to management and problem solving.

The army chief of staff shared the air force's concerns and ordered a review of the Army ROTC program in 1961 to "make the program more productive and appealing to students and institutions, and more compatible with Navy and Air Force programs, while still fulfilling Army requirements."[8] Those in charge of ROTC concurred that the program needed "an entirely new look." They also agreed that the first step in creating that new look was to repeal the 1916 NDA, which they deemed "inconsistent with current . . . requirements."[9] In the course of the ensuing debates among Congress, the ROTC staffs, and the Pentagon, each agency revealed its own goals and hopes for ROTC.

The task of reforming ROTC focused most urgently on numbers. As already noted, fifty-nine AFROTC and sixty AROTC units ended the compulsory feature of their programs in the early 1960s. While defenders of those decisions continued to insist that voluntary programs alone could produce enough officers, those at the top of the command structure had reason to be concerned. Despite predictions to the contrary, enrollments and, more important, commissions, were falling below established minimum standards.[10] In the fall of 1963, as the debate over compulsory ROTC was being settled, the Illinois AROTC unit expected 170 juniors to enroll in advanced ROTC; only 101 actually did.[11]

On a national level, the picture was much the same. The army failed to make its 1963 enrollment goal and the air force expressed concerns about its ability to meet future goals. Army ROTC enrollment fell "alarmingly" from 169,000 in the academic year 1962–63 to 158,016 in 1963–64 to 157,303 in 1964–65.[12] An air force survey of eighty-eight AFROTC units found fifty-one experiencing falling enrollments, many of these by as much as 20 percent.[13] The army noted, "This is a disturbing trend and if it continues it will have a serious impact on the readiness of the Army to fulfill its role in national defense."[14] Moreover, the need for officers was expected to become more acute in the coming years as the huge cohort of men who received their commissions during World War II and the Korean War retired after completing twenty years of service.[15] The army predicted that officer shortages could reach as high as 7,000 per year between 1963 and 1969.[16]

The services and educators primarily focused on four theories, in addition to the end of the compulsory programs, to explain the drop in enrollments. The first theory contended that a lessening of the national Cold War hysteria, beginning with the death of Josef Stalin and the end of the Korean War in 1953, had reduced the urgency men felt to join the military. The Geneva Summit of 1955 and the "Kitchen Debates" of 1959 served to further thaw, if not melt, some of the Cold War tensions. As the possibility for war seemed less imminent, this theory held, fewer men signed up for military training.

The second theory argued that the power of the draft as a motivating factor had waned, causing fewer men to look to ROTC as a means of evading conscription. A 1961 presidential order that placed married men "at the bottom of the [draft] call sequence" had given men another way to defer their military obligations. The order had been designed to reduce "an overabundance of young men" eligible for conscription. Similarly, the system encouraged automatic deferments for college students who passed their courses.[17] Many men continued to look for ways to deal with the capricious draft system, but by the early 1960s that system looked less threatening to some than it had been in the 1950s, when even national celebrities like Elvis Presley and Willie Mays were called to serve.

Third, some educators argued that increased demands on student time

made ROTC, which required at least five hours per week, simply too onerous. Collegiate curricula were becoming more demanding, and adding
ROTC made a student's schedule that much more hectic. And fourth, some
observers believed that the college student of the 1960s was more interested
in making money and less interested in serving his country than his predecessors had been. Philip Caputo noted that his fellow students in the early
part of the 1960s "thought of joining the army as the most conformist thing
anyone could do, and as the service itself as a form of slavery."[18] Similarly,
a University of Illinois senior named Roger Ebert told *Newsweek* in 1964:
"Most of us just want to get through school, get to work, get married, and
get out to the suburbs."[19]

Of these four theories, the first reflected the military's autonomous effort
to reposition itself in a world that it now saw as less bipolar than during
the Cold War. The other three were related to manpower and recruitment
issues. None of these explanations was directly connected to antimilitary
or antiwar sentiment on the campuses, though they were all certainly connected to the new student indifference and unwillingness to join the program.

The services, especially the air force, hoped to address the enrollment
drop by increasing the pool of men eligible to become ROTC cadets. To do so,
the air force focused on "the restrictive features of existing legislation (that)
inordinately limit the selection base for our commissioning program."[20] The
1916 NDA had required any man seeking a commission to serve in ROTC for
all four of his undergraduate years. The services wanted this feature re-
pealed and a two-year ROTC program created (for the student's junior and
senior years) to take advantage of four groups of men barred from service
under the NDA:

1. Transfers from senior colleges without ROTC units and the growing
   number of junior colleges, which accounted for 800,000 of the
   nation's 3.1 million undergraduates in 1963. Junior college
   populations, moreover, were expected to grow throughout the 1960s.
   The services especially targeted this group, which constituted 64
   percent of the junior-year male student population in a 1962–63
   sampling of AFROTC host schools.[21]
2. Students who attended schools that did not themselves host ROTC
   units but were located within an easy commute to an ROTC host.

3. Students who had to work to earn money for school and therefore could not afford to make a four-year commitment.

4. Students who decided late in their college career to join ROTC.[22]

University administrators, through the Army Advisory Panel on ROTC Affairs and the National Association of State Universities and Land-Grant Colleges, supported these ideas and favored "a bold move rather than . . . a creeping approach" to the enrollment problems.[23] They proposed that the air force and army lobby for legislation authorizing them to grant full scholarships to their ROTC students as the navy had done since the DOD's approval of the Holloway Plan in 1946. The educators believed that the Holloway Plan made the NROTC program less susceptible to enrollment fluctuation and better able to attract high-quality men. The new scholarships, the schools hoped, would "be made available to all cadets, without discrimination, whether enrolled at an institution conducting the four-year program, or the modified two-year program."[24]

The army and air force also hoped to get scholarship authorization, but they put less faith in scholarships than the universities did, knowing that Congress would give them only the *authority* to award scholarships (as it had done for the navy); it would not provide additional money to make the scholarships a reality. Consequently, the services believed that the initial impact of the scholarships would "almost surely be rather limited."[25] The services did, however, push to raise the monthly ROTC stipend, which had been at $27 per month since 1947, to $50 per month.[26]

Many military and civilian officials liked the idea of the two-year program so much that they proposed abandoning the four-year version altogether. The two-year program, they argued, would be less expensive and encourage wider student participation by reducing the time demands, allowing students with heavy academic commitments to fit ROTC more easily into their college schedule. The Air Force ROTC senior staff favored the elimination of the four-year program; the University of Illinois's Military Affairs Committee officially concurred in 1963.[27] An informal survey conducted by the air force found that 120 of the 182 schools hosting AFROTC units backed dropping the four-year program in favor of the proposed two-year program.[28]

The AROTC and AFROTC staffs strongly favored offering only the two-year program but promised to give schools the option of choosing to host the two-year program, the four-year, or both, depending on the desires of the school. Whatever their choice, the ROTC senior staffs told the schools that they could look forward to fewer ROTC contact hours. They had determined that they needed to reduce the students' "intolerable burden" of 480 contact hours, especially for the engineers that Secretary of Defense Robert McNamara coveted.[29] Therefore they proposed that much of the ROTC's technical preparation be moved to summer camps.

After coordinating its plan with the army and navy, the air force submitted a proposal to the Bureau of the Budget in 1962 that involved four major features: a raise in the ROTC stipend; a reduction of on-campus training in such technical subjects as drill and tactics; the opening of two-year programs (if desired by the host school); and the authority for each service to offer 8,000 scholarships annually.[30] Few expected that the army and air force would take immediate advantage of the scholarship authority, but the air force saw the opportunity to get such authority and have it securely protected from any future budget cuts.

The DOD and the Bureau of the Budget granted quick approval of the air force plan and sent it to the House Armed Services Committee, under the sponsorship of Louisiana Democrat F. Edward Hébert, in time for the 1963 legislative session. The bill, House Resolution 9124, had the unanimous support of educators, whose spokesman, NASULGC executive secretary Russell Thackrey, wrote to the committee: "I would like to *emphasize* that we are strongly in favor of the enactment of HR 9124 . . . Believe me, the ROTC needs the kind of revisions this bill provides. It has not been brought up to date since it was started and is beginning to suffer."[31]

Educators and military officers agreed on the important features that the new legislation should contain: scholarships in the existing four-year program *and* the proposed two-year program in order to include, among others, "the great development of 2-year institutions whose transfer students have not been eligible for ROTC"; a reduction of the teaching of military subjects such as drill on campus; and a raise in stipend for all cadets.[32] Such changes would halt the recent reduction in "the potential and actual effectiveness of the Reserve Officers' Training Corps programs" and create a "comprehensive program compatible with the educational objectives of the colleges and universities and adequate to assure meeting the qualitative and quantitative needs of the respective services."[33]

The general consensus that the highest officers of the military and academia had reached concluded nearly fifteen years of harmonious relations. Tensions certainly existed, but enough agreement on fundamental issues also existed to permit the two institutions to present a bill to Congress with one voice. The bill tried to create a program that met the educators' desires for a more educationally sound program and the military's desires for cost-effectiveness and greater participation from white undergraduate males. Despite this general level of agreement, however, the ROTC Vitalization Act ran into immediate difficulties with members of Congress, who had quite different goals for ROTC. The resulting legislation, instead of continuing the quest for harmony, set the goals of the military and the university at odds, unintentionally helping to create the crisis that would come at the end of the 1960s.

"More as a Means of Teaching Americanism"

The debates over the ROTC Vitalization Act lasted for two legislative sessions.[34] In the course of these debates, Congress altered or jettisoned many central features of the air force plan, which had focused on ways to make the program smaller, easier for students to fit into their schedules, and less technical. The congressional product focused more on citizenship training and visibility. The final Vitalization Act substantially altered the ROTC program in ways that solved some problems, left others unresolved, and created some unintended legacies for later years.

Congressional leaders took issue with certain features of the air force plan for the reform of the ROTC program. Representative Hébert argued that the program should be designed to provide good order on campus.[35] He therefore favored the full four-year program over the service's preferred two-year program. He also opposed the closing of "low-producing" units, as well as the conversion of units to voluntary enrollment, believing that the patriotic value of these units on campus justified their existence, despite their higher per capita costs. Similarly, he opposed the air force's plan to remove military training from campus on the grounds that more, not less, military presence on campus was desirable.

Hébert thus conceptualized the ROTC program as a large and visible program for all male undergraduates at participating institutions. As he said on the House floor during the debates, "As I envision this program, it is something which will bring about a resurgence in this country toward making our youth, not from the cradle, but certainly from the playground on up, conscious of their duty to their country and eager to perform in the service of their country and to be motivated by the highest ideals of citizenship."[36]

Some headquarters officers in both the army and the air force also opposed their ROTC staffs on the issue of on-campus military training. The staffs had hoped to remove such training to summer camps to free up time on campus for other subjects. To many ROTC officers, drill seemed anti- quated; junior officers in the more managerial military environment of the 1960s did much less marching than their predecessors had done and were subjected to much less formal discipline. As a 1964 AFROTC report declared, "Today's Air Force has little time or need for yesterday's emphasis on drill."[37] Military managers, in Morris Janowitz's formulation, relied on "the techni- cal proficiency of their team members" not the "formal authority structure" of years past.[38] As the new military was based much more on consensus than authority, devoting hours of valuable on-campus time to drill seemed wasteful. Moving the teaching of drill to summer camps could leave campus ROTC instructors with more time to teach military management, decision making, and critical-thinking skills.

Nevertheless, those at army headquarters pushed for such training to con- tinue on campus "in order to preclude the loss of prestige for the ROTC pro- gram and its becoming an extracurricular activity leading to its possible dis- continuance."[39] Some officers in the army also believed that to remove drill and other military subjects would marginalize the program: "It is felt that the importance of drill and ceremonies in the cadets' training is such that it must be a part of the curriculum . . . It is anticipated that morale and esprit of the cadets and, in turn, effectiveness of the training [are related to drill] . . . [Removing these subjects] may lead to the ultimate removal of the ROTC program from some campuses."[40] To these officers, abandoning drill meant abandoning the very heart of military training. These men were older, and almost all of them were veterans of the authoritarian military. According to them, removing drill meant eliminating the martial foundations of military training and risking irrevocable damage to the entire chain of command.

To emphasize the continued importance of the four-year program, Hébert authorized the 8,000 scholarships per service called for in the air force pro- posal, but he added a provision that these scholarships be made available only to students in the four-year program. A two-year program would be created, but its students would receive only a stipend, not the tuition assis- tance given to selected four-year students. The bill thus opened ROTC to transfer students and men who decided to join ROTC later in their career. However, the four-year program remained the heart of ROTC. Only ten AFROTC units and five AROTC units dropped the four-year program, be- cause to do so meant abandoning access to scholarship money.[41]

The headquarters officers believed, like Hébert, in the principle of universal military service that had been the basis of the draft laws of the 1950s. ROTC service should be visible, they believed, because it was a badge of pride, indicating an individual's commitment to his country. As army headquarters stated: "Every young man has an obligation to contribute to national defense. The college-educated man can best serve his country and his personal interests by earning a commission and fulfilling his obligation as an officer."[42] Reducing the four-year programs, drill, and the visibility of ROTC seemed to threaten a denigration of the principle of military obligation.

The service headquarters officers in the Pentagon were also closer to Congress and more sensitive to broad budgetary issues. Because of this sensitivity and their ideology of universal service, they went against the advice of their ROTC staffs, who counseled them to keep the program small, efficient, and inexpensive. Instead they concurred with the congressional view of the program as a citizenship training course that had to be visible to serve as a model of loyalty and patriotism. The ROTC staffs were primarily interested in a program to produce junior officers. The Congress and the service headquarters wanted that and more.

The law as finally passed had five main features:

1. The addition of a two-year, nonscholarship program.
2. The authorization of 5,500 full scholarships per service for four-year students.
3. The increase of monthly stipends to $50.
4. The authorization of the "cross-enrollment" of students from nearby schools that did not have ROTC units.
5. The reduction of contact hours from 480 to 360.

Three other features of the legislation that were added almost as afterthoughts are illustrative of the difference discussed above between the ROTC staffs and the Congress. Congress required that all advanced ROTC cadets enlist in the reserves. Should the cadet leave ROTC before graduation, he would then become subject to immediate call-up to enlisted service in the reserves. This provision closed a loophole that had permitted students to accept a scholarship, then walk away from ROTC weeks before graduation. The bill also required that contracts with host institutions specify that the highest ranking ROTC instructor be granted the title of professor and, finally, that the institution award "appropriate credit" for ROTC classes. The ROTC staffs had not asked for these features in any of their proposals.

The final bill legislated twice the number of total contact hours in the four-year program than the air force plan had called for (360 as opposed to 180). Furthermore, the law did not specify, as the AFROTC planners had hoped, that the reduction in contact hours should come at the expense of technical military subjects like drill. Reduction of contact hours was at the discretion of unit commanders. Army headquarters recommended eliminating the substitution of civilian-taught courses for those taught by uniformed personnel (see below) and reducing the time spent on academic subjects such as military history, which, of course, contravened the desires of educators.[43] The new curricula, then, affirmed the centrality of technical, military subjects at the expense of liberal arts courses.

These alterations did not damage support for the bill among educators, who rallied to assure passage. University of Illinois president David Henry wrote to Brigadier General William Lindley, "We strongly share your hope that the new ROTC legislation, HR 9124, will be approved by Congress this session," and Kent State president Robert White wrote to Ohio senators to say that he "unreservedly hope[d] for enactment of so-called ROTC bill."[44] Their support was based on a patriotic expectation that the program would be improved by the new legislation, the possibility for greater student participation promised in the bill, and the hope that the new scholarships would mean more money coming from the DOD to the university community. Although the Senate reduced the scholarship authorization from the House's 8,000 per service to 5,500 per service, this was still a dramatic improvement from the previous authorization of 5,500 *total* scholarships, limited to the fifty-three schools with NROTC units.

Still, the bill demonstrated that Congress had different goals for ROTC from those of educators or even some military officers. These differences created a legacy of visibility and adherence to technical military subjects that neither educators nor many ROTC instructors desired. *Newsweek* summed up the debates over the Vitalization Act well when it reported that "some Congressional patriots view the ROTC more as a means of teaching Americanism than of turning out officers."[45]

The Impact of Vitalization

Hébert told the House that his bill would "be the salvation of the free world and a free nation as we know it."[46] While it may not have been exactly that, the Vitalization Act did give ROTC the "new order of battle" that it needed to bring it in line with the mission it had already assumed.[47] It was not, how-ever, exactly what the services and the schools wanted. Those on Capitol Hill and in the Pentagon emphasized the visibility of ROTC and therefore were unwilling to reduce drill or compromise the four-year program, despite rec-ommendations from the program's administrators. To the politicians and headquarters staffs, ROTC represented idealized patriotism and committed self-sacrifice among the nation's college students. They were therefore will-ing to reject the advice and recommendations of those senior officers di-rectly in charge of the ROTC program.

Those officers wanted to make the program available to more students, and they also wanted a program that would be more acceptable to the uni-versity hosts. The hosts wanted to see less drill, both because of its visible contrast to other university programs and because even many ROTC in-structors acknowledged that "close order drill in many instances drives men away from the program."[48] The high visibility that the Vitalization Act legis-lated was an important legacy because it established a priority that educa-tors, and even some military personnel, did not share.

The services' desire to maintain high standards for on-campus technical military preparation meant that reduction in contact hours would have to come from academic subjects. This lack of priority for academic subjects influenced the 1964 ROTC curricula introduced by both the army and the air force. The new curricula deemphasized liberal arts courses and autho-rized the end of the substitution experiments of the late 1950s. The immi-nent reduction in the total number of contact hours meant that the services had to make some choices about what they wanted their cadets to learn. They chose to emphasize nonacademic military subjects because they be-lieved that deficiencies in these areas made postcommissioning training more expensive. They also believed that academic subjects were only tan-gentially related to the military and to the successful completion of the mis-sion of the American junior officer.[49] Before the Vitalization Act, the services had been willing to devote portions of the ROTC curriculum to academic subjects, but when the act mandated a reduction of contact hours, the ser-vices demonstrated their preference for nonacademic, military courses.

University administrators, however, were "highly disposed toward this idea of substitution" and were reluctant to give it up.[50] Michigan and Prince-ton officials argued that the kinds of cognate courses that had been substi-tuted in the past were indeed military in that they were concerned with the political, cultural, technical, and social environment within which military officers operated. Substitution had the additional virtue of making ROTC "fit in with the 'social fabric' of the university campus." At Princeton, this fit meant that ROTC cadets studied such subjects as economics and non-Western societies. Princeton president Robert Clifford protested the end of substitution to Secretary of the Army Stephen Ailes by arguing that "the Army must allow a degree of flexibility in the implementation of the new program so that it may be adapted to individual campus conditions. Each college must be encouraged to participate in the teaching of such courses in so far as its faculty talents permit."[51]

University of Michigan officials also protested the end of substitution, saying that the program had been a "terrific boon" to Michigan ROTC students. Michigan had been in the process of negotiating the substitution of two more courses into the AFROTC curriculum, Aeronautical Engineering and Business Administration, when it was informed that all substituted courses would be removed from the curriculum. Michigan administrative dean Robert Williams told the air force, "Some years ago the Air Force was the leader in this move toward the utilization of one course for two purposes, and it is the judgment of our group that the discontinuance of this practice can result only in harm to our combined efforts."[52]

Their protests fell on deaf ears. The Vitalization Act mandated a drop in contact hours from five to three per week, and the services had decided that technical military courses were more important to their mission than the civilian-taught courses that schools such as Princeton and Michigan wanted to remain a part of ROTC. The original architects of the bill wanted to see the technical courses moved to summer camps in order to continue the substitution programs, but congressional intent promoted the teaching of these subjects on campus to give ROTC visibility and vitality.

The 1964 cancellation of substitution echoed the debates over the initial introduction of substitution in the late 1950s. Those debates had touched on the larger issue of whether ROTC instruction was to be based on education, the general preparation of the cadet's talents through instruction in subject areas with more ecumenical applications, such as non-Western societies and business administration, or training, the more narrow preparation of individual ability to perform such tasks as drill, marksmanship, and map reading. American universities had been moving away from training in undergraduate instruction, even in specialized areas such as engineering and architecture, preferring instead to focus on more general problem-solving and management techniques.

This broad trend had the support of philanthropic groups such as the Ford Foundation, which dispensed $100,000,000 in grant money in the early 1960s through its Special Program in Education. The goal of the Special Program was to encourage "the humanities, natural sciences, and social sciences in cultivating the thoughtful leadership and independent opinion essential in a free society." Five of the six largest recipients of Ford Foundation Special Program in Education grants hosted ROTC programs.[53]

Substitution had thus been extremely popular with educators because it inclined the ROTC program toward the education model they preferred. The termination of substitution demonstrated that the services, despite occasional rhetoric to the contrary, were still inclined toward military training as the heart of their program. This dissonance underscored ROTC's growing divergence from the general trend in higher education. Educators attending a joint army-civilian ROTC meeting at Ohio State University in 1965 warned the army of the growing conflict: "ROTC on the campus is a 'paradox' to many students, since it gives heavy stress to 'training' (drill, rifle practice, map reading, etc.) at the same time instructors in other subjects are attempting to develop the student's conceptual powers through liberal education."[54] Michigan administrative dean Robert Williams warned the ROTC instructional staff in Ann Arbor that ROTC programs could not continue to exist at variance with changes in the general development of higher education:

> I am fully convinced that in the foreseeable future educational philosophy in all areas will demand more and more emphasis on 'principles' and less on 'how to do it' courses. If this be true, the competition for the time of the undergraduate who may wish to secure a commission through ROTC activities will require, in my judgment, (1) full recognition of ROTC courses as general electives within degree requirements, and (2) the critical review of the course content which justifies full utilization of the courses for degree programs.[55]

Close observers of the ROTC program might have noted that in reducing contact hours and endorsing a two-year program, the services were acknowledging that the program was indeed of marginal quality. The services were in fact admitting that they could turn out the same quality product with significantly fewer contact hours. All three ROTC programs developed six-week summer camps to be attended before the student's junior year for men entering the two-year program. This meant, of course, that the services thought that they could teach the first two *years* of the ROTC program in just six *weeks.* And indeed the six-week camp proved adequate; by all accounts, the two-year cadets were every bit the peers of the four-year cadets by the time they reached their senior year.[56]

The addition of the two-year program proved to be a moderate success by providing "greater flexibility in meeting the needs of students interested in obtaining Air Force commissions."[57] The air force claimed that within two years of the Vitalization Act's passage, the new program had served to boost enrollments by attracting men from all four targeted areas. The air force had hoped that the majority of the two-year cadets would come from junior colleges, but air force data indicated that the biggest appeal of the two-year program was to nontransfer students who decided to join ROTC at some point in their freshman or sophomore year. Seventy percent of the AFROTC two-year cadets were nontransfers; only 15 percent came from junior colleges.[58] Evidence from individual units supports this conclusion; by 1966 all of the two-year cadets from Kent State's army ROTC unit were four-year, on-campus students.[59]

The two-year program was more important for schools like the University of Pittsburgh, which then had a system of four regional campuses. The addition of the two-year program allowed the many University of Pittsburgh students who transferred from a branch campus to the Pittsburgh campus to enroll in ROTC in their final two years. Between 1965 and 1967 Pittsburgh's Army ROTC enrollment jumped 50 percent and the instructional staff subsequently grew from six to nine. Pittsburgh professor of military science Lieutenant Colonel Benjamin Hollis credited the two-year program with the enrollment increase.[60] In the same time period, the University of Washington's Army ROTC enrollment rose from 334 to 696, the first rise since Washington had dropped compulsory ROTC in 1962.[61]

The Vitalization Act fulfilled its main quantitative task: in 1967 the air force predicted that ROTC would begin to overproduce by 500 officers and that only twelve units were still producing unacceptably low numbers of officers.[62] But the act also sent some uneasy messages to the careful onlooker. It reduced time spent in the academic cognate courses that civilian officials saw as central to the mission of higher education and maintained the emphasis on the technical, military showpiece courses that the universities saw as most antithetical to their mission. Moreover, the act did not address some important abiding concerns, such as instructor qualification and credit for ROTC courses. Nor did it address the widely held perception that ROTC was so out of step with the new American university that it could not attract men and keep them interested long enough to convince them to pursue military training.

The Life of the Cadet

The main goal of the Vitalization Act was to attract significant numbers of students from groups previously excluded from serving. Even as the ROTC programs were trying to attract new men, however, they were suffering a period of quiet crisis among the men they already had. On campuses nationwide, people concerned with ROTC noted that the enthusiasm of cadets was low and that the program was having trouble keeping students motivated. One observer noted that "quite a few ROTC units wear their uniforms and drill with the precision of fat ladies exercising at the YWCA."[63]

One analysis of this problem argued that the sagging enrollments and enthusiasm were a function of the program's not being sufficiently martial. In this vein, some Army ROTC units, including the one at Rutgers, created Ranger units.[64] Other army units, such as that at the University of Illinois, increased field training and introduced training in airborne and special warfare in order to add "challenge" and "realism" to the ROTC experience.[65] Similarly, the University of Texas AROTC unit added a counterinsurgency branch in 1966.[66] The Illinois unit also established a military counseling office to advise students on the options open to them if they chose a military career.[67]

Another interpretation argued that as graduation requirements increased, students simply had less time and energy to devote to ROTC. The logical solution, of course, would have been to encourage the greater use of substitution, which effectively allowed one class to count twice—once for ROTC credit, once for graduation credit. But of course the services' interpretation of the Vitalization Act discouraged substitution.

If the participants at the 1965 Ohio State conference were right, then many students were having trouble understanding the role of ROTC on the campus. As noted, ROTC was not keeping pace with the general pedagogical trend at American universities of developing student talents through liberal education models. Indeed, the subjects the military and Congress preferred, such as drill and marksmanship, were ill-fitted to such a model.

The ROTC cadets of this era fell largely into two groups. One group of students joined ROTC primarily out of a desire to join the military and perhaps to make the armed forces their career. For this group, ROTC was a means to a commission and, for some, a scholarship. They were particularly attracted to the airborne and special warfare programs started at Illinois, Rutgers, Texas, and elsewhere. A commission in a special warfare unit had become an extremely prestigious military accomplishment since President Kennedy's championship of the Green Berets.

The second group joined ROTC primarily to avoid the draft. By most measures, this group accounted for just under half of the ROTC cadet population.[68] While it is true that until 1970 a student in good standing received a virtually automatic draft deferment, the expanding needs of the American military for manpower owing to the war in Vietnam created uncertainty about the security of student exemptions. In 1952 only 210,693 men were exempted from the draft due to student deferment (known as a 2-S), but by 1965 the explosion of college enrollments meant that 1.8 million men (or 10 percent of the total draft pool) were 2-S. Selective service officials consistently considered the removal of the student deferments as a way to increase the draft pool and lessen the class-based inequities that student deferments implied. By 1967 many politicians, including Massachusetts senator Edward Kennedy, were advocating a random "lottery" system for the draft that would end all blanket exemptions.[69] And of course student exemptions were never permanent; they ended after graduation.

University of Pittsburgh professor of military science (PMS) Lieutenant Colonel Benjamin Hollis explained that the enrollment increase at his unit in 1966 was partially a function of "more sweat being put on the students" by local draft boards.[70] The draft boards, Hollis believed, were putting increasing pressure on students in the lower half of their class by making conscription seem to be a more tangible reality. Consequently, those in the bottom half hoped that ROTC would give them "an additional assurance that they [would] be able to finish college."[71] Such pressure had the paradoxical consequence of encouraging the best students to avoid ROTC while holding out ROTC to the remainder as a means of avoiding conscription.

This dual motivation for ROTC enlistment explains the seemingly contradictory situation of declining enthusiasm on the one hand and the introduction of special warfare training at some units on the other. At least among a portion of the ROTC cadets, interest in the military was not waning; membership in ROTC honor societies was at record levels.[72] Still, on most campuses, a large minority of cadets, many of them not among the best students, were in ROTC primarily because of an interest in *avoiding* military service. It was largely due to the insouciance of this group that outside observers noted increased sloppiness and apathy in ROTC training. This quiet crisis for ROTC was exacerbated by the inability of the universities and the military to resolve many of their abiding concerns over academic issues.

Sometimes the actions of ROTC units themselves reinforced negative stereotypes, confirming the antimilitary beliefs of some and driving some young men away. In 1966 the Army ROTC unit at Worcester Polytechnical Institute held a "mock invasion" of the town of Middleboro, Massachusetts. At dawn on a May morning, ROTC cadets in full uniform moved through the town carrying weapons. The unit, however, had failed to inform town officials, resulting in "a police switchboard jammed with calls from frightened residents reporting suspicious looking characters in the neighborhood."[73]

The Middleboro incident and an incident at the University of Washington in 1967 both made national news and created significant negative publicity for ROTC. Washington cadets had received a secret briefing (no notes and no outside discussion permitted) on "subversive" groups at the university, including SDS and the civil rights group the Student Nonviolent Coordinating Committee (SNCC). Then, in "an attempt to add realism to our Brigade Staff training," cadets were ordered to collect posters and information on the groups and any students or faculty who belonged to such groups.[74] One cadet refused to participate and may have been the individual who leaked the story to the American Association of University Professors (AAUP) and the American Civil Liberties Union (ACLU) in Seattle.

Once the story became public, Washington president Charles Odegaard ordered that the "spy" exercise be stopped. The Washington PMS at first denied that any such operation had been ordered, then recanted when a brigade S-2 (intelligence) file on "left wing activities" emerged. The ROTC file told cadets that persons or groups that opposed the war in Vietnam "were in fact our enemies." The PMS later refused to show President Odegaard the briefing materials on the grounds that they were secret, because the university was then in the process of removing credit for any course (including two NROTC classes) that used classified materials.[75]

Despite attempts by all parties to keep the scandal out of the spotlight, the case made national news, appearing in newspapers from San Francisco to New York. In Seattle, the fallout over what became known as the "duck scandal" proved to be quite damaging for ROTC.[76] The duck scandal produced the first serious challenge to military training in the University of Washington's history. Professors and students charged that ROTC had "violat[ed] the canons of academic freedom, especially the principle of free and open exchange of knowledge."[77] The controversy eventually blew over, but it left a shadow on ROTC at the University of Washington and elsewhere that contributed to an overall unease with military training on civilian campuses.

Abiding Concerns

Of the issues left unresolved from the Cold War era, academic credit and instructor qualifications were the two most often debated. ROTC instructors were not more formally educated than their counterparts from the 1950s had been, despite service protestations to the contrary, and they were not the "top flight" men the services needed in order to improve relations with the host schools.[78] The services assumed that "men who have discharged responsibilities successfully in other assignments will do so in this one."[79] Moreover, as information and education both grew more complex, the need for technically proficient and experienced instructors became even greater. After passage of the Vitalization Act, all three services added programs to teach their instructors how to teach, but these programs were usually perfunctory two- to three-week courses that hardly provided the academic credentials of collegiate teaching experience and advanced degrees.

Of the 196 officers assigned to AFROTC duty in 1964, only 36 (18 percent) had an advanced degree; this figure was actually much lower than the 27 percent of ROTC instructors already on assignment that year who possessed an advanced degree. The air force continued to hold to the idea that it was more important to assign young officers than to assign formally educated ones. No officer assigned to AFROTC duty that year was older than forty-eight; only one had attained the rank of full colonel.[80] The navy was only slightly more able to assign officers with advanced degrees; 28 percent of its instructors were so qualified in 1965.[81]

The services had taken great pains to advertise that ROTC duty was "definitely not a 'last assignment' before retirement," as it had once been.[82] Nevertheless, the services used ROTC duty as a reward for men who had recently completed an overseas tour of duty; volunteers for ROTC assignments continued to get priority. Eighty-five percent of AFROTC officers took their appointment while completing an overseas tour of duty, meaning that the universities were unable to interview the candidates and that factors other than qualifications and teaching experience determined assignments to ROTC units.

The services and the universities agreed that the assignment of formally educated officers was an important goal and would, if attained, improve military-university relations. Two successive University of Illinois professors of military science argued in their annual reports that the university should insist on men with master's degrees, as they would be "ambassador(s) for the United States Army."[83] They further argued that men with advanced degrees made the job easier by becoming more a part of the university and its value system: "Officer personnel should either possess graduate degrees or be qualified and interested in graduate study. It is essential to overcome the objection that our officers lack professional academic credentials. Those officers who possess graduate degrees are more acceptable to the professional academicians, and those officers who pursue graduate study are invaluable as intelligent advocates of the program on the academician's home ground."[84] Those at AFROTC headquarters, while not placing a priority on formal education, understood that the job of the PAS "takes them into areas of [the] academician while remaining a professional Air Force officer. This requires the utmost in background, interest and versatility to properly fit into this academic environment."[85]

But if a general consensus existed that formally educated officers made the ROTC-university relationship easier and instruction better, the services still made no determined effort to assign more ROTC officers with advanced degrees. Two problems inhibited such assignments. First, the services simply did not have many officers with master's degrees whom they could assign to ROTC units. While the 28 percent of NROTC instructors with a master's degree in 1965 may seem itself a small number, only 12 percent of all naval officers had a master's degree.[86] Simply put, the number of officers who had an advanced degree was very small, and many of them served in highly specialized areas from which they could not easily be reassigned. Thus even when the services and the universities could agree on the necessity and value of formally educated officers, personnel realities meant that, in the words of a joint university-navy board, "the achievement of this goal [was] going to take time."[87]

Second, the personnel assignment calculus, difficult under ideal circumstances, became even more chaotic as officers were assigned in greater number to Southeast Asia. The war changed officer assignment priorities and forced the universities to an initial position of lenience toward the services. If the services needed officers for the war, the universities could hardly insist that ROTC assignments take precedence over providing leadership for what was then seen by many as a war against communism. As the University of Illinois provost told the army in 1966, "While we normally expect that faculty nominees at the assistant professorial level possess doctoral academic credentials or, at a minimum, the equivalent of a Master's Degree, I am in agreement with our Professor of Military Science that an exception may be made at this time because of the severe personnel problems generated by the situation in Viet Nam."[88]

All universities had to deal with the limitations of the service personnel systems. The services genuinely wanted to assign "only officers of demonstrated competence, vigor, and initiative" to ROTC units, but they were constrained from doing so.[89] To compensate for the comparatively low level of instructor education, some schools began or expanded seminar programs that featured lectures by civilian faculty on issues relevant to global military systems. In 1966–67, the Illinois seminar program featured talks entitled "The Indian Army and India's Military Potential," "The Role of the United States in Southeast Asia," "Soviet Attitudes," "Military-State Relationships in Germany," "The Role of the United States in World Affairs," "Soviet Foreign Policy," "Military-Civilian Relationships in Latin America, and "Chinese Foreign Policy."[90]

Because instructor qualifications did not rise as the universities had hoped, resolution of the question of academic credit remained difficult. The services had also reduced time spent on academic subjects while maintaining the number of contact hours in courses, like drill, that the universities had determined were least worthy of credit. According to national ROTC curriculum models, drill and military ceremony were to constitute one-third of the cadet's total contact hours.

Academic opinion of ROTC course quality dropped significantly when the new curriculum models were introduced. A 1965 review of the ROTC programs at the University of Washington found the new programs "not rigorous in the usual academic sense." Washington officials pushed for NROTC instructors to audit civilian courses in order to "be introduced to new teaching methods." ROTC courses, they alleged, focused too much on "approved solutions" and "housekeeping chores." Cadets and midshipmen, they argued, were "indoctrinated," not taught. Their analysis found that ROTC graduates were "not capable of . . . sophistication of argument" and received inflated grades. In one quarter, 72 percent of ROTC grades were A's and B's, when the College of Arts and Sciences only awarded 44 percent A's and B's. That same quarter, only 2 percent of ROTC students received D's and F's; 16 percent of students in the College of Arts and Sciences received D's and F's.[91]

The new evaluations contrasted with the enthusiasm the services them-selves had for their curricula. The services advertised their courses as follow-ing the creative model of liberal education, not the "how to do it" model of the past. Still, the goals of ROTC were narrower than those of civilian edu-cational programs. The air force introduced its 1964 curriculum thus: "[AFROTC's] emphasis is on education—*professional education*. The basic goal of this professional education is to provide the military knowledge and skills needed by the cadets on the day they become Air Force second lieuten-ants."[92] The services nevertheless argued that their courses were enough like civilian courses to merit academic credit on the same basis.

The ROTC staff officers, however, were of mixed opinion as to exactly *why* it was important that the universities extend full credit to ROTC courses. On the surface, of course, it seemed intuitive that maximum academic credit would encourage more students to enroll and would also make ROTC a more central part of the school's general academic offerings. At the same time, insisting too forcefully on more credit carried with it the risk of offend-ing university faculties who jealously guarded their right to determine which courses merited credit, the ultimate stamp of official approval. Fur-thermore, both the air force and the army had conducted studies that ar-gued that the amount of credit awarded bore no relation to the quality of ROTC graduates produced and affected enrollment only in engineering pro-grams.[93]

The army's official policy, then, was for a PMS to press for more credit only if such a move would clearly benefit the program, although on a na-tional level the army still lobbied educators for credit as recognition of the ROTC curriculum's educational merit. The air force and navy, however, were more insistent. The air force had determined that only 50 of its 170 host schools awarded "full effective credit" in all degree programs, and it pressed for an increase nationwide at the 1966 meeting of the AFROTC Ad-visory Panel:

> We believe that the Air Force has a responsibility to both the students and the institutions to offer courses that have academic substance and are pre-sented in a manner in harmony with the educational goals of the host insti-tution. We think that students taking ROTC courses on the campus should receive academic credit for these courses on the same basis that they would for other campus offerings. We recognize that academic credit is a matter for local faculty determination and we seek only to have our course offerings examined on their merit.[94]

With one-third of the AFROTC curriculum dedicated to drill and military ceremony, the air force's plea for evaluation of its courses "on their merit" made it easy for university faculties consistently to deny service requests to increase credit, although reductions in credit were also rare.

The universities continued to insist that if the services wanted their ROTC programs to carry more academic credit, they would need to be strengthened. The Army Advisory Panel on ROTC Affairs meeting in 1967 was almost wholly dedicated to the issue of credit. Educators told the army that to receive more credit, its courses would need to devote more attention to academic subjects, be taught by men with advanced degrees, and "serve an education need for future leaders, civilian as well as military." The panel suggested that the army fund programs in "team-teaching," classes taught by both civilian and military instructors, until enough officers with advanced degrees arrived on ROTC staffs.

Civilian faculties resisted giving ROTC credit for courses that they believed could be better taught in regular university departments. Thus, in 1965 the University of Texas College of Arts and Sciences Course Committee rejected a proposed basic AFROTC academic program that included courses that overlapped with offerings in the history and government departments: "The Committee does not consider that certain portions of the subject matter content of these courses should be taught by professional military officers. It is the contention of some members of the Faculty that the subject matter in question (Democracy, Communism, etc.) is purely academic and that an objective presentation of it could not be given by military personnel obligated to conform to establish[ed] Defense Department policy.[95] University officials proposed that the air force either return to substitution to allow civilian faculty to teach these courses or develop a purely technical curriculum for which the university would grant credit. The University of Texas was thus willing to give ROTC credit for teaching military subjects within the range of the instructor's expertise, but not for academic subjects generally understood to be outside their purview.

In other words, the universities, despite general official support, informed the services that if they wanted ROTC to receive more academic credit, they would have to improve the academic value of the program. The centrality of ROTC to national security warranted the program's survival, but it no longer provided sufficient justification to merit further university concessions to the program. These debates were unrelated to the growing, but still minor, opposition on campuses nationwide to the expanding war in Southeast Asia. Rather they were issues that remained from the Cold War. The war in Vietnam was, however, coming to occupy more of the nation's energy and drawing more attention from critics.

Vietnam's Early Impact on ROTC

President Lyndon Johnson's decision in August 1964 to ask for a congressional resolution to prosecute the war in Vietnam provoked few immediate negative reactions on American campuses. Congress passed the resolution with only two dissenting votes, and by all accounts the American people were in agreement. According to one poll, 67 percent of the American people supported Johnson in February 1965 after he ordered the series of punitive bombings known as Rolling Thunder in retaliation for a Viet Cong attack on an American airbase.[96]

By the end of 1965 American planes had flown 25,000 sorties and dropped 63,000 tons of bombs on Vietnam. In July President Johnson had promised General William Westmoreland 100,000 American troops, in addition to the 40,000 already in Vietnam, to allow Westmoreland to begin "search and destroy" operations against the Viet Cong.[97] These events still had no demonstrably negative impact on ROTC units nationwide. The University of Illinois Army ROTC unit even noted "a definite trend towards improved attitudes towards ROTC" in the fall of 1965.[98] The only immediate impact of the war may have been to boost enrollments; many analysts cited students' attempts to avoid being conscripted into the war, not the Vitalization Act, for the rising ROTC enrollments.

Still, as the war casualties and questions mounted, so did student opposition. ROTC instructional staffs endeavored to stay out of campus debates. In September 1965, when an antiwar poster was glued to an ROTC bulletin board at the University of Pittsburgh, Lieutenant Colonel Benjamin Hollis chose not to take any action himself; instead he handed the poster over to university police and told the chancellor that he hoped to "avoid publicity." Hollis argued that most members of the University of Pittsburgh community were either supportive of or indifferent to ROTC and that to seek a confrontation would only play into the hands of the antiwar students and faculty.[99]

The New Left, which led the antiwar movement, had not yet begun to oppose ROTC because of the program's connection to the war in Vietnam. At schools such as Kent State, ROTC cadets had the unenviable job of presenting colors to the next of kin of a local soldier or airman killed in Vietnam, but no other visible links yet existed. ROTC cadets had not yet begun to go to

Vietnam in large numbers, and few Vietnam veterans had returned from overseas to serve as ROTC instructors. Initial campus opposition to ROTC, then, was not focused, as it would be later, on ROTC's production of officers necessary for the war.

Instead, student opposition to ROTC focused on those traditional points of conflict that remained from the 1950s. A fall 1967 rally at the University of Pittsburgh featured signs that read "No Tenure for Sergeants" and "Intellectualism, Not Militarism."[100] Even Pittsburgh's most implacable ROTC foe, psychology professor James Holland, took his stand not because of the war but "because [ROTC] is so out of step with University policy."[101] Similarly, at Rutgers, student body president Ray Korona spoke out against ROTC's teaching methods rather than its link to the war in Southeast Asia.[102] While the war may have made ROTC foes more assertive, it did not initially provide new reasons to call for the program's reform or abolition. The principle objections to ROTC remained those based on the basic discrepancies between ROTC and other university programs.

Until 1968 the American people, including most of those in university communities, generally supported the war. As late as October 1967, 53 percent of Americans favored *escalation* of the war.[103] Most campuses were not hotbeds of activism during this early period of antiwar sentiment. For example, the Rutgers chapter of SDS received only five responses to its mass mailing of a student referendum on ROTC in 1967.[104] Still, a growing number of people were coming to challenge American intervention in Vietnam. The problem was not yet serious enough to cause ROTC staffs to address the problem on a national level, but ROTC unit heads were beginning to take note.

The question of the appropriate response to antiwar demonstrators was a topic of much informal conversation at the 1967 conference of professors of military science, held at Ft. Meade. Kent State's PMS expressed the consensus of the conference in a letter to Kent State president Robert White:

> To my knowledge no overt opposition to our programs has been evident [as a result of anti-Vietnam feelings]. My position to both my cadre and cadets is that we will avoid any confrontation with campus groups which might demonstrate or harangue against us—I would hope that we could totally ignore them . . . [Kent State] is not a military reservation or defense installation and groups have every right to their existence in order that each student and faculty member may have a wide range of ideas from which to

choose—the right to question is fundamental. Excuse the soapbox, but I want to do everything possible from my position to prevent, before it is even a possibility, any fracas between hotheads on both sides.[105]

The same year, the PMS at Rutgers defended the rights of twenty-seven demonstrators who blocked an ROTC drill period. He also supported the mild punishment (disciplinary probation) given by the university's disciplinary board.[106]

ROTC officers were caught in a difficult position. If they made statements deemed contrary to the aims of the military, they were in violation of the values of their profession and possibly faced sanction from above. If they remained silent or stuck to the rhetoric emanating from the Pentagon, they were accused of not tolerating academic freedom or objectivity. Most officers, anticipating that their futures were as military professionals, not academics, chose silence. This tactic was more than a product of self-interest; it was also intended to keep ROTC out of campus debates. Instead, however, it opened ROTC officers to new charges of anti-intellectualism. Military officers across the nation hoped to keep antiwar sentiment from affecting ROTC programs. Until 1968, they were largely able to do so. But after 1968 the visibility that the Vitalization Act mandated would contribute to the sternest challenge in the history of the program to the place and order of ROTC.

The debates over the passage and implementation of the ROTC Vitalization Act demonstrate two important points. First, serious problems in ROTC predated later challenges that were related to anti-Vietnam sentiment. Even without rising antiwar sentiment, the program was approaching a period of crisis in terms of the quantity and quality of cadets produced, its relations with the university hosts, and the direction of the ROTC curriculum. The problems that ROTC encountered after 1968, then, were not entirely new. They had roots that went back to the 1950s and were encouraged by major changes that accompanied the Vitalization Act of 1964.

Second, the Vitalization Act shows that the military, Congress, and higher education had different goals and directions in mind for ROTC. Several military officers lobbied for changes that reflected the civilization, innovation, and diversification that Janowitz has described. They argued that as the United States military began to assume a more constabulary role (both at home and abroad), junior officers would need to have a better understanding of politics, history, and management.[107] For the most part, educators were sympathetic to this view because it was more in line with their own understanding of how the on-campus portion of military training should be conducted.

This view, however, was at odds with an older position that emphasized military ceremony and drill as a means of achieving order and discipline. Proponents F. Edward Hébert and others were less interested in increasing the efficiency of the armed forces than they were in using the authority and hierarchy that they saw in the military to promote patriotism and civic virtue. Drill became a focal point in the debate, symbolizing either outdated, automatonic mindlessness or orderly ceremony.

The compromise between these two viewpoints delayed the implementation of an ROTC curriculum centered around problem-solving educational techniques similar to those used by civilian faculty. By maintaining an outdated image of the military, the Vitalization Act highlighted the most objectionable features of ROTC. Furthermore, by contravening or ignoring the wishes of the air force architects of ROTC reform, the bill also left several critical problems unresolved. As a result, ROTC was poorly positioned for the battles ahead.

CHAPTER 5

ROTC from Tet to the All-Volunteer Force

Those who fear the rise of an American Foreign Legion, loyal only to its own officers, must see that the fastest way of bringing such an organization about is to abandon the ROTC. For America's sake, let's strengthen the ROTC, not destroy it.

—Georgia Tech *Technique*, May 17, 1970

Before the 1968 Vietnamese lunar new year, known as Tet, the majority of Americans believed the proclamations of the American military and political establishments that the war, while not yet won, was clearly under control and that victory was certain. However, within hours of the start of what became known as the Tet offensive on January 30, millions of Americans had reason to doubt all that they had been told. On hearing early reports of the attacks, one of America's most respected journalists, Walter Cronkite, shouted, "What the hell is going on? I thought we were winning the war!"[1] As the bombing of Pearl Harbor had done a generation earlier, Tet changed the American approach to war almost overnight and, eventually, ended Robert McNamara's reign as secretary of defense, General William Westmoreland's position as head of American forces in Southeast Asia, and the Johnson presidency itself.

The Viet Cong used American overconfidence as well as the noise, heavy traffic, and thirty-six-hour cease-fire for the Tet holiday to disguise a series of well-coordinated attacks on five of South Vietnam's six largest cities, thirty-six of South Vietnam's forty-four provincial capitals, sixty-four of its district capitals, Tan Son Nhut Airport, the presidential palace in Saigon, and the headquarters of the South Vietnamese general staff. Nineteen Viet Cong soldiers even got inside the new American embassy in Saigon.

The Tet offensive created a psychological collapse in the United States and a dramatic shift in attitudes toward the war. Robert Kennedy argued that Tet had "finally shattered the mask of official illusion with which we have concealed our true circumstances, even from ourselves."[2] Some opposition to the war had been steadily growing throughout 1967 as the personnel needs of the army had forced the conscription of recent college graduates and as the financial costs of the war had ballooned to $33 billion per year, provoking inflation.[3] Tet, however, was the watershed; in March 1968, for the first time, the percentage of Americans calling themselves Doves exceeded the percentage calling themselves Hawks.[4] After Tet, support for the war fell sharply among Republicans, Democrats, and Independents alike.[5]

Of course, Tet alone did not create the "dissolution of consensus" on American campuses in the late 1960s.[6] Civil rights issues and questions of university procedures regarding defense contracts had already caused contention. But Tet marked a dramatic turning point that "breathed life into languishing American liberalism" and forced a complete reexamination of both the war and the place of the military in American society:[7] "What mattered to the American public what that this [supposedly] defeated enemy could attack anywhere and was attacking everywhere more fiercely than before. The winning of the war was not coming 'into view.' The war in Vietnam was never going to be won. Nothing had been achieved by the outpouring of lives and treasure and the rending of American society. The assurances the public had been given were the lies and vaporings of foolish men."[8] After Tet, the battles in Southeast Asia and the debates on American campuses took on a whole new dimension.

"Like an Embassy on Foreign Soil"

Just as the American public's response to the war changed sharply as a result of Tet, so too did university attitudes change toward ROTC. As noted earlier, ROTC's position on the campus had always been somewhat uneasy, but official approbation and the perception of ROTC's contribution to national security had provided it with, if not universal support, a general level of approval at best, indifference at worst. Tet cast a shadow of doubt on the national security justifications of the American military system in general and on ROTC as a manifestation of the military. On the campuses, this sentiment produced an air of suspicion and incertitude. By the end of March, ROTC officers were beginning to talk about their unit in words similar to the army's professor of military science at Michigan State, who likened his assignment to being at "an embassy on foreign soil."[9] The level of outright hostility and violence varied significantly from campus to campus, but on most campuses ROTC's prestige dropped significantly after Tet.

Tet also enlivened and accelerated the politicization of college students, many of whom were already active in such causes as the civil rights movement. Many radical students were, in Tom Hayden's words in October 1968 to the National Commission on the Causes and Prevention of Violence, "moving toward confrontation" as a means of protest, and many less radical students were paying increasing attention to controversial issues on campus and across the nation.[10] Political views on many American campuses were moving to the left, challenging the status quo and the nature of university links to the military, the intelligence community, and the giants of the defense industry, to name but a few.

As a manifestation of this sentiment, forty-five AFROTC units reported "verbal abuse, sit-ins, placards, pamphlets, and anti-ROTC articles in both official and unofficial campus newspapers" between February and June 1968.[11] Most protests against ROTC were peaceful; national events, such as the assassinations of Martin Luther King in April and Robert Kennedy in June, created heightened tension but no real violence. The ROTC cadre's policy of not getting involved in campus confrontations surely helped to keep protests nonviolent.

But just as some military officers had predicted, the visibility of drill and military ceremony legislated into ROTC through the 1964 Vitalization Act (see Chapter 4) made ROTC more of a target than it might otherwise have been by highlighting exactly the features of the program that were most objectionable to university communities. Outdoor drill sessions were the scene of virtually all of the anti-ROTC activities reported by AFROTC units to air force headquarters in 1968.[12] While these confrontations rarely provoked violence, they added to the tension and mutual mistrust that was building between on-campus military personnel and student protesters.

For the most part, ROTC officers and cadets remained apart from the protests. Only on rare occasions did they confront student protesters, and when they did the results were quite damaging to the already declining status of ROTC. To cite one example, in October 1968 an army master sergeant assigned to the University of Pittsburgh ROTC staff approached a protester who was wearing a jacket adorned with army medals he had purchased at a military surplus store. The sergeant demanded that the protester remove the medals. The protester refused but invited the sergeant to cut them off if he was offended; the sergeant did.

The incident seems minor enough in retrospect; there was no violence and it did not incite further action from either side. Still, the reaction of the university community gave ROTC units a sufficient reminder of why they should try to be nonconfrontational. The Pittsburgh student newspaper reported the incident as "ROTC versus 'Democracy'" and argued that the event served as a vivid example of why ROTC had no place on campus. "This blatant act of assault, without any legal authority to act, was shocking to everyone who witnessed it. But in effect, the action taken by [the] Sergeant . . . is a microcosmic example of the problem that ROTC presents to this university in particular, and to the entire higher educational system in general."[13]

Interestingly, Pittsburgh's PMS, Colonel David Clagett, did not defend the sergeant or try to justify his actions. Instead, he reiterated the position of his department: "The policy of the Department of Military Science has been and is that members of the department will not in any way interfere with students or student activities. This is the first time such an incident has occurred and it will not be repeated." That same day, the sergeant apologized to the student, saying that he had "acted *as an individual* and did exercise poor judgment."[14] The position of ROTC units, then, was clear. They would try, despite the visibility Congress had mandated into the program, to remain apart from antiwar activity. The mood on college campuses was becoming ever more hostile to the military; confrontations only aggravated the problem.

The air force also counseled its ROTC instructors not to use a "response of force" to protesters, but to try a "peace offensive" characterized by "curiosity, open-mindedness, and empathy." Through these actions, the air force argued, "we can contribute to the remodeling of the military image in the eyes of students, publicize the mission of the AFROTC, and in on our small way, help close the barrier between adults and youth in this critical generation."[15]

For many members of that generation, the link between ROTC and the war in Vietnam had come to symbolize the Faustian militarization of many American institutions, including the universities. For others, the war and attendant antimilitary feelings on campuses nationwide had dramatically reduced the prestige of the military and inclined many against pursuing a military career. Even those already in ROTC were chafing at the program's discipline more than they had in the past. Both by demanding a new approach and by simply staying away from the program, undergraduates were pushing for change.

Total ROTC enrollments fell dramatically, from 218,466 in October 1968 to 161,507 one year later, a drop of more than 25 percent.[16] After producing a record number of commissions in 1968 (largely as a result of the reforms introduced by the Vitalization Act) ROTC enrollments declined in 1969 at all but two schools nationwide, Kearney State (Nebraska) and Southern Colorado State.[17] The ninety NASULGC schools reported a 22 percent drop in ROTC enrollments among member institutions.[18] University of Michigan ROTC enrollments fell 31 percent from academic year 1967–68 to academic year 1968–69; in the same time period University of Illinois enrollments fell 38 percent.[19] Evidence from freshman enrollments portended even more serious problems in the future. One hundred seventy-four freshmen had enrolled in AFROTC at the University of Pittsburgh in the fall of 1968; only 34 freshmen did so one year later.[20] At Illinois, total freshman ROTC enrollments fell from 376 in 1968 to 182 in 1969.[21]

Some military officers tried to make a simplistic connection between the end of academic credit for ROTC at many schools and the lower enrollment levels, but it is clear that much more was happening. Enrollments dropped just as sharply at schools where the amount of credit awarded did not change. More important than credit, ROTC had ceased to carry the prestige it had in the past. Only one in four AFROTC cadets surveyed in 1968 described the prevailing attitude toward ROTC cadets on their campus as "highly favorable" or "mildly favorable."[22] The *Wall Street Journal* noted in 1968 that "a few college girls wouldn't be caught dead dating an ROTC cadet."[23] Once a badge of patriotism, ROTC had become a stigma. Even at Georgia Tech, where "anti-ROTC peer pressure was minimal," the army's PMS asked that campus security guards, not cadets, lower the American flag at the end of each day to "lessen the military profile on campus to the minimal reasonable level."[24]

Furthermore, after Tet, the character of the war in Southeast Asia itself changed. With the official goals of the war and sanguine proclamations of progress largely discredited (along with the beginnings of troop withdrawals in 1969) fewer men went to war because of an ideological belief in the purpose of American involvement. Many soldiers fought simply to remain alive, not to achieve murky military and political goals. After Tet the war became bloodier, racial tension among American forces became rampant, drug use among the men soared, and discipline in some units broke down entirely. In 1970 alone, 2,000 incidents of "fragging," attacks by enlisted men on their own officers, were reported.[25] As Neil Sheehan, a careful observer of the war from its outset, noted:

> The riflemen who had fought with Hal Moore in the valley of the Drang [in 1965] and at Bong Son [in 1966] would not have recognized the U.S. Army of 1969. It was an Army in which men escaped into marijuana and heroin and other men died because their comrades were "stoned" on drugs that profited the Chinese traffickers and the Saigon generals. It was an Army whose units in the field were on the edge of mutiny, whose soldiers rebelled against the senselessness of their sacrifice by assassinating officers and non-coms in "accidental" shootings and "fraggings" with grenades.[26]

Before Tet, many men had joined ROTC out of a desire to have some control over their military service, not to avoid it. After Tet, service in ROTC was seen to carry with it the possibility of assignment to the more brutal, less meaningful war of the post-Tet era.[27]

The introduction of the draft lottery in 1969 meant a further change in the quality and quantity of ROTC cadets. The lottery system ended the blanket service exemptions previously given to undergraduates in good standing. Instead, in December 1968 the selective service system randomly assigned a draft number to each day of the year and then to each man between age nineteen and twenty-six, based on his date of birth; thereafter an individual's chance of being drafted depended on his draft number. Men born on June 8, for example, no longer had anything to fear from conscription, for they had the highest number, 365.[28]

The lottery brought an end to much of the speculation that had characterized the draft. Now a man knew more precisely his chances of being drafted. For men with high draft numbers, ROTC no longer had to serve as a means of avoiding military service. One DOD study concluded that one-third of ROTC cadets nationwide dropped out after the lottery system was introduced and that the overwhelming majority of those men held high draft numbers.[29] In 1971 only 13 percent of AFROTC cadets had draft numbers higher than 280.[30]

For men with low draft numbers, conversely, ROTC could serve as a way to avoid conscription. In 1970, nearly half (46 percent) of AFROTC sophomores said that they had joined ROTC because "it was AFROTC or the draft."[31] One year later, 33 percent of AFROTC cadets had draft numbers lower than 80; that is, one-third of the cadets were among the one-fifth of males most likely to be drafted.[32] Enrolling in ROTC offered an option to those who found other means of evading the draft unappealing. ROTC might keep a man on campus long enough for the war to end, or, if military service was inevitable or desirable, at least give the man some say as to which branch of the service he entered. Army ROTC experienced the sharpest enrollment declines, partially because of the perception that the army and marines bore a heavier casualty burden than either the air force or the navy. To many, a commission in one of the latter two services seemed to offer a way to fulfill one's military obligation with less risk. As the saying went, "There ain't no Viet Cong submarines."

The services were certainly aware of the impact of the lottery system; the ROTC units often used it as recruitment tool "woo[ing] university students with promises of safe assignments and deferred enlistments."[33] The University of Pittsburgh Army ROTC unit even displayed a poster in 1969 that read, "Want to Beat the Draft? Enroll in the 2-Year ROTC Program."[34] The two-year program became especially popular with sophomores who had just drawn a low draft number and were therefore suddenly more vulnerable to conscription. Georgia Tech's AROTC program advertised that for two-year cadets, "a draft deferment is authorized and takes priority over a previously issued draft notice."[35] In other words, enlisting in ROTC could defer the draft notice that had arrived in a young man's mailbox the day before.

University officials, like Georgia Tech president Arthur Hansen, understood that "draft pressure is overwhelmingly the primary reason for ROTC enrollment."[36] Most studies concluded that anywhere from 35 percent to 60 percent of ROTC cadets were motivated by the draft. One study argued that only 31 percent of ROTC students from schools in the Northeast and 45 percent of ROTC students from schools in the South were "true volunteers" who would have joined ROTC in the absence of the draft.[37] Using ROTC to control the timing and nature of one's military service existed before this era, but now perhaps half of the cadets were using ROTC primarily to avoid the draft.[38]

Given that so many ROTC students enrolled primarily to avoid the draft, it is not surprising that the character of the program changed. Yale president Kingman Brewster argued throughout this period that a system of conscription with student exemptions had turned the nation's colleges and universities into a draft haven, thereby creating "sourness" toward both higher education and the military.[39] This sentiment certainly made it down to ROTC units. Just as the blanket student exemptions had caused many men to enter or remain in college to avoid the draft more than to learn, so did the draft cause significant numbers of men to join ROTC to avoid the war more than to satisfy a desire to be in ROTC. As more of these men joined ROTC units and as the prestige of these units on campus fell, cadets began to object to many ROTC requirements that made them stand out from their peers and thus made them easy targets for ridicule.

Not surprisingly, cadets focused on hair and uniform requirements as the two military regulations that most visibly separated them from their non-ROTC classmates. One study of AFROTC dropouts at the University of Massachusetts found that half of them left the program because of appearance requirements and their "unwillingness to wear the uniform on campus."[40] Similarly, University of California officials noted that uniform requirements were cited most frequently in cadet complaints about ROTC.[41] In 1970, two AFROTC cadets from Michigan State University wrote a seventy-four-page paper "challenging the morality, legality and practicality of Air Force regulations governing permissible coifs, mustaches, and beards," an act of recalcitrance unthinkable before Tet. Their report was intended to demonstrate that the military's insistence on crew cuts was not only irrational but also counterproductive: "The cadets cite evidence indicating that students with crew cuts are at a disadvantage with girls and that they are subject to the ridicule of fellow students and teachers. They also allege that the corps' image, which is under attack at Michigan State and many other campuses, would be improved if hair were left a matter of individual preference and that the recruiting of candidates would become easier."[42] Or, as the girlfriend of one University of Pittsburgh cadet warned his instructor, "Your stupid haircut regulations are going to break up our relationship!"[43]

"Those Which Are Hardest to Defend"

The most radical students and faculty held to a position, vocally espoused by groups such as the Students for a Democratic Society, that the goals of ROTC and the goals of the American university could never be reconciled. ROTC, they argued, "is not only antithetical to the ultimate purposes of higher education, but contrary to basic pedagogical principles as well [because of] the unquestioning submissiveness endemic in the rigidly hierarchical structure of military education."[44] They sought expulsion of ROTC, not reform, because in their eyes ROTC was "an island of indoctrination in a sea of academic freedom."[45]

The radicals also opposed ROTC because, they argued, the program turned the university into an "officer factory." SDS contended in 1970 that "ROTC . . . produces the officers essential for continuing the United States' genocidal war in South East Asia."[46] At a 1969 rally at the University of Washington, SDS members argued that "ROTC is as much a part of the exploitation in Latin America as the United Fruit Company. In order to help the liberation struggles in the Third World we must fight the military as well as the corporation."[47] The logical extension of this argument was that the universities were complicit in the immorality of the war in Southeast Asia (and elsewhere) by permitting the services to train future officers on campus:

> If the university's role in cooperating with ROTC is the production of officers, our universities have become, in part, mere extension schools of our government's military establishment . . . The university continues to provide the tools to make possible policies such as those which led the U.S. into war in Asia . . . The university has granted the government the same moral sanction that the Krupp Industries gave the German government during World War II when it supplied the Reich with arms and munitions.[48]

The radical position occasionally found violent outlets, especially in 1969 and 1970 (see Table 5.1). The number of AFROTC units reporting hostile activity rose from 45 in academic year 1967–68 to 131 in 1968–69.[49] Eighty-two units reported physical damage to their buildings in 1970.[50] The type and amount of anti-ROTC activity varied widely from school to school. Of

Table 5.1   Anti-ROTC incidents reported by AFROTC units, by type and academic year

Type of incident	1969–70	1970–71
Major damage/injury	55	16
Minor damage/injury	138	34
Disruptive demonstrations	37	4
Official studies	175	59
Threats of disruption or violence	90	54
Nonviolent demonstrations	180	74

Source: "AFROTC/Host Institutional Activities" (1972), University of Illinois Archives, President John Corbally Papers, Box 33, ROTC–Air Force.

the universities studied most systematically here, the University of Michigan experienced by far the highest number of violent disruptions. In 1969–70 alone, Ann Arbor ROTC units reported six major incidents, including a dynamite explosion, a fire, a three-day occupation of the ROTC building, severe damage to ROTC vehicles, and a night of demonstrations that left the ROTC building with forty broken windows.[51] At Kent State, protesters burned the ROTC building and cut the hoses of fire fighters sent to douse the flames, just two days before the Ohio National Guard shot and killed four KSU students, including, ironically, an ROTC student who was observing the demonstration. Georgia Tech, Kansas State, Pittsburgh, and Illinois, however, reported no incidents of similar severity. In fact, a "Smash ROTC" demonstration planned at Illinois in response to the Kent State shootings failed to yield enough students and was canceled.[52]

But as newsworthy and visible as radical student attacks were, the military and most university administrators paid little formal attention to them. Plenty of reliable evidence existed that the protesters constituted a small, if vocal, minority on all campuses. University of Michigan president Robben Fleming "never thought there were more than 20 or 25 really disruptive, violent people around campus."[53] Two polls taken at the University of Pittsburgh in 1968 showed 70 percent of undergraduates were in favor of continuing ROTC with credit.[54] Even at Kent State, a poll taken in 1970 *after* the shootings in May showed three in four students in favor of retaining ROTC and half in favor of its remaining accredited.[55] At only one of the ninety NASULGC member schools, State University of New York (SUNY)–Buffalo, did a student referendum show a majority of students opposed to ROTC's continuance.[56]

The University of Colorado experienced incidents of both student activism and sustained support for ROTC. In March and April of 1970, Colorado's ROTC unit was firebombed, a student sit-in aimed partly at ROTC attracted 1,000 people, another anti-ROTC rally attracted 300 people, and the faculty voted to end credit for ROTC classes in the College of Arts and Sciences. All of this turmoil and publicity notwithstanding, support for the idea of ROTC remained high. Table 5.2 shows the results of two Colorado referenda conducted just two weeks after the Kent State shootings, along with the results of a similar poll taken at Rutgers in March. At Colorado, 78.7 percent of the student body and 82.3 percent of the faculty favored keeping ROTC, though not all wanted ROTC to remain accredited. At Rutgers, an almost identical 80 percent of the student body wanted ROTC on campus.

Table 5.2   Results of student and faculty referenda at the University of
Colorado and Rutgers University

Type of referendum	No. of respondents	Abolish ROTC	Keep ROTC, remove credit	Keep ROTC, retain credit
Student referendum, University of Colorado, May 13– 15, 1970	6,388	21.3%	39.3%	39.4%
Faculty referendum, University of Colorado, May 18, 1970	741	17.1%	29.0%	53.3%
Student referendum, Rutgers University, March 1970	1,949	20.1%	21.2%	58.7%

Source: "War and ROTC Related Events 1969–," (n.d.), University of Colorado at
Boulder Library, Archives, News Media Relations Office, Box 1, Student Disturbances,
Folder 2; "Students Favor ROTC," *Targum*, Mar. 18, 1970. Faculty numbers do not add
up to 100% because 0.6% of the faculty voted for ROTC to be compulsory for men.

On a national level, the picture was much the same. The 1969 National
College Poll found that "most students . . . are antiwar. They are not necessarily antimilitary. There is quite a distinction between the concepts."[57] Indeed, this distinction is crucial. The National College Poll found that 60 percent of the nation's undergraduates believed that America was wrong in
sending troops to Vietnam but that 80 percent (exactly the same percentage
as at Colorado and Rutgers) were at the same time in favor of voluntary
ROTC programs, and 59 percent were in favor of their receiving academic
credit.[58] Thus a considerable amount of evidence demonstrated two important points: that the student radicals did not speak for the vast majority of
the nation's undergraduates and that anti-Vietnam sentiment did not necessarily correlate to anti-ROTC sentiment.

The services devoted much more attention to the numerous formal investigations that faculty committees made into ROTC than they did to addressing the concerns of student radicals. As the Air Force ROTC commandant
told university representatives in 1969, "While the threats and actual incidents of violence are by far the most dramatic manifestation of the anti-
ROTC sentiment, the sixty-seven institutional investigations of the AFROTC

curriculum [in academic year 1968–69] are considered more significant by AFROTC."[59] By June 1970 forty-six of the ninety members of the NASULGC had formal studies under way to investigate ROTC and its place on campus.[60] Illinois, Kent State, Michigan, and Pittsburgh produced a total of nine such reports between April 1968 and September 1971.

These reports were either written by ad hoc faculty senate committees given the specific task of examining ROTC and its relationship to the university or by education and curriculum committees that had official supervision over university courses and faculty appointments but had not customarily exercised that authority over ROTC in the past. These reports represented the faculties' chance to reassert that leverage. They revealed that the central concerns of the majority of the university communities were the same concerns that had been expressed in the 1950s. In short, the turmoil accompanying the protests against the war in Vietnam increased the attention faculties focused on ROTC, but it did not fundamentally change the issues or even introduce new ones.

Rather, Vietnam gave the universities the motive and the opportunity to correct long-standing anomalies presented by the ROTC programs. Critics later charged that academics set conditions that were solely intended to make it impossible for ROTC to remain on campus; this was simply not the case. Instead, the faculties issued reports that challenged ROTC to reform itself to become more a part of the university according to the same criteria applied to other programs. When the dean of Rutgers College reviewed the report of the Rutgers faculty in 1968, he did not describe it as the first step of a program to eliminate ROTC; rather he said that the "faculty did everything it could *to bring ROTC into the mainstream of Rutgers College as a regular department.*"[61]

Sensitivity among the faculty to ROTC also reflected a growing tension in higher education between the image of the "multiversity" capable of fulfilling the vocational and nonvocational needs of the nation and the image of the university as a place for nonvocational liberal arts training for a variety of disciplines, such as that supported by the Ford Foundation in the early 1960s (see Chapter 4). The latter position favored, in the words of Yale president Kingman Brewster, "the squeezing out of vocational courses generally in university colleges of the highest standing. As knowledge becomes more complicated and more demanding, there is less room for the 'how to do it' courses in the best universities."[62] This trend had been accelerating on some campuses since the 1950s and had long been a source of contention among some civilian faculty. ROTC, they argued, focused on the "how to do it"

124 **Making Citizen-Soldiers**

model of instruction. One such critic opined that "the problem analysis and decision-making [of ROTC courses] can be learned in a brick-laying course."[63]

The most common feature of the faculty reports recommended that the university (especially liberal arts colleges) no longer sanction ROTC through the blanket awarding of academic credit. Engineering colleges presented a different situation because they received their accreditation from the Engineers Council for Professional Development (ECPD). This group, according to Michigan professor of engineering M. J. Sinnott, had a policy for "25+ years that engineering degree programs not be diluted by giving credit toward graduation for ROTC courses."[64] This system of accreditation, combined with the shared professional emphasis of engineering curricula and military education, rendered the question of academic credit in engineering colleges either moot or incontestable.

The recommendations of no academic credit in the colleges of liberal arts were largely related to the faculties' opinion of the quality and content of ROTC courses. As a common prelude to open discussion of ROTC, faculty subcommittees reviewed ROTC courses to determine how their quality matched up to those in the regular university offerings. They unanimously criticized ROTC courses for being, in the words of Michigan's 1969 Gindin Committee, "shockingly bad . . . simply inappropriate to a liberal arts education . . . appalling . . . conjectural, non-analytical, cheaply moralistic, and often blatantly propagandistic."[65] Pittsburgh's Student Affairs Committee further criticized ROTC as lacking "humanistic or political analyses."[66]

The reports also argued for the imposition of more university control over ROTC, whose faculty, they contended, were selected under different criteria from those that applied to civilian faculty. Furthermore, ROTC faculty had to answer to an outside agency and, the faculties charged, were therefore incapable of pursuing objectivity and freedom of inquiry. Princeton's 1969 Ad Hoc Committee on ROTC argued that "the ROTC courses of instruction are prescribed and conducted under procedures incompatible with those which normally govern the establishment of courses and the selection of faculty at Princeton."[67] Or, as the University of Illinois faculty senate argued: "It is clear that certain organizational and procedural aspects of ROTC on the campus presently are not closely parallel to those normal to other academic or professional programs."[68]

These reports argued that the ROTC courses were dissimilar enough from regular university offerings to warrant some formal distinctions, including the removal of credit for ROTC courses. In some cases the committees removed credit for any course connected to ROTC, but more commonly they demanded that ROTC courses receive credit only after passing faculty reviews. The University of Illinois Faculty Senate in 1970 recommended that credit be awarded only after "subjecting that course of instruction to our normal procedure of academic review and approval. To do otherwise would only intensify the growing concern of many members of the academic community over control of university functions and prerogatives by agencies outside the university."[69]

Given the most recent evaluations of ROTC courses by Illinois faculty, this recommendation was effectively the same as a blanket denial of credit, but it did leave open the possibility of credit restoration in the future. Michigan also left such a door open in 1970 when the Literature, Science, and Arts faculty removed ROTC credit for any course not cross-listed with an academic department. Therefore, if a regular university department could find disciplinary or interdisciplinary merit in an ROTC course, that course could receive credit. Similarly, a spokesman for the University of Pittsburgh committee that recommended denying credit to ROTC students in the College of Arts and Sciences declared that "if members of the faculty were to participate in restructuring the program's curriculum towards academic acceptability, ROTC might again receive academic credit."[70]

A university did not need to remove all credit to make a statement about its impression of the quality of ROTC courses. University of Texas officials told the air force that "as long as the ROTC courses contain material of University caliber and are taught at University level by properly qualified individuals, they will continue to receive our maximum support."[71] Nevertheless, the Texas faculty voted in 1969 to reduce credits given for ROTC courses from a maximum of twenty-four to a maximum of nine. They also voted to end a policy that permitted ROTC to serve as a substitute for the American history graduation requirement.

Many of the reports also recommended, in the words of the faculty of Rutgers University, "that courses not specifically military—e.g., history, political science—[should] be taught by appropriate civilian academic departments."[72] Such a recommendation recalled the substitution programs of the late 1950s that academics had lauded (see Chapters 2 and 4). Substituted courses, taught "under the auspices of one of the degree granting colleges or schools," would, of course, receive full credit.[73]

The reports also challenged the academic titles universities gave to military personnel. Titles are the closest academic parallel to military rank, and therefore, like degree credit, they are more than just a formality; they signify the faculty's approbation and formal sanction. As noted in Chapter 4, ROTC contracts stipulated that the head of an ROTC unit receive the title professor of air (or military or naval) science. Junior officers had customarily, although not contractually, received the title associate professor or assistant professor. Military instructors, however, were not professional academics, they rarely held advanced degrees, and they usually lacked teaching experience. The faculty committees, therefore, were generally united in arguing that the officers were unworthy of holding academic titles.

During debates at Boston University, one group of radical faculty proposed that the PMS be known by the title "Coach of the Back Bay Chowder and Marching Society."[74] Some of the more mild reports suggested qualifying the titles granted to ROTC officers. At Pittsburgh, the Student Affairs Committee recommended adding "clinical" or "adjunct" to the titles. At Princeton, the Ad Hoc Committee voted to change the titles of ROTC officers to "Lecturer with the Rank of Professor."[75] At Michigan, Harvard, and the University of Illinois at Chicago Circle, however, the faculties voted that officers should not have any academic title and thenceforth should be known only by their military title.[76]

The reports also argued for more civilian oversight of the program. Yale stated that the necessity of more civilian control was "almost beyond challenge. Military officers certainly listen to a different drummer."[77] The type of oversight varied from having civilian faculty serve as advisors to military courses to requiring that all ROTC courses be approved each semester by the faculty. At Kent State, supervision of the program changed hands from the faculty of the College of Arts and Sciences to the Provost Office, in the hope of assuring greater centralized control over ROTC appointments and course offerings.

At Cornell, Michigan, and Princeton, faculty committees also recommended changing ROTC from a department to a "program." The committees argued that the change would formally, and correctly, acknowledge ROTC's place on the campus. The Princeton committee said the change would end "what the Committee believes has been an inappropriate status for ROTC. Departments . . . characteristically have undergraduate concentrators and recommend candidates for degrees."[78]

The issues of drill and military procedure arose in several reports. Drill was singled out in many reports as being especially antithetical to the mission of the university and unworthy of credit because it had no "appeal to intelligent students."[79] Many faculties therefore wanted to remove drill from the curriculum or at least remove it from the visible public centers on campus. The University of Pittsburgh moved drill practice from a lawn in the heart of campus to the confines of nearby Forbes Field.[80] Kent State similarly recommended that all ROTC drill courses be conducted inside the campus football stadium and that "military courtesy procedures be eliminated on campus except in the formally designated drill and drill-related areas. No rifles, swords, or other potentially lethal weapons be permitted on campus at any time except in the drill and drill-related areas. Because KSU does not have a dress code, voluntary wearing of the uniform will not be restricted. However, *involuntary* wearing of the uniform on campus except in the drill and drill-related areas will not be permitted."[81] Princeton and the University of Illinois at Chicago Circle went a step further and voted to ban both drill and lethal weapons from the campus.[82]

These changes were designed to soften the most martial aspects of ROTC, but they were also a response to real questions of officer training and preparation. To some military and civilian leaders, Vietnam had demonstrated that tactical preparation alone was insufficient for American officers fighting a war of liberation. The war in Vietnam was as much a war for the "hearts and minds" of the Vietnamese people as it was a war for territory and tactical advantage. Substitution was the universities' answer to reform ROTC and its officer preparation by introducing more understanding of the history, culture, and politics of the world's peoples.

As a package, then, these reports argued for consequential reform in the operation of ROTC. For all of the many changes recommended by these faculty committees, however, what is perhaps more significant is what the faculties did not recommend. Only one faculty report, that from Dartmouth College, recommended that ROTC be removed from the campus. Elsewhere, motions and petitions demanding that the university sever all ties to ROTC were routinely defeated by margins of five to one or more. Even recommendations that ROTC retain ties to the university but be moved off campus were soundly defeated. Furthermore, on some campuses, faculties recommended reform only for certain issues. In 1968, for example, Johns Hopkins faculty voted to deny credit for ROTC but to allow ROTC instructors to keep their academic titles.[83] Some individual faculty members saw these moves as a first step toward removing ROTC from the campus, but the faculty committee reports did not argue that ROTC was an all-or-nothing venture. They could, and did, make recommendations designed to make ROTC fit into the fabric of their campus community.

Indeed, despite the changes they recommended, the faculty committees remained firmly committed to their traditional support of ROTC. The NASULGC's Special Subcommittee on ROTC Policy rejected the idea that "the civilian academic community, public or private, is antithetical to association with national security affairs."[84] The Princeton and Pittsburgh reports explicitly supported ROTC because it prevented the formation of a military caste and infused the military with civilian ideas. At Colorado an initial motion for ROTC reform failed to pass a faculty vote. A rewritten version began: "ROTC should continue to have a place on the campus of the University of Colorado." The second motion passed easily.[85] These reports, then, argued not for abolition of ROTC but for reform. ROTC's traditional strengths continued to outweigh the faults academics saw in the program. Therefore they made a series of recommendations designed to bring ROTC in line with regular academic offerings and produce a program worthy of remaining on the campuses on its own merit.

The student movement had a mixed impact on these faculty reports. It would be erroneous to assume that the faculties considered these issues only because of pressure from students. As the previous chapters indicate, faculties since the 1920s had investigated the role of ROTC on the campus; at least in part, the post-Tet reports represented the fruition of years of inquiry. Faculties had their own sense of what did and did not merit inclusion in American colleges and universities, and their ideas did not necessarily overlap with those of students.

Radical faculty were less interested in ROTC per se than they were in using ROTC as a means of repudiating the military and university ties to the military. The faculty reports, however, did not share the logic of the radical formulation that an anti-Vietnam position necessarily equated to an anti-ROTC, or even an antimilitary, position. Richard Jessor, the most important faculty critic of ROTC at the University of Colorado, was "dismayed" to learn that students received credit for ROTC, but he did not view the ROTC problem as an antimilitary issue. The faculty Jessor represented and the student radicals had a "sharp difference of perspective despite having a common concern." Although he disagreed with the academic and procedural issues connected with ROTC, Jessor saw the civil-military connection that ROTC provided as "healthy" for both parties.[86]

Jessor's position was not unusual. Arval Morris, a professor of law at the University of Washington, argued on behalf of the Washington chapter of the AAUP that ROTC "is unquestioningly non-curious" and "corrosive of the ideal of the university as a community of scholars." Nevertheless, the

AAUP believed that ROTC was "clearly preferable" to a system of officer training directed solely by the military. ROTC, Morris argued, "must be preserved . . . It is no answer to say: 'Throw ROTC off campus and be done with it.'"[87] Faculty could, and did, argue for significant change for ROTC while concurrently supporting the concept of officer training on civilian campuses. Similarly, a Harvard faculty member elucidated his support for officer training but not the ROTC status quo when he said, "Some faculty members (including myself) do indeed believe that it is legitimate for students to participate in reserve officer training activities, while rejecting the notion that certain courses taught by military officers form a solid part of the educational process which we work hard at maintaining."[88] A vote against ROTC accreditation therefore did not necessarily equal a vote against military training.

Furthermore, the student movement pushed significant numbers of faculty, many of them senior faculty, to a hard-line position in opposition to student radicals. This position inclined many to support the ROTC status quo in order not to give in to the student radicals. The faculties, they argued, should not "placate a minority of yahoos on the left who had threatened confrontation unless [the university] cleansed itself of its infectious association with an ill-defined but presumably insidious military establishment."[89]

Although opinions and faculty declarations varied from campus to campus, a consensus emerged that ROTC should be changed, not expelled. An observer of Michigan's 1969 Buttrey Committee, which produced one of the harshest anti-ROTC reports, noted that "no member of the committee supported ROTC as it now exists throughout the nation. There was, however, no desire on the part of the committee to recommend abolition of ROTC."[90] The recommended reforms pertained to the long-standing anomalies inherent in the creation of ROTC as a vocational military officer preparation program that existed under different regulations from those that governed other university programs. The services received this flood of reports with concern because of the sheer weight of changes proposed therein, but many of the reports' key features were in accord with an officially stated position that emerged in 1969 from the new Nixon Pentagon.

The Benson Report

It would be misleading to assume that all of the initiative for reform of ROTC came from the universities. As indicated in previous chapters, many uniformed and civilian officials in the armed services had long agreed that reform of the ROTC program was necessary if it was to retain its vitality. Now President Nixon's support of a zero-draft military added greater urgency to the problem of ROTC. Many in the new Nixon administration believed that reform would be critical to ROTC's future if and when the draft, a major motivation for enrollment in the program, ended. In this vein the new secretary of defense, Melvin Laird, created the Special Committee on ROTC in the first few months of his tenure, to report on the most serious problems facing the program and to make recommendations for its reform.[91] George Benson, president of Claremont College, chaired the committee; the remainder of the panel, which became known as the Benson Committee, included administrators from Stanford, John Jay College, Tulane, Purdue, and Illinois, and the highest uniformed officer in charge of ROTC from each of the four services.

In September 1969 the committee produced the "Benson Report," a sixty-one-page exploration of the major issues connected to ROTC.[92] It made twenty-one recommendations to the secretary of defense, many of which argued for less change than the university faculty reports. For example, while acknowledging that credit was the exclusive prerogative of university faculties, the report recommended that "appropriate academic credit be given for ROTC courses" other than drill, that ROTC instructors should keep their academic titles, and that "uniforms and drill are a part of the military profession and should remain on campus."

The report did, however, recommend some changes. It advised that universities should assume more responsibility for the hiring and firing of ROTC instructors, encouraged greater use of substitution, and recommended the creation of "high level faculty-administration committee(s) to oversee and work with the ROTC programs."[93] The report argued that ROTC was "clearly in the national interest," and it strongly favored continuing the program, but with some changes in operating procedures. It rejected the radical position that ROTC had no place on civilian campuses, but it did acknowledge ROTC's dissonance from other college programs: "ROTC is the only instructional program on campus whose curriculum and method of instruction is largely determined by an external body, whose instructional staff is furnished by one external source, and which prepares young men for a single employer."[94] Consistent with a century and a half of university experience with military training, the report firmly argued that it was important to keep ROTC intact, even with its anomalies. "If ROTC were to be removed from the nation's campuses there would be grave danger of isolating the services from the intellectual centers of the public which they serve and defend."[95]

The report was endorsed by the DOD and most universities as an appropriate starting point for negotiations. The NASULGC noted that the Benson Report marked a "positive approach to the improvement of officer education programs."[96] A year later, the association's Council for Academic Affairs "commend[ed] the Benson Report of the Department of Defense regarding ROTC and urge[d] the implementation of the recommendations made therein," especially, the council noted, the recommendations to permit the host institution to "determine its own policies and procedures in educational matters, such as the amount of credit to be granted for the ROTC programs."[97]

The Benson Report provided general guidelines, not a boilerplate to be implemented nationwide. Still, it became the seminal document for ROTC policy in the Nixon Pentagon. The report's final recommendation was the creation of "an office in the Department of Defense to secure coordination of service ROTC rules which may affect the relationship of ROTC as a whole within the academic world."[98] The DOD responded by creating the office of assistant secretary of defense (education) in 1970 and naming Benson to the position. Through the Benson Report, the DOD made a commitment, as the universities had, to work to save ROTC. It is therefore worth examining in greater detail the motivations that both the universities and the services had for negotiating a re-formed place on campus for ROTC.

Why Save ROTC?

If ROTC was so out of step with the goals and procedures of higher education, why not, from the university perspective, throw out this distasteful manifestation of a sordid connection with the military? Or, from the service's perspective, why not abandon Michigan, Illinois, Pittsburgh, Colorado, Kent State, and any other campus that wanted to force reform and instead open larger, postgraduate Officer Candidate Schools where the services could run their officer preparation programs without the interference of interloping civilians?

The answer was that, for all its faults, ROTC provided real, tangible benefits to the campus and the services. These benefits overlapped in many cases. Both institutions had an interest in attracting the highest quality student possible. The ROTC host schools were some of the finest colleges and universities in the nation. ROTC thus provided an on-campus recruitment and training office that many in the services believed was crucial to attracting high-quality cadets. Due to the selectivity of the ROTC scholarship programs, ROTC had the potential to bring full-scholarship students onto the campuses who were at least the equal of their non-ROTC peers.

Furthermore, the services and the universities had legislative bodies to placate. All state legislatures, as well as the United States Congress, favored retention of the ROTC program. If the universities and the services could negotiate away the major problems surrounding ROTC, they could keep the elected officials who had oversight over the budgets of both institutions out of the reform process.

Two additional factors impelled the military to negotiate a reformed, but certain, place on campus. First, cost effectiveness played a considerable role. In 1969 the average ROTC officer cost $4,320 to produce. By contrast, officers produced through Officer Candidate School cost $8,406 each on average, and service academy graduates cost $47,136 on average. ROTC was a bargain even when one considered factors such as the higher attrition rates and post-commissioning training costs of ROTC-trained officers. One study of ROTC and Naval Academy graduates from 1962 found that total training costs per 100 officers still in service ten years after commissioning were $2.9 million for NROTC graduates and $8.9 million for Annapolis graduates.[99] Given that the services projected that ROTC would be relied on to produce as many as 80 percent of the post-Vietnam officer corps, ROTC represented potential for enormous savings.[100]

Second, not all military personnel believed that civilian criticism had harmed the program. Rather, many understood that most civilian academics were committed at least to the *idea* of ROTC. They recognized that much of the criticism of ROTC, such as that of course content, was directed at improving the program, not discarding it. Furthermore, some uniformed personnel had long agreed that some aspects of the program, such as the emphasis on drill, needed to be changed. To these officers, the faculty reports signified a genuine desire on the part of the universities to work to find ways to make ROTC stronger. The stereotype of the conservative, rigid military officer did not always fit the reality. Many ROTC commanders, such as Colonel Wayne Bridges at Georgia Tech, saw the demands for change as "justified" and believed that a fruitful, open dialogue with university administrators could prove beneficial to ROTC.[101]

Three major factors impelled university administrators to negotiate with the services, despite vocal protests on campus for the absolute removal of ROTC. Without question the most important of these considerations was a long-standing ideological belief in the importance of citizen-officers and the role of ROTC in assuring the supply of such officers. Administrators, especially those from state-supported schools, felt that higher education had an obligation to produce officers. Furthermore, they remained convinced that ROTC's greatest advantage was that it served as a hedge against the creation of a military elite exclusively trained at the service academies.[102] To these men, ROTC did not mean the military's presence in the university, but the university's presence in the military. Ralph Huitt of the NASULGC noted that his group "believe[d] that officers in the military should come from institutions all over the country, and that this diversity of background helps to maintain a democratic leadership in the military. This is a principle which we would not surrender lightly."[103]

Second, although many universities themselves lost money conducting ROTC programs, their students often depended on ROTC's scholarship authorization.[104] In 1966 NROTC, the smallest of the three ROTC programs, paid $93,500 in tuition to the University of Illinois.[105] In the 1968–69 academic year, ROTC meant close to $1 million to the University of Michigan; direct scholarship payments to Michigan students accounted for more than $400,000 of that figure.[106] More subtly, DOD research money was a significant source of income at these schools. Keeping the services happy had financial benefits beyond officer education.[107]

The third reason involved leaving a career option open for those students who desired it. Many young men (and, increasingly, young women as well) wanted to become military officers. The university had an obligation, many faculty and administrators argued, to assure that such a career option remained open. The NASULGC concluded in 1969 that "it is appropriate for institutions . . . to offer courses and programs of interest to those wishing to serve as officers in the Armed Forces, as they do for other occupational fields."[108]

For all these reasons university administrators supported the idea of ROTC, if not in the program's current form. Their view agreed, in broad outline, with the consensus of the faculty reports. The task at hand, then, was for the administrators—serving both as representatives of the individual schools and as faculty delegates—to build on their agreement with the services as to the necessity of ROTC reforms in a way that would serve the interests of both parties.

"A Disposition on Both Sides to Find Common Ground"

The reform of ROTC revolved around a dialectical process of negotiation, heretofore absent in discussions of the issue, that had formally existed between the schools and the military since the creation of regular ROTC advisory boards in the 1950s. Between August 1969 and November 1971, Michigan president Robben Fleming and vice president Robert Williams met several times with Secretary of Defense Melvin Laird, the uniformed heads of the NROTC and AFROTC programs, an assistant secretary of the navy, an assistant secretary of defense, two deputy assistant secretaries of defense, the head of the Navy Bureau of Personnel, and the chief of naval operations, always exclusively on the topic of ROTC. In 1970 the Association of American Universities surveyed its member schools on the issue of negotiations with the DOD and found "evidence of a disposition on both sides—the military and the universities—to find common ground on which ROTC programs can be continued . . . Most of the universities seem to be approaching the issue with a readiness to adjust and compromise with the services in order to preserve ROTC programs in some form."[109]

To be sure, this process was accelerated—but not created—by Vietnam and the attendant turmoil on the campuses. Without the student movement, it is unlikely that officials of such importance would have involved themselves personally in the issues. But these men did not bring a radical agenda with them to the negotiations. They aimed to reconcile basic inconsistencies and contradictions between the goals of military training and higher education. The discussions, between the highest academic and military officials in the country, kept the issue of ROTC reform alive until settlements could be reached.

With Nixon's reduction of American forces in Vietnam, the military began to prepare for fundamental changes.[110] During the Vietnam War era, many officers had received their commissions through Officer Candidate School, which had been expanded to meet the increased demands of the military for junior officers. While most of these officers performed their duty admirably, several university and military officials believed that the six-week crash preparation offered by OCS was markedly inferior to ROTC. As George Benson noted in 1970, "We cannot doubt the importance of a high degree of education for our officers. A half hour of immaturity on the part of one ill-educated junior officer can affect our whole national image adversely."[111] Benson's comment about the ill-educated junior officer is a thinly veiled reference to army Lieutenant William Calley, who was tried for the March 1968 massacre of 350 Vietnamese civilians in the village of My Lai.[112] One explanation of that massacre was that the services had accepted too many "substandard" men into OCS; only one of the eight officers charged as principals in the massacre had a college degree. Calley himself had had only one checkered year of junior college. He later told an interviewer that he left for Vietnam "with the absolute philosophy that the U.S.A.'s right. And there was no gray . . . there was just black or white."[113]

Many military men themselves argued that ROTC provided a humanistic counterbalance to OCS- and academy-trained officers. University of Colorado class president and ROTC cadet Glenn Porzak told an assembly of students that "ROTC is vital for keeping dissent within the Army by officers with a liberal education."[114] One American soldier told an interviewer in Vietnam in 1969, "Believe it or not, there're a lot of young officers, especially a lot out of ROTC, who really preach against the genocidal thing."[115] Many academics, students, and military officers believed that ROTC had the potential to infuse the services with better educated men who had been exposed to the diverse ideas of the modern university rather than more narrow ideas of OCS. A college education, they contended, imparted more of the maturity and refined, "gentlemanly" qualities idealized in military officers than did the six weeks of training in OCS.

To many academics, then, reform of ROTC, not abolition, held the potential to create a military that more closely shared the values of American society. To reject ROTC, they believed, would only serve to place the military out of reach of academic and civilian influence. Many academics thus took a keen interest in the discussions revolving around ROTC. In August 1970, the NASULGC senate met in a special session to discuss three issues related to the relationship between higher education and government, including "revision of the ROTC program to make it academically stronger." Such revisions, members argued, would assure that the primary means for academics to influence the military would survive.[116]

One year later, they forcefully reiterated this position in a resolution approved by the NASULGC member institutions and later by the Association of American Universities. Their statement captures the consensus of university administrators in this era:

Recently the desirability of civilian educational institutions participating in the education of those who may serve as officers in the Armed Services has been subject to question. Some charge that this involvement contributes to the "militarization" of our society. We believe that the opposite is true. The continued availability in substantial numbers of officers for the Armed Services from a variety of civilian educational backgrounds actually is one of the surest guarantees against the formation of a military caste or establishment . . . It would be highly undesirable for officer education to be restricted to the service academies, or to be carried on entirely in programs removed from college or university campuses.[117]

The military shared this view, but for slightly different reasons. Military officers viewed ROTC reform as a critical part of reestablishing good relations with American society in the aftermath of Tet and the graduated withdrawal from Vietnam. One way to replenish a diminishing fund of legitimacy was to create an officer corps that shared the values of the society it served. To many, ROTC played a critical role in this process, as cadets were exposed for four years to civilian peers and instruction from civilian professors. This pattern offered a better opportunity for the interaction of civilian and military ideas than the more isolationist pedagogical model of the service academies or OCS.

University administrators, usually provosts or vice presidents, had the job of relaying the major features of the faculty committee reports to the services and negotiating with the uniformed and civilian heads of ROTC programs to implement the faculty recommendations. In many cases, these recommendations violated the spirit or the letter of the 1964 Vitalization Act or existing university-service ROTC contracts. Additionally, where the recommendations of a faculty report violated the Benson Report, they also stood in opposition to the officially stated DOD position.

The administrators generally agreed with the recommendations contained in the faculty reports, which, after all, brought up many of the issues they had been dealing with for years. They shared the general goal of reforming ROTC, as Michigan president Robben Fleming demonstrated:

> As to the larger question of whether ROTC ought to be on the campuses, I tend to favor it despite my own connection with civil liberties causes. My reasons are that I fear a professional army in a democracy; that I think the infusion of officer talent from non-professional ranks promotes the concept of a civilian army; that in twenty-two years on three campuses which have ROTC programs, I have yet to find the faintest hint that somehow the military is dominating the campus; and I believe that officer standing is a legiti-

mate outlet for those students who must serve some time in the military anyway.[118]

Even in cases where the administration disagreed with the faculty, the diffuse nature of university administration and power distribution meant that there was little they could do. Issues of credit, for example, were in almost all cases the exclusive prerogative of the faculty. A university president could not simply order that credit be awarded, and in several cases, the administrators realized that trying to use political clout to sway a faculty vote ran the risk of producing a rogue outcome. Knowing all this, University of Pittsburgh chancellor Wesley Posvar, himself a West Point graduate and former Air Force Academy department chairman, told the Pennsylvania state legislature that he would not try to change his faculty's vote to drop credit for ROTC courses, despite the legislature's threats to cut funding to Pittsburgh by 25 percent and Posvar's belief that ROTC deserved elective credit.[119]

The academic authority structure, of course, was nearly the polar opposite of the military pattern. Administrators who assumed the job of negotiating with the services and state legislatures to implement reform often had a very difficult time explaining that they simply could not order faculties to change their recommendations. Threats from Michigan and Pennsylvania legislatures and Congress to cut funding to the universities if they dropped ROTC credit therefore put administrators in an awkward position. They obviously had to pay attention to real budget issues, but they could not circumvent faculty votes with which they disagreed.

Furthermore, presidents and their representatives had their own supervisors to consider. University trustees and regents commonly favored the status quo regarding ROTC programs and looked with great suspicion at any move that might call the university's commitment to the nation into question. Robben Fleming knew that at Michigan "there was not a single vote among the Regents for abolition of ROTC . . . Thus if the [Buttrey] Committee made such a recommendation, it would fail before the Regents. If I did not support the recommendation, the faculty would reject me. If I supported it, the Regents would nevertheless turn it down, and my influence with them would be greatly diminished, perhaps to the point where I should resign."[120] Of course, the committee made no such recommendation, but Fleming's words indicated the sensitive position sometimes occupied by university administrators.

Within this background, formal discussions about ROTC between the universities and the military began in mid-1969, soon after the Nixon administration had established itself at the Pentagon. In an interview shortly after he became secretary of defense, Melvin Laird said that he was willing to see military ceremony reduced and the substitution of regular academic courses for military ones broadened, but said, "We are not prepared to see the ROTC program degraded in any way."[121]

Similarly, the uniformed services were quite willing to discuss possible changes to the program, in large part because many of the faculty recommendations, such as the reduction of drill and the assignment of instructors with advanced degrees, were in line with suggestions they had made as early as 1960. They also understood that other changes, such as qualifying the academic titles used by ROTC instructors, need not affect the program unduly. AFROTC staff told their instructors that "even out of the turmoil, some good will come. Some legitimate needs for change will be made and even in some of the colleges where opposition has been the greatest we may find more faculty support and involvement after they examine our program and have an opportunity to input their ideas for an improved program."[122] These negotiations, then, were not always as acrimonious as the backdrop of faculty reports and student demonstrations might lead one to believe. To be sure, hard-liners existed on both sides, but most negotiators understood that both sides also shared the goal of finding a way to keep ROTC on the campuses.

Drill: "The Program's Worst Enemy"

The issues that were reformed most quickly and easily were those on which some general level of agreement already existed, such as the visibility of drill on campus. Other issues, such as the awarding of academic credit for ROTC courses and academic titles for ROTC instructors, were more contentious because the services saw changes in those areas as a threat to the status and quality of the program. In addition, general agreement existed on some issues, such as instructor qualification, but structural problems inhibited easy solutions. In these cases, the services and the universities worked to find creative temporary solutions until permanent ones could be implemented.

As noted, some military criticism of drill had been building since 1960. Observers in the late 1960s continued to criticize drill as outdated, irrelevant, mindless, and embarrassing to the student. Survey evidence suggested that drill was even unpopular among people who supported all other aspects of the ROTC program.[123] Reducing the importance of drill promised to reduce a source of tension for both supporters and opponents. "Leadership laboratory," noted one army officer, "may well be the program's worst enemy."[124] And as a navy officer argued, "It's the weapons and the drilling that get up their dander, so, hell, let's throw them a crumb."[125] This officer's casual willingness to abandon drill indicates that its training value was minimal, a mere "crumb." The services had few problems accepting the faculty recommendations for removal of academic credit for the drill portions of the ROTC curriculum, and some officers were willing to consider removing drill from the campus altogether.

At least initially, the services and the universities had to negotiate around the desires of powerful members of Congress, who held that the arguments against drill were "without merit." A House Armed Services Subcommittee, led by F. Edward Hébert, declared, consistent with the logic that had produced the Vitalization Act five years earlier, that it intended to see drill continued on the campus. Drill, the subcommittee determined, instilled leadership and "training in the ability to accept orders."[126] Nevertheless, negotiations between the universities and the services to reduce the amount of drill continued undaunted. The services did, however, begin to lobby Congress to explain the changes in ROTC policy and try to convince congressmen that drill did not form a necessary part of ROTC training.

Indeed, the congressional lobbying paid dividends. Meetings in March 1970 between F. Edward Hébert, Assistant Secretary of Defense Roger Kelly, and the three uniformed heads of ROTC convinced Hébert that the changes to the program, including a reduction of "some of the weapons and tactics orientation," were intended to strengthen ROTC. Army Brigadier General C. P. Hannum noted immediately after the meeting, "I consider the briefing with Congressman Hébert a total success . . . This effort should serve to finally clarify to the [House Armed Services] committee that what the Army is doing to revitalize the ROTC program is truly progressive change rather than 'knuckling under to the dissidents,' as some members of the committee now believe."[127] Hannum succeeded in convincing Hébert that the authoritarian military model the congressman so admired was not the direction that ROTC had gone in the recent past, nor was it the direction that it would head in the future. To succeed in the new American military system, ROTC had to focus less on drill and more on assuring its place on the campus through congruity with the goals of higher education.

Knowing that the consensus of informed opinion within the military had become decidedly receptive to a reduction of drill, University of Michigan vice president Robert Williams led off a meeting with the Bureau of Naval Personnel by saying, "Let us begin by dismissing the drills, spit and polish, corps activity, or whatever you care to call it as a vital [and] necessary part of the ROTC program."[128] In a similar vein, University of Illinois provost Dayton Pickett told a representative of the Army War College, "That portion of military leadership skills acquired through participation in drill is seen as a highly questionable component of a university curriculum."[129]

Because many uniformed and civilian military officials agreed that drill was overemphasized in the ROTC curriculum, they did not strenuously object to university desires to deny credit for drill or to reduce the number of hours spent on drill. Indeed, many military officials had opposed the changes of the Vitalization Act that made drill as much as one-third of the curriculum's total contact hours. Thus this issue became the easiest to resolve. The hours devoted to drill became the common target of military and educational officials who were pushing to reintroduce substitution.

Substitution and the "New York Plan"

As noted in earlier chapters, substitution had been a popular program from the late 1950s until 1964, when ROTC curricula returned to a more technical emphasis. The services reacted to initial substitution suggestions in the late 1960s by allowing the ideas to germinate on the individual campuses. The proposals varied significantly in scale and scope nationwide. MIT, for example, replaced drill with cadet presentations on aspects of engineering and physics relevant to the military.[130] Elsewhere, substitution ideas were more complex. In 1969 the army authorized all professors of military science to introduce substitution, encouraging the substitution of courses from the following areas: American military history, world military history, diplomatic history of the United States, political geography, American government, international relations, geopolitics, studies of developing countries, international trade and finance, psychology, sociology, group dynamics and human relations, calculus, chemistry, biology, physics, geology, foreign language, political philosophy, organization and management, computer science, and statistics.[131] "This is a forward move, in my judgment," noted Michigan's Robert Williams, "and it is my understanding that the departments concerned and the assistant deans in the college who work with the students and their programs are delighted about this movement."[132]

Most universities introduced some form of substitution, but the University of Michigan introduced the most elaborate series of curricular changes nationwide. Michigan introduced substitution for army and air force drill periods for the 1969 fall semester. Air force freshmen took political science, juniors took two courses in aeronautical engineering, and seniors took international politics and either two industrial engineering courses or two business administration courses.[133] Army cadets in their freshman year substituted political science and speech, and sophomores substituted geography and history. For the 1970–71 academic year, the navy agreed to require its midshipmen at Michigan to take American military history, national security policy, calculus, physics or chemistry, and computer science.[134] The air force also selected Michigan to be one of four campuses to test a new "alternate curriculum" that made more elaborate use of substitution ideas than had previously occurred anywhere. In place of Air Science 102 (United States Military Forces), freshmen cadets selected a course from the following list: Humanities 101 *(Iliad, Oedipus, Canterbury Tales)*, Humanities 102 *(Hamlet, Candide, Civil Disobedience)*, Freshman Composition, Shakespeare, Creative Writing, and Great Books. Introduction to International Politics replaced Air Science 201 (Introduction to Defense Policy) for sophomores.[135]

The services generally supported the idea of a limited amount of substitution, because they saw value in having junior officers with a broader education and a firmer grounding in areas like engineering, administration, and even the humanities. They did, however, urge that a significant amount of the corps training activity remain the sole preserve of uniformed officers. As the University of Pittsburgh PMS told the administration: "Although the Military Science Department could expand its use of the University courses provided they met the overall objectives, a course composed solely of University courses is not desirable," because the ROTC faculty needed to know their cadets well enough to evaluate their ability to succeed in the military. Pittsburgh's ROTC instructional staff proposed instead a "team" approach wherein civilian instructors would teach the academic portion of the curriculum and military instructors would teach the corps-preparation aspects.[136]

The University of Illinois also supported the team-teaching concept and introduced team-taught courses in the following areas: military map and photo analysis, United States defense establishment, American military history, principles of military instruction, military law, and principles of military leadership.[137] The services generally showed more enthusiasm for team teaching than for substitution because team teaching allowed the ROTC staffs to maintain more contact hours with their cadets. It also meant less fundamental change to the program; team teaching had already existed informally on some campuses in the form of guest lectures from civilian faculty.

Their utility notwithstanding, team teaching and substitution could not help the ROTC units respond to criticisms that their instructors were unqualified to teach at American universities. As noted earlier, the ROTC headquarters staffs had long desired to have master's degree holders assigned to ROTC units, but the personnel realities of the armed forces and the need for officers in Southeast Asia had constrained them from doing so. After 1968, the need for highly qualified officers became even more acute; having highly qualified officers could improve relations with host schools and increase the chances for restoration of academic credit. Furthermore, some schools, like the University of Texas, had established new criteria for accepting officers as ROTC instructors and had begun to reject candidates who failed to meet these criteria.[138]

Knowing that a permanent solution was still some time away, the universities and the services teamed up to create a temporary solution through New York University's National Security Information Center (NSIC). Beginning in May 1968, with funding from the private sector, the NSIC began to conduct an ROTC Enrichment Program that had three goals:

To give added depth and perspective to instruction in politico-military subjects in the ROTC curriculum.

To assist ROTC in maintaining standards of study that merit academic accreditation.

To assist ROTC instructors in broadening the academic base of their teaching.[139]

The "New York Plan," as it became known, paid guest lecturers to give talks to ROTC cadets, most often at times formerly devoted to drill, to enrich the level of ROTC instruction. The original list of 233 lecturers included Zbigniew Brzezinski, Walt Rostow, and various university professors, as well as officials from Los Alamos National Laboratories, the RAND Corporation, the White House National Security Staff, and other national security organizations.[140] The NSIC designed the New York Plan to supplement ROTC instruction for a period of four years, by which time it anticipated that instructors with advanced degrees would be the norm. With the help of General Motors, the NSIC also sponsored two-day training programs in which a total of 263 ROTC instructors participated. Eventually, 11,000 cadets at 201 schools heard lectures supported by the NSIC.[141]

Some ROTC units drew inspiration from the NSIC and created their own programs. Georgia Tech's ROTC programs developed the Atlanta Forum on National and International Affairs (AFNIA), designed with ROTC in mind but open to all students from nine colleges and universities in the Atlanta area. AFNIA sponsored a conference on Sino-American relations in 1971 that featured speakers from the Brookings Institute, the State Department, the Japanese Embassy, Johns Hopkins University, Dartmouth College, and George Washington University.[142] The following year Dean Rusk gave the keynote address at an AFNIA conference on the Middle East.[143] Similarly, at the University of Washington the Carthage Foundation and Claremont College supported a program of ROTC guest lecturers on such topics as nuclear proliferation, Russia's relationship to Eastern Europe, the Berlin crisis, and American foreign policy. These seminars met in the time period formerly devoted to drill.[144]

With the New York Plan and local variants like the AFNIA helping to upgrade instruction, the services took their own steps to assure that they could assign officers with advanced degrees in the years to come. They ended the policy of giving volunteers priority in ROTC assignments and began treating ROTC as a regular assignment to assure that the quality of instructors would improve. One AFROTC instructor recalled: "The feeling I had was I wondered what I had done wrong to be selected [to teach ROTC] . . . Somewhere along the line I understood that it would be helpful to the ROTC program if they had someone who was competitive for promotion to general in the role of a detachment commander in ROTC."[145] Or, as Colonel Glen Watkins, University of Pittsburgh PAS, noted in 1969, "It's time for people with experience and motivation to come to the college campuses. The Armed Forces have always put their best men in Southeast Asia and the Pentagon."[146] Watkins was among the many ROTC instructors who were sent to their alma mater in the hope of further improving the standing of ROTC instructors and their relationship with the host schools.

The services still had to find a way to get around the structural problem of not having a large supply of men with master's degrees. The army demonstrated its commitment to solving this problem when it introduced the Civil Schooling Plan, under which officers would spend two years, on full salary, earning a master's degree, then three years teaching ROTC at the same school.[147] The assignment of formally educated officers was a special priority of Admiral Elmo Zumwalt, chief of naval operations, who instituted navy programs similar to the army's Civil Schooling Plan to assure that men with high professional qualifications were sent to NROTC campuses.[148]

By 1970, these programs had paid off. After that year, all ROTC instructors assigned to Michigan, Illinois, Kent State, Georgia Tech, and Pittsburgh had advanced degrees. This pattern was partly due to the increased assertiveness of the universities; Michigan turned down two candidates at this time because of their inability to qualify for admission to Michigan graduate schools.[149] But even on a national level the number of officers with advanced degrees was increasing. All but four AFROTC instructors assigned to a detachment in academic year 1970–71 had an advanced degree.[150] All four services stabilized the tours of duty of men with advanced degrees at three years to keep qualified instructors on the campuses.

Official Recognition and Meaningful Perquisites

While the formal qualifications of ROTC officers were improving, university faculty and administrators on some campuses continued to push for a change in the academic titles given to ROTC officers. At Michigan and the University of Illinois at Chicago Circle, the faculties voted to remove their academic titles altogether, while at Pittsburgh the faculty voted to add "visiting" to the title. They argued that military officers, having climbed a different career ladder than academics, did not merit professorial titles. Michigan astronomy professor and navy reserve captain Freeman Miller told Senator George Kuhn:

> Academic appointments are won by members of the faculty the hard way—year after year of teaching and scholarly study and research. It simply comes down to the fact that a promotion to lieutenant colonel or commander is earned by one kind of endeavor and a professorship by another . . . [H]aving traversed the two quite different routes to a navy captaincy and university professorship, I can testify that neither qualifies one for recognition by a title or rank in the other area.[151]

The services initially resisted this change but amended their stance after the civilian leadership of the DOD accepted the position that the titles themselves were not important but the status they conferred was. Secretary of Defense Melvin Laird told the Senate: "I would see no objection to calling an officer by his military grade if he had the official recognition and meaningful perquisites of the academic rank of professor—other than tenure, of course. If an institution does not agree to this, then it cannot have an ROTC unit on its campus."[152]

These perquisites included having the ROTC instructor "listed in the institutional catalog on the same basis as other professors and shar[ing] the same faculty voting and committee responsibilities as other professors."[153] In the Big Ten schools, of course, such perks also included access to the schools' two most precious commodities—parking spaces and football tickets.[154] The schools had never planned to remove the perks or status, just the titles. The maintenance of fringe benefits and listings in the course catalogs helped convince DOD officials that dropping the titles did not necessarily denigrate the ROTC programs. To them, the issue of titles was cosmetic if it did not affect the formal functioning of the officers on campus.[155]

The debate over changing the ROTC units from academic departments to programs followed similar lines. Michigan and Illinois at Chicago Circle faculty voted to remove ROTC's departmental status because "department [is] inappropriate due to [ROTC's] nonpreparation of its own budget, only nominal control over curriculum, exterior funding and nonrecruitment of its own staff."[156] As with individual academic titles, the universities proposed not a reduction in ROTC status but a change in its formal position to "recognize the distinction (in no way derogatory) between the typical University department and an ROTC unit."[157]

Again it was a high-level meeting, this one at Maxwell AFB, between Brigadier General Ben Cassiday and Robert Williams, that produced agreement. Williams "made clear in all statements that the University was in no sense 'downgrading' ROTC" in changing ROTC to a program. Michigan, he told Cassiday, simply wanted to acknowledge ROTC's distinctive nature. The change would not affect ROTC's listings in course catalogs, the ability of ROTC officers to participate in university administration, or the secretarial and custodial support the university provided to ROTC. Cassiday accepted the Michigan position, and thereafter the ROTC units at Michigan and Illinois-Chicago Circle became known as Military Officer Education Programs (MOEPs).[158]

Academic Credit

The services and the universities reached easy resolution on the preceding issues because of the general agreement that had already existed. Achieving resolution on other issues, however, proved to be more difficult. The arduous problem of academic credit remained the most hotly contested issue. Virtually all of the faculty reports discussed above recommended the removal of academic credit for ROTC courses in the colleges of liberal arts because, in the words of a University of Illinois committee, "The content of courses and the qualification of the instructors appear sufficiently marginal that such offerings are not commensurate with the College's traditional goals. The assignment of a limited number of hours or advanced ROTC course work for graduation credit seemed a dereliction of duty if the educational quality of the service programs are to be enhanced."[159]

In the 1960s, in an Illinois ROTC class on navigation, a cadet (who happened also to be an astronomy major) correctly identified a constellation as "Cassiopeia." The sergeant who graded the exam marked the answer incorrect, telling the cadet that the army manual called the constellation "The Big M" and that "no other response was acceptable." When the civilian academics in the astronomy department learned of the problem, they reacted by protesting against the "basic inflexibility and oversimplicity of the Army ROTC program."[160] Incidents such as these helped to produce a consensus among academics that the levels of credit awarded for ROTC classes were not at all justifiable.

Whereas the universities were in general agreement on this issue, three distinct military opinions emerged. One was that losing credit would adversely affect enrollment, since students would be less inclined to take ROTC classes. Lack of accreditation would therefore damage the program's ability to recruit and keep students. "Unless we can give credit where credit is due," noted Pittsburgh PMS David Clagett, "then our enrollment figure will continue to drop to such an extent that the university['s ROTC unit] will become non-productive. The possibility then arises that the unit could be removed."[161] This position was most common among ROTC unit heads, who saw their enrollments plummeting and looked to credit as a means to stop the flood of students leaving the program. Academic credit, they hoped, would make their recruitment task that much easier.

A second position, related to the first, was that a loss of credit would constitute "prima facie evidence that [the University] has downgraded the services."[162] The issue, then, was one of image not credit. Lack of credit, some argued, would demonstrate that the university, and especially the liberal arts colleges, wanted to put ROTC "on the fringe."[163] This argument implied that the problems created by the loss of credit would go far beyond enrollment; such a vote would indicate that faculties were repudiating the military and the military model for organization and authority. Traditionalists like Congressman Hébert and some in the civilian leadership of the navy held most adamantly to this position, fearing that any weakening of the military's authority would portend disaster both for good order on the campuses and for the good order they saw dissipating in society more generally.

The third position, subscribed to by those DOD officials most interested in finding a basis for negotiation with the universities, was that losing credit would not necessarily harm the program. Melvin Laird argued, "We have found over the years that many well-supported and highly productive programs have given little, and in some cases no, degree credit for military courses in the ROTC program. Where overall institutional support is strong, the issue of degree credit has not been a bar to a successful program."[164] Those who held to this position noted that engineering schools rarely gave any academic credit to ROTC, yet several engineering colleges, like Georgia Tech, supported strong and vibrant ROTC programs.

Obviously the third position left the most room for negotiation. Faculty and administrators were for the most part unconvinced by the first two arguments. They held to their positions that ROTC courses were the intellectual inferior of standard university courses and, if ROTC sought accreditation, it would have to improve the course quality. University of Pittsburgh professor Peter Karsten argued, "Other [students] may not come because we offer no credit for Cuban guerrilla warfare training, John Birch Society readings, or underwater polo. Those are risks we take when we construct . . . curricula that we believe has merit."[165] The services' arguments about enrollment declines also failed to convince most university officials. "I doubt whether the Army wants officers who entered the service merely because they could get a few hours of academic credit toward their degree," one provost told a trustee, calling it a "hardly defensible motivation."[166]

The DOD derived its official stand on the issue from Laird's argument that lack of credit was not necessarily a hindrance to a successful program and the Benson Report's determination that credit awarded should be the prerogative of the faculty. Lawyers from the DOD and the Association of NROTC Colleges and Universities had agreed that "appropriate credit" could legally mean no credit if so determined by the group with authority to make such a judgment—namely, the faculty.[167] The services (despite some initial resistance by the navy) thus concentrated their energies on upgrading their courses and instructors so that ROTC courses could receive accreditation on their own merits; such a course of action, if successful, would fully satisfy all parties. In 1971 the air force nominated Colonel Marvin Grunzke, who held a Ph.D. in experimental and industrial psychology from Yale, to the position of PAS at Michigan in the hope that he could attain an adjunct professorship in the psychology department (see Chapter 7). Such an appointment would thus accredit all courses taught by Colonel Grunzke.

The navy initially fought to retain all credit, but later modified its position. It threatened to pull its units out of Colorado, Michigan, and Illinois, as well as Minnesota and Northwestern, where faculties had made similar recommendations, and replace them with schools from its NROTC waiting list of sixty institutions. This threat failed, however, because Assistant Secretary of Defense Theodore Marrs and Secretary of Defense Melvin Laird were opposed to the navy's leaving any Big Ten school; also, the Navy agreed with DOD and Michigan officials that there was not "an equivalent to . . . any one of the institutions in the Big Ten with NROTC units" on that waiting list.[168] Nevertheless, in 1971 the navy directed that no NROTC scholarship student be permitted to enroll in a liberal arts college that had removed credit. This policy remained in effect for one academic year while an irate Association of NROTC Colleges and Universities successfully appealed the "mortmain" directive.

This debate over credit indicates that the services—even the navy, which fought hardest on this issue—preferred having no-credit programs at schools like Michigan and Illinois to having full-credit ones at less visible, less prestigious schools. The services continued to push for the restoration of credit (see Chapter 6) but never again threatened removal of a unit as ultimate sanction. Instead, they accepted the universities argument that to be accredited they needed to have the approval of an academic department.

The debates over these abiding issues reflected the general consensus between university and military officials that the ROTC program was indeed worth saving, but that it needed serious reforms to "place ROTC within the regular academic framework of the University and make ROTC much less an adjunct unit than it has been."[169] By the end of this period, working compromises had been reached to permit ROTC programs to exist with the frameworks laid down by university faculties. At the end of 1971, University of Illinois chancellor J. W. Peltason described the debates of the past few years thus:

> Vigorous support of academic programs on the campus of any major university does not imply unquestioning allegiance to traditional modes of

instruction and curricular patterns. The proposal recently considered and approved by our Senate represents a serious attempt at increasing the academic quality of our three ROTC programs without substantially diluting that measure of professional military officer contact with the cadet or midshipman absolutely necessary to programs of this type . . . I can tell you honestly . . . that these conversations [between administration and military], as well as others conducted in the same vein are designed not to weaken or degrade programs which we already consider to be good ones, but rather they are intended to strengthen our ROTC programs, and to place them more within the regular academic framework of the campus than has heretofore been the case.[170]

These resolutions were sufficient to placate most faculty and administrators. Whether the ROTC units could attract enough undergraduates to make the program viable, however, remained to be seen.

Resolution of some of these key issues did not mean that ROTC's continuance was assured. The military, while agreeing as an institution to many fundamental changes to the program, still had many members, such as the navy's director of educational development, who saw the compromises as "inexcusable" and "less than satisfactory."[171] Similarly, many in the universities remained suspicious of the military despite the conclusion of negotiations on favorable terms to academe. After his battles with the navy, Robert Williams told Admiral Kinney, "It would be appropriate during the coming year for each party to watch the other in the same manner that the American Navy and the Russian Navy are watching each other in the Mediterranean."[172] Furthermore, although working compromises had been agreed to in principle, they still had to demonstrate that they could provide a lasting harmony for ROTC on American campuses.

More fundamentally, the compromises would be rendered moot if enough undergraduates did not find the ROTC program sufficiently important and interesting to join. Even increases in the number of scholarships could not stop the plummeting enrollments. The army increased the number of scholarships it awarded from 4,759 in academic year 1969–70 to 5,500 (the ceiling established by the Vitalization Act) the following year.[173] Still, even many large universities were turning out far fewer officers than they had in previous years. Michigan, which had produced fifty-nine army, twenty-eight navy, and twenty-seven air force officers in 1969, produced only thirty army, seventeen navy, and nine air force officers in 1972.[174] Nationally, the figures were equally dramatic. In 1968, the freshman AFROTC enrollment had been 25,966; by 1972, it had fallen to 8,147.[175] After 1973, a zero-draft environment meant that a major force for sustaining ROTC enrollment levels was gone. For ROTC and the all-volunteer force concept to survive, the American military system would have to make fundamental changes in the education and training of American officers in the post-Vietnam era.

CHAPTER 6

ROTC in the Era of the All-Volunteer Force, 1972–1980

Margaret Snyder has a job waiting for her when she graduates: she is going to be a marine.

—University of Washington *Daily,* 1976

The antidraft pressures of the Vietnam War and traditional American anxieties over conscription combined in 1973 to produce a new "zero-draft" military environment; for the first time since 1948, the United States military would rely exclusively on volunteers. The draft had served as a primary motivator for recruitment in all branches and grades of the armed forces for a quarter century by giving men a way to control the nature and timing of their otherwise capricious military service obligations. Similarly, the draft had served to boost ROTC enrollments by offering men the possibility of service in the more prestigious and higher-paying officer grades. Nixon's jettisoning of the draft meant that the freefall in ROTC enrollments caused in large measure by the Vietnam War would not immediately correct itself after the withdrawal of American forces from Southeast Asia. The zero-draft environment portended fundamental change to ROTC and to the entire system of military personnel procurement.

Criticisms of the draft that led to its abandonment were twofold. One argument against the draft was that, with its system of deferments and exemptions, it was biased against young men from low socioeconomic backgrounds. The very poorest members of society were relatively infrequently drafted due to their tendency to do poorly on physical and mental tests, but "among those who were found to be qualified, the poor were more likely to be drafted than were men of higher social status."[1] Also, draftees were more likely than volunteers to see combat.

The second argument recalled traditional American anxieties over conscription. The draft, many said, amounted to a conscription of labor. Forcing an individual into military service had always been inconsistent with American cultural and economic beliefs, but in times of war and national emergency, such as the Cold War that had inspired the 1948 draft law, this inconsistency could be tolerated.[2] In the aftermath of a humiliating defeat, however, it could not. The 1970 Gates Commission, which was assigned by President Nixon to examine the concept of a volunteer force, began its report by arguing that "a return to an all-volunteer force will strengthen our freedoms, remove an inequity now imposed on the expression of the patriotism that has never been lacking in our youth, promote the efficiency of the armed forces, and enhance their dignity."[3] Higher wages and better working conditions, it argued, not conscription, would attract men into the American armed services.

After the Gates Commission issued its report, the all-volunteer force became a virtual inevitability, and the services began planning for the transition. Furthermore, because the Nixon Pentagon called fewer draftees for Vietnam after 1969, the AVF was functionally in place even before its official creation in 1973. Supporters of the all-volunteer concept argued that market incentives, such as higher pay, would keep the services supplied with enough highly motivated men. But for the AVF to work, the services would have to make some fundamental changes in the nature of the military to attract volunteers, including raising pay and improving the quality of military life.[4]

ROTC units faced the same dilemma. Without the draft to induce men to join, ROTC training had to be redesigned, in the words of George Benson, assistant secretary of defense for education in 1971, "to make [ROTC] attractive enough in an era of volunteer armed forces."[5] ROTC now had to induce men to volunteer in an absolute sense. This structural necessity, combined with movements in American society more generally, created changes in the program that did not result from faculty reports or student demonstrations. Eventually these reforms forced a change in the very definition of the groups in American society that were qualified to be military officers.

The AVF was the third major cause for declining ROTC enrollments in an approximately fifteen-year period. The first cause had been the conversion of many compulsory units to voluntary status in the late 1950s and early 1960s. The services had supported that drop because the draft, the foundation of ROTC enrollments, was still compelling enough to push many men into the program. The second cause for enrollment decline had been the consistent erosion of the power of the draft itself as a motivating factor, beginning with the 1961 exemption of married men. Throughout the 1960s, young men found other ways of beating the draft, most of them inspired by a desire to avoid the war in Vietnam.[6] The introduction of the lottery system in 1969 formally removed large numbers of men from the draft; a large subset of those men were concurrently able to eliminate ROTC as an option for evading conscription. The AVF represented the impetus for the third, and most essential, major decrease in ROTC enrollments.

As Table 6.1 indicates, ROTC enrollments were on the decline even before the abandonment of the draft was widely contemplated. Now, for the first time in the history of the program, a majority of units, some of them large units with long traditions of officer production, were unable to meet their contractual obligation of having seventeen juniors enrolled. In 1974 the army put 140 of its host schools on probation for failure to meet this minimum standard.[7] Even a school as large as Michigan spent much of the 1970s on probation for enrollment reasons. Similarly, total University of Illinois ROTC enrollments fell 82 percent from 1966 to 1974; total University of Texas ROTC enrollments fell 66 percent in the same period.[8]

ROTC thus faced a monumental challenge with the end of the draft. It also faced uncertain campus and political climates. The formal agreements dis-

Table 6.1 ROTC enrollments 1968–1975, by service

Academic year	Army ROTC	Naval ROTC	Air Force ROTC
1967–68	141,495	9,443	44,987
1968–69	125,126	9,063	40,533
1969–70	87,122	7,708	27,978
1970–71	62,647	6,528	23,070
1971–72	45,130	6,445	21,201
1972–73	34,773	6,898	18,724
1973–74	31,363	6,765	17,464
1974–75	38,228	6,546	15,993

Source: Department of Defense Manpower Statistics, various years.

cussed in Chapter 5 created a truce on those campuses that had most vocally called for change in the 1960s, but the long-term success of that truce was still in some doubt. ROTC had become less visibly distinct from the civilian programs with which it coexisted, but even after 1972, it still had the distinction of being a vocational, military program. The *Princetonian* spoke for many when it reported: "Students may have a right to learn the techniques of warfare, but it is not the responsibility of the university to make such instruction available to them."[9] The truces and curricular changes to the program notwithstanding, ROTC's vocational and military emphases continued to make it an anomalous, and therefore controversial, university program.

Universities also had to face an increasingly watchful federal government in an era of what administrators experienced as "adversarial regulation."[10] Universities had become the target of increasing federal attention through the Buckley Amendment, which limited the universities' right to distribute information about their students, and Title 9 of the Education Amendments of 1972, which prohibited gender distinctions in all educational programs and activities. The proponents of Title 9 did not consider ROTC per se, but the law certainly implied that all educational programs would have to promote gender equality.[11] These new laws "proceeded from the conclusion that universities were guilty of violating the public interest" by being too exclusive.[12] Through these and other laws, universities in the 1970s had to deal with a significantly more intrusive federal government than they had in the 1960s.

Furthermore, university and government budget concerns grew more serious in the 1970s than they had been in the 1960s. The level of public support given to higher education began to fall after the oil crisis of 1973, even as inflation and the costs of computing, facilities expansion, and financial aid programs were rapidly increasing.[13] These financial crises forced universities to scale back commitments and focused attention on the cost-effectiveness of university support for ROTC units. At the same time, military budgets were tightened; the services opted to close unproductive training units and spend the money saved on the creation of new units, fundamentally changing the nature of the ROTC hosts.

All was not gloomy for ROTC's future, however. As we have seen, formal agreement existed on some of the most contentious issues, and support for ROTC among university administrators was generally high. Furthermore, American confidence in the military began to rise again after 1973, even as faith in other institutions was waning. Between 1973 and 1976 the percentage of Americans expressing "a great deal" of confidence in military leaders rose from 33 percent to 42 percent, while the percentage of Americans expressing "a great deal" of confidence in educational leaders fell from a high of 50 percent in 1974 to 38 percent just two years later.[14] The degree of confidence expressed by college-age people was even more remarkable. Between 1973 and 1975 (the first three years of the AVF), the percentage of eighteen- to twenty-three-year-olds reporting "a great deal" of confidence in the military rose from 28 percent to 44 percent. The percentage of that group who reported "a great deal" of confidence in education grew much more slowly, from 34 percent to 38 percent.[15]

There was therefore some indication that the military as an institution still held the confidence of many Americans, some of whom were concurrently losing faith in other American institutions. That confidence might help the services reestablish good faith with the general public, but it would not in itself be enough to guarantee ROTC enlistments or good faith with university communities, whose values did not necessarily overlap with the public's on military matters.

Furthermore, some of the problems that had confronted ROTC in the Vietnam era were absent in the era of the AVF. If Kingman Brewster's argument that the draft created a feeling of "sourness" on the campuses was valid, it might then be presumed that without the draft that sourness and the concurrent threat to life and career patterns would produce far less campus opposition and disruption. Indeed the vocal, and at times violent, antiwar protests began to dissipate by 1971 and were totally absent the following year. Even at schools with radical traditions, such as Michigan, anti-ROTC rallies after 1972 failed to generate significant numbers of protesters.[16] The lower levels of visible protest on military issues led some observers to talk of a new "post-Vietnam" era of university-military relations even while American soldiers were still in Vietnam. "Remember the 1969–70 protest days on the American college campuses?" queried a 1973 Army ROTC publication nostalgically, "Indeed those were dreary days for Army ROTC."[17]

The desire to place Vietnam safely and squarely in the recesses of memory, combined with the rapid turnover among undergraduate populations, also led some observers to talk of a new kind of college student. In 1975 an officer reflecting on his four years' experience as an ROTC instructor noted, "The wild radical is gone. Replacing him is the serious-minded student who knows he is here for a purpose and wants to get as much out of his college education as possible."[18] Such widespread proclamations gave some observers cause for renewed faith and optimism, but the American college student had not changed quite so rapidly. What had changed rapidly was the nation's abandonment of conscription and the concurrent shift to market incentives as a means of military recruitment.

The volunteer environment of the 1970s meant a new challenge for officer procurement. Market incentives—such as higher pay, better conditions, and the inducement of a genuine, rather than half-coerced, patriotism—combined with a new sense of worth in the military as a profession, would have to replace the draft as the primary means for getting men into ROTC. The Gates Commission had optimistically (and erroneously, in view of the heavy role the draft played in determining enlistment rates) predicted that with such incentives and an improved public image for the military, ROTC could begin to overproduce officers by 1975; this judgment appears even more sanguine in retrospect, when one considers that the Gates Commission never seriously contemplated an expanded role for women or African Americans in the AVF-era ROTC program.[19] As we will see, however, market incentives were entirely insufficient to induce enough college students to sign up for ROTC, threatening the viability of the program so long as it continued to prefer white males.

The Gates Commission's rosy predictions notwithstanding, ROTC administrators and observers saw only steadily declining enrollments. "ROTC survived demonstrations, sit-ins, and trashings in the late sixties," noted Michigan's *University Record* in 1974. "Now it is on the verge of succumbing to something less dramatic—disinterest."[20] Instead of waiting for the better times the Gates Commission predicted, the services responded to the enrollment crisis with a series of new tactics. They expanded the pool of potential officers by responding to the desire of women to join the program and by making serious efforts to recruit higher numbers of African Americans into ROTC. These changes, while coincident with a growing sense of egalitarianism in higher education and in American society more generally, were themselves only partly its product. None of the faculty reports of the 1960s and 1970s had criticized ROTC for excluding women and African Americans, despite attempts by those faculties to seize the moral high ground. Universities in the Vietnam era expressed a great deal of concern over issues of credit and procedure, but not ROTC demographics. In the latter case, the interests of the military, which was itself moving (albeit slowly) toward equality, and the demands of the AVF pushed for a change that all parties could agree was the "right thing" to do.

Rather than being prompted by university communities, these demographic changes emanated both from a simple need to fill the junior officer ranks in an era of declining enrollment from traditional sources and from the desires of previously excluded groups to enter what they perceived as the advantageous job environment of the armed forces. Women and African Americans were also concurrently entering new sectors of the civilian economy in increasing numbers. To be sure, federal legislation and the complementary interest in equal opportunity programs emanating from the universities themselves provided a synergy that increased the potential success of these integrations. But the military embraced the idea of a broadened base for officer recruitment even in the absence of direct pressure from university administrators and faculty, because of its own belief in its wisdom and utility.

"The Intent and Spirit of National Policy"

The 1948 law that had made women a permanent, if auxiliary, component of the American military system had established that no more than 2 percent of the American officer corps could be female. Since the mandated percentage was so small, before 1969 American military planners had only once considered opening ROTC to women, in 1956. With the single exception of that failed experiment, the American military trained its women officer candidates at sexually segregated female officer candidate schools both to separate them from men and because the focus of women's training was administration, not combat. Once trained, women served in separate units—the army's Women's Army Corps (WAC), the air force's Women in the Air Force (WAF), and the navy's Women Accepted for Voluntary Emergency Service (WAVES)—which had separate promotion lists and a clear noncombat ideal.[21]

On most campuses, however, women participated indirectly in ROTC events through women's auxiliary units. As early as 1927 such an auxiliary existed at Kansas State, where sixteen women competed for the positions of honorary colonel and honorary major.[22] These auxiliaries sponsored teas, helped cadets type theme papers, served as hostesses for ROTC events, and helped to plan the annual military ball. They also existed to make "indoctrination a little more bearable, a little more appealing" for the men.[23] The air force female auxiliary, called Angel Flight, became a national organization in 1957, and within nine years it had more than four thousand members at 113 schools.[24] Membership in the University of Pittsburgh Angel Flight was a prerequisite for election as queen of the military ball; in 1961 there were twenty candidates for the honor.[25]

The explicitly feminine emphasis of these auxiliaries was in part a conscious attempt to emphasize by contrast the very masculine qualities that ROTC was designed to instill (Angel Flight selection criteria included "scholarship, personality, appearance, and leadership"[26]). In 1960 Army ROTC headquarters advertised that "the Army's primary job is to develop MEN, poised, alert and capable of taking full advantage of the progress thus far achieved in organization of units and development of materiel."[27] Indeed, the strong masculine emphasis of ROTC culture—as a reflection of the larger military culture—made the inclusion of women on anything but an auxiliary basis difficult. Official marching cadences (called "Jody Calls") at the University of Colorado in the 1950s included, "There ain't no use in looking down / There ain't no women on the ground" and "I don't know but I've been told / CU women are mighty cold."[28]

In 1956 ROTC had made a formal attempt to enroll women when the air force opened ten ROTC units to women on a trial basis in order to boost WAF officer ranks. Penn State, Butler, Miami (Ohio), George Washington, and the Universities of Maryland, Texas, California, Southern Illinois, Georgia, and Florida tested the new Women's Air Force Cadette Pilot Program, which was to commission ten WAFs per unit per year. Consistent with the auxiliary status of the WAFs, the conditions of ROTC training for women "cadettes" was designed to be unequal. The male and female programs were legally separate, and WAF commissions technically came not from ROTC but from direct commissioning.[29] The women received no scholarships, were not permitted to take weapons training, and enrolled with the knowledge that they could withdraw at any time without penalty, meaning they had a way out if they decided that they preferred raising a family to having a military career.[30]

The program did not last long, in part because it offered a clearly second-class (and nonscholarship) status to the prospective cadettes, thereby deterring enlistment, and in part because of the air force's insistence on separate training for female officers, necessitating the assignment of female instructors.[31] The program stirred some limited interest in the WAFs but commissioned only seven officers. It never got past the trial stage and was formally canceled in July 1960.[32] Thus the first attempt to enlist women in ROTC ended. To the extent that women were connected to ROTC before the 1960s, then, they served primarily as auxiliaries to men.

Shortly after the Cadette Pilot Program foundered, however, a fascinating process of militarization began among small groups of college women, altering the relationship between collegiate women and the ROTC program. One manifestation of this evolution is evident in the changing nature of the female auxiliaries. Careful observers of the ROTC program noted "the accelerating rate of participation by young women in collegiate military societies" in the early 1960s.[33] These societies were themselves becoming more martial in their orientation.

In 1960 two "girls drill teams" were among the twenty-eight teams that competed in the Twelfth Illinois Invitational Drill, marking the first time that women participated in the event.[34] Four years later the University of Illinois Angel Flight auxiliary had a fifty-woman drill team, led entirely by women, and in 1966 the University of Texas AROTC rifle team accepted its first female member.[35] To be sure, the traditional auxiliaries continued to exist, but elements of change were undoubtedly mixed in with the continuity. In 1967, for example, Kent State's female auxiliary, the Army ROTC Sponsors, changed its name to the less ancillary-sounding Coed Cadets (note also the 1960s' spelling of *Cadets*, compared with the 1950s' spelling, *Cadettes*) and purchased military-style uniforms; membership subsequently rose from eight to thirty-one.[36] Women's societies were taking a much greater interest in military matters on several campuses, and they were taking on responsibilities much more martial than typing the theme papers of their male peers. These changes foreshadowed an integration of women into ROTC that was vastly more successful than anyone in power had believed was possible.

Evolving definitions of women's place in America drove many of these changes. The "separate spheres" of the 1950s gradually began to yield to more complex gender definitions. Among the important events of the early 1960s were the publication of Betty Friedan's *The Feminine Mystique* and President Kennedy's establishment of a Commission on the Status of Women, both in 1963. Three years later the National Organization for Women (NOW) released its statement of purpose, endorsing "true equality for all women in America, and [movement] toward a fully equal partnership of the sexes."[37] Surely, not all women shared the goals and ambitions of groups like NOW, but across the nation the rebirth of feminism called into question traditional views of men's and women's roles.

Individual women reacted to these changes in a wide variety of ways. Many daughters of World War II veterans were coming of college age, and they took great pride in the accomplishments of their fathers and wanted to

make some patriotic contribution of their own. They had grown up understanding, in the words of Lynda Van Devanter, who entered nursing school
in 1965, "the obligation we all had to be of service not only to our family,
community, church, and country, but to all of mankind." The military
seemed to her the way to fulfill that obligation and to answer the challenge
of President Kennedy's call for the "chosen" generation to change the
world.[38] From World War II to the AVF, women had consistently been more
interested in joining the military than the military had been in recruiting
women. On one level, the evolving nature of the military auxiliary societies,
and the creation of organizations such as the gender-integrated Peace Corps
in 1961, were reflections of this process.

More important to policymakers than the changing nature of women's
military auxiliaries was a legislative change in 1967 (Public Law 90-130)
that removed the 2 percent ceiling and promotion restrictions that had been
imposed on female officers in 1948. The immediate impulse for the legislation was twofold. Since, in the words of the Marshall Commission on Selective Service, "women willing to volunteer for military duty exist in far
greater numbers than the services will accommodate," lifting the ceiling
might allow the military to relax the numbers of men who had to be in-
ducted.[39] Also, the promotion restrictions had created a bottleneck of valuable female officers who had joined the armed forces during World War II.
Before Public Law 90-130 these women were significantly behind their
male peers in terms of rank, and because their promotion possibilities were
so constrained, they were leaving the services in high numbers.[40]

Public Law 90-130 meant that there was now no formal ceiling on the
number of women whom the services could recruit. Informal ceilings, however, still existed, since women were banned from all combat operations and
therefore could not legally hold some military jobs. Still, the number of support personnel the services needed was sufficiently high to permit women to
qualify for a much larger number of jobs than they were then filling. In
other words, after 1967 there suddenly existed a large number of jobs in the
military for female officers and no ceiling to prevent them from taking those
jobs. The services' initial response to these changes was mixed. Public Law
90-130 had lifted the legislative ceiling, but it had not required the services
to take any action to raise the percentages of women in uniform. Because
there was then no formal mandate for increasing the number of female
officers, Public Law 90-130 need not have had an impact on ROTC units.

The ROTC staffs responded to Public Law 90-130 as early as 1968, when an air force feasibility study found "no insurmountable obstacles to the re-cruiting, selection, preparation, and commissioning of WAF officers at se-lected AFROTC detachments." Still, the air force initially found it "costly," due to anticipated low enrollments, and "undesirable," due to the need to assign a WAF officer to each detachment, to enroll women in AFROTC.[41] The air force, consistent with the logic of its Cadette program about a decade earlier, had assumed that women could not be integrated into ROTC on the same basis as men because of their auxiliary status, thus necessitating the as-signment of a WAF officer to each detachment. The university representa-tives on the 1969 Air Force ROTC Advisory Panel gave the air force little en-couragement to think otherwise, noting, "We are not convinced that a WAF ROTC program would settle any major problems for the Air Force."[42]

The problems of training and cost, however, would be rendered moot if ROTC opportunities were made available to women on the same basis that they were already available to men. Under this scenario, assigning WAF officers to all detachments would not be necessary; women could be trained under essentially the same procedures as men. Colonel Jeanne Holm, the WAF Director, believed that "coeducationalizing" AFROTC was "essential to expanding career roles for women," and she pushed for full gender integra-tion of AFROTC.[43] Theodore Marrs, under assistant secretary of the air force for reserve and ROTC affairs, agreed with Holm, indicating that opening ROTC to women also had the benefit of being consistent with "the intent and spirit of national policy."[44] The air force's need for officers, its tradition of comparatively liberal attitudes toward female officers, the enrollment cri-sis in ROTC, and such legislation as Title 9 and the Equal Rights Amendment combined to produce an environment singularly congenial to reform rather than conservative retrenchment.

In 1969 the air force began a pilot coeducational, two-year AFROTC pro-gram, identical to the male program in curriculum, at Ohio State, Auburn, Drake, and East Carolina; if successful, the air force planned to expand the program to six more units in 1970. The air force further directed that the officers produced from AFROTC would count in addition to, not in place of, the 225 women officers produced annually from OCS.[45] No ceiling therefore existed on the quantitative success of the air force program.

Women responded immediately to the opportunity to experience ROTC training. Fifty Ohio State University women signed up for ROTC in the first year.[46] At Temple University, which was not part of the pilot program, eight women signed up for ROTC in 1969 in response to a "routine university announcement" that such courses could be used as a substitute for that university's physical education requirement. Because the program was unrelated to the air force integration experiment, the women could not qualify for a commission even if they desired one. Nevertheless, they took marksmanship and tactics courses along with the men.[47]

The surprising success of the pilot program caused the air force to abandon plans for a gradual expansion and immediately begin gender integration in the two-year and four-year programs at all units. In the fall of 1970, eighty-one AFROTC units enrolled more than five hundred women officer candidates—a modest 2 percent of the AFROTC total, but impressive for a trial program. The quantitative success of the Women in the Air Force Reserve Officers' Training Corps (WAFROTC) program was evident to the army and navy as well. "At a time when male disillusionment . . . ha[d] thinned the ranks," women represented a source of a rather large number of new cadets.[48] This is not, of course, to argue that women were any more or less disillusioned with the military or America generally than men, simply that the disillusionment itself argued for opening military service to the one-half of the American population theretofore clearly marginalized.[49]

The army and navy programs, lacking the active support of people like Holm and Marrs, were characterized more by acquiescence than action. The navy agreed to a test program on four campuses for women in 1972 "as a compromise," in the hope that the Naval Academy could remain all male.[50] The army was also hesitant, but due to "pressure generated by the other coeducational ROTC programs, particularly that of the Air Force," it also opened a test program in 1972.[51] Not surprisingly, the air force took a definitive early lead in the integration of women and thus began to see the most immediate positive effect on enrollment. In 1972 the navy had 17 female midshipmen on 4 campuses and the army had 212 female cadets on 10 campuses, but the Air Force already had 1,427 women enrolled on 156 campuses.[52]

While some men had difficulty responding to the dramatic expansion of women into ROTC, the success of female cadets could not be denied. At the University of Illinois, where female enrollments lagged behind national patterns for a few years, male cadets found that the biggest advantage of having women in the unit was "to make sure we have something more to look at than just the cadre when we attend AFROTC functions!"[53] These attitudes notwithstanding, women were proving themselves the equal of men in units nationwide, much to the surprise of some men, who had expected them to fulfill a quite different role.

The army gave the ten units selected to test the integration of women in 1972 "little guidance on whether or not to modify their program." The cadre at the University of Hawaii, assuming that women's roles would expand in the coming years, made no curriculum changes; women completed rappelling exercises and M-16 rifle training alongside men. Twenty of the unit's 69 cadets were female; 3 women joined Hawaii's arduous Ranger unit. The Hawaii women outscored the men in small-unit operations and behavioral sciences tests, and the senior cadets (all men) gave the outstanding cadet award to one of the women. The Hawaii cadre told the army that it was "extremely impressed with the enthusiasm demonstrated by the young women. At the outset they were much more inquiring, energetic, ambitious, and outspoken than their male counterparts."[54] The army understood the success of the female cadets to be a function of their exceptional dedication, suggesting that women who decided to join ROTC came from a self-selected group.

The air force, army, and navy all increased the pace of their integration programs faster than initially planned, largely due to the demand of women to sign up. The army found the response to its ten-campus pilot program "greater than expected and hundreds of women expressed their desire to enroll in Army ROTC at the [nonpilot] institutions offering the course."[55] By 1973 the Air Force ROTC Advisory Panel, which in 1969 had recommended against opening the program to women, had "wholeheartedly support[ed] long-range relationships between the Air Force and the academic community in regards to acceptance of ROTC on campuses and to the effective recruitment of women."[56] The increasing interest in, and commitment to, military life among a subset of American female college students provided the justification for a rapid expansion of women's place in ROTC.

At some schools, such as the University of Pittsburgh, women accounted for more than one-third of new enrollments and a large share of the high-quality enrollments.[57] In 1975, 42 percent of female Army ROTC cadets from the fourth region (the Northwest) were number one or two in their class. Only 15 percent of the men were so qualified.[58] Women cadets soon became heads of their units at several schools, including the army ROTC unit at Ohio State.[59] By 1976 women held three of the nine offices in the University of Illinois AFROTC honor society and the Outstanding Basic Cadet award at the University of Texas.[60] The following year women won battalion commander honors and the Army ROTC Gold Medal at Illinois.[61] These accolades indicate that women were not only interested in the financial benefits of ROTC but also sought to excel as female pioneers in a formerly all-male bastion.

Women's motivations for enlisting in ROTC ranged from the simple desire for a challenge or "to do something different" to the more practical reason that the military job environment offered equal pay scales to women within grades, a rare condition in the civilian economy.[62] ROTC also allowed women to break out of traditional roles in dramatic and visible ways, providing leadership opportunities and, for those who sought it, weapons and flight training. In a 1980 survey, four in five female ROTC cadets said that ROTC gave them more opportunities for personal growth than any other campus activity.[63]

As noted earlier, the success of women in ROTC units was coincident with a changing social and legislative environment. By early 1973, thirty of the necessary thirty-eight states had ratified the Equal Rights Amendment; the DOD assumed that the imminent passage of the amendment would force major changes in the nature of the American military system. A 1972 DOD task force noted that "it is likely that *after* the Equal Rights Amendment is ratified, all laws and Service policies which treat women differently than men will be challenged on grounds of unconstitutionality."[64] The services and the DOD hoped that if they were able to make changes "in an orderly way" they could avoid being forced to make drastic changes by the courts, which were already forcing gender equality in military family and benefits policies.[65] The integration of women was also helped along by the belief of some men, such as the PNS at the University of Washington, that opening training to women was the proper course of action. "Training military officers without regard to sex is an idea whose time has come," he noted. "The Navy needs female officers, and we have the facilities for graduating female officers. It's as simple as that."[66]

It may not have been quite as simple as that, but the surprising ease with which women were integrated into ROTC programs was critical to keeping the program viable. "Only the participation of women in ROTC," noted the DOD in 1980, "has been responsible for keeping enrollments on the increase."[67] By 1980, 2,080 women had been commissioned via the AFROTC program and almost 4,000 more women were enrolled in the program, including 1,102 scholarship winners.[68] The success of female ROTC cadets mirrored, and in turn contributed to, the success of military women more generally. Their ability to succeed in a previously all-male realm led to the gradual disbanding of the WAC, WAF, and WAVES auxiliaries between 1973 and 1978 and the integration of the service academies in 1976.

Two trends combined to create the reforms that made the integration of women into ROTC possible. First, the interest women were showing in ROTC was a reflection of their expansion into other previously male-dominated professional fields, such as engineering, where women's share of the profession rose from 9.1 percent to 13.4 percent between 1972 and 1978, and in fields analogous to the military, such as law enforcement, where in the same period women's share rose from 2.6 percent to 5.9 percent.[69] To be sure, the military was not alone in blazing new trails; other significant gender integrations included the Secret Service in 1970 and the New York City Police Academy in 1972. Women's own changing sense of appropriate careers, reflected both in the changing nature of the auxiliary societies and the trend of female employment nationwide, therefore increased the supply of qualified women for ROTC. Second, a change in the American personnel procurement system reduced the number of available male officer candidates and increased the demand for women to fill the void. The successful integration of women into ROTC depended on both of these changes.

"An All-Out Effort to Correct Such Inequities as May Have Existed in the Past"

The integration of African Americans into ROTC mirrored the integration of women in timing, causation, and outcome. The desire of more African Americans to enter the armed forces, changing legislative and social environments, and a structural change in manpower policies combined to produce reform. There were, however, two key differences between the integration of women and the integration of African Americans. First, African Americans had a history of greater rates of participation in the military than women. Thus the integration of African Americans built on an earlier tradition, and rising rates of participation by African Americans in ROTC represented an acceleration of an existing pattern, rather than the creation of a completely new one. Second, many charged that African Americans had borne disproportionately high casualty rates in Vietnam, in large part because of their overrepresentation among the enlisted ranks and underrepresentation in leadership positions.[70] The services thus hoped to use ROTC to increase African American representation in the officer corps, which stood at just 2.2 percent in 1971, compared with 10 percent among the enlisted ranks.[71] Therefore, the recruitment of more African American officers for ROTC received far greater institutional support from the military than had the integration of women in this same period.

All four services understood the racial integration problem to be serious, especially in light of racial violence on ships and bases worldwide in the early 1970s. In 1971 the DOD created the Defense Race Relations Institute at Patrick Air Force Base and set a goal of sending all air force personnel through the program in four years. The following year, the Marine Corps banned race as a consideration for housing or personnel assignments. According to historian Bernard Nalty, the program was more than just words. Marine Corps Commandant General Cushman enforced the new directives with a force sufficient to demonstrate "that he meant what he said."[72] In the hierarchical environment of the military, firm support from a commander can make a world of difference.

These programs and others like them reflected a recognition among many political and military leaders that old understandings of the place of African American soldiers had to be discarded. The notion that white southerners, who supposedly knew how to "deal with" African Americans, should be in command positions over them faded. The military came instead to understand that having African American noncommissioned officers (NCO's) and regular officers was critical to both the operational efficiency of the military and to the creation of the more just and equal environment that military leaders like Cushman and Admiral Elmo Zumwalt, chief of naval operations, wanted to create. To achieve this goal, however, the services would need to find a way to get more African American officers in uniform.

Production of African American officers had fallen by more than 50 percent between 1967 and 1972, largely due to the low prestige of the military among African Americans during the Vietnam era and the wider opportunities available to African Americans in the civilian sector as American corporations developed equal opportunity programs. In 1971 the navy, under Zumwalt, set a goal of raising the percentage of African American officers to 12 percent in five years.[73] The army and air force also set goals to increase the percentage of African American officers to a number commensurate with their representation in the service populations as a whole, but since the service academy classes were relatively small and were themselves only 2.2 percent African American in 1970, raising the percentage of African American officers required "an all-out effort to reverse [past] trend[s] and to correct such inequities as may have existed in the past."[74]

With the academies largely unable to make a dramatic impact on racial balance and with the OCS program on the ropes following the My Lai incident (see Chapter 5), ROTC emerged as the obvious solution. Universities, of course, were themselves undergoing a revision in racial composition, and they represented a source of high-quality minority officer candidates. The major currents of reform centered around two complementary approaches. The first approach focused on opening new ROTC units at historically black colleges and universities and other schools with high minority populations. In this period, the navy added units at Florida A & M, Prairie View A & M, Savannah State, and Southern University. The air force established units at Grambling, Mississippi Valley State, Fayetteville State, and Tennessee State. The army added units at Alabama A & M, Fort Valley State, Alcorn State, Jackson State, St. Augustine's, Benedict, Bishop, and Norfolk State.

The historically black schools already had some experience with ROTC programs. The twelve Army ROTC units created before 1950 had provided nearly 9,000 officers to date. Some of these schools were land-grant institutions and were therefore mandated to have military training programs. Schools such as Southern University (ROTC unit activated in 1916), Howard University (activated in 1921), and Tuskegee Institute (activated in 1941) had ROTC units that long predated the Vietnam era.[75] Their administrations saw access to military training as "a significant stride forward" for African Americans. While many civil rights leaders had bitterly opposed the war in Vietnam, they had not necessarily become antimilitary. African American leaders had traditionally seen the military as a means for African Americans to demonstrate loyalty, reliability, patriotism, and courage, as well as a place to gain valuable training and access to good jobs. The student bodies of these schools supported the establishment of ROTC units, indicating that they shared the view of the military as a means of advancement for the African American community, for themselves personally, or both.[76]

For African Americans, ROTC offered several important advantages. While the overall job environment in the United States appeared to be improving, the job market continued to offer fewer opportunities for African Americans than it did for whites. As a result, African Americans were "more willing to subject [themselves] to the demands of life in the armed forces in return for the combination of pay, allowances, and the promise of training and travel."[77] Enlisting in ROTC offered the additional benefit of a free or subsidized education and service in the officer corps. The military job environment was also one of the rare situations in America where African Americans could be in positions of authority over whites.

In a racist society the military can, at times, stand out as a model of racial harmony. When field and company grade officers took military directives on equal treatment seriously, military service was color blind. Authority in theory, often in practice, derived from criteria utterly unrelated to race. A reporter for *Ebony* magazine observed the high reenlistment rates of African American soldiers and commented, "The Negro has found in his nation's most totalitarian society—the military—the greatest degree of functional democracy that his nation has granted to black people."[78]

Over time, the military job environment improved for all employees in terms of pay and conditions. For African Americans, especially, however, the military job environment looked more appealing as racial animosity eased. Bernard Nalty argued that by 1973 "two or more blacks no longer constituted a potential riot in the view of whites" and that off-base encounters between African American and white service personnel were "no longer as overtly antagonistic toward each other as before."[79] This is not, of course, to argue that all of the racial tension of the past decades had suddenly dissipated; rather, it is to say that as volunteers replaced draftees and as the military made a genuine commitment to improve the lives of African American service personnel, the military became a less hostile working environment for African Americans. This improvement in the working conditions of the military helped ROTC recruit officer candidates at old and new units alike.

The new units to be hosted at historically black schools were selected according to a formal application procedure and a series of on-campus visits by military personnel. The services seem to have been particularly attracted to conservative schools such as Prairie View A & M, where the administration still enforced curfews and hair regulations for students; the administrators had also considered changing the sports nickname of the school from the Panthers after the confrontational Black Panther Party grew in popularity among African Americans at universities nationwide. However chosen, the success of these units was a high priority for the services. The first Prairie View PNS came to his post from a similar position at Harvard, and Secretary of the Navy John Chafee personally administered the oaths of service to the school's first group of NROTC graduates.[80]

The second approach to integrating the officer ranks centered around increasing the presence of African American cadets at existing ROTC units. The army understood that the most important step to be taken in this direction was improving the image of the military in the eyes of African Americans, both civilian and military. Nationally, the services ran advertisements in African American magazines such as *Jet* and *Ebony*, and they vigorously sought the support of African American leaders through lobbying the NAACP and the Urban League. On the campuses, improving the image of the military meant assigning more African American officers to ROTC units as instructors. The services especially tried to make such assignments at schools, such as the University of Pittsburgh, where the minority representation was increasing. In 1970 the army assigned Captain Alvin Officer to Pittsburgh. Provost Charles Peake noted that Officer's assignment would "be of considerable help in strengthening the rapport between the Military Science Department and black students."[81]

These efforts paid dividends almost immediately, especially for the army. In 1973, 12.9 percent of those attending ROTC summer camp were African American, up from 9.1 percent in 1972 and 4.9 percent in 1971.[82] Within ten years African American students accounted for 25 percent of AROTC cadets, 10 percent of NROTC midshipmen, and 18 percent of AFROTC cadets. By 1980 many of the historically black schools had become prolific producers of junior officers. Prairie View A & M's unit was the nation's second largest by 1982.[83] The twenty-one historically black schools that hosted Army ROTC units produced a total of 551 officers in fiscal year 1979; these units were responsible for 9 percent of the total Army ROTC officer production and more than half of the total minority officer production.[84] As was the case with the integration of women, the pressures of the AVF, the desires of African Americans to join the military, and a growing sense of a need for African American officers combined to create significant demographic change. Because of its role as the primary source for active-duty officers, ROTC was in a position to make a more immediate and dramatic impact on the demographics of the American officer corps than the smaller service academies could. The campuses felt this impact as well. In 1971 Duquesne University's graduating ROTC class chose as their motto: "Our numbers here at Duquesne are many . . . white and black . . . long hairs and short."[85]

The gender and racial integration of ROTC mirrored ideological trends in American higher education in the 1960s and 1970s. Roger Geiger has recently argued that the pressures of federal legislation were a relatively minor factor in assuring the success of affirmative action programs. As early as

1965 many schools had begun considering the admission of more women both as a way to stop losing qualified male students to coeducational schools and as a way "to have larger and academically more talented undergraduate student bodies while also alleviating their financial burdens with additional tuition."[86] In short, admitting women made sense both for the universities and for ROTC, because they offered a way to increase enrollments without reducing existing standards.

Furthermore, many schools had internal commitments to affirmative action that exceeded federal goals. For these schools, the addition of women and African Americans to ROTC fit smoothly into overall plans. The University of Michigan, for example, "established [affirmative action] goals for some departments that were not deficient and overall targets for minorities that were unrealistically high. The ascendant ideology and local coalitions of [faculty] activists induced universities to go beyond the legal minimum in implementing affirmative action . . . It was this internal conviction of the correctness of affirmative action that ultimately propelled university policy."[87] Thus, although university faculties did not demand demographic change in ROTC, such change nevertheless fit nicely into ideological currents in both the military and higher education. Academics thus received federal changes to ROTC demographics not as evidence of intrusion but as evidence of agreement.

Shifting the Geographic Balance of ROTC

To solve the problem of lower ROTC enrollments, the services also opened new units at schools that did not necessarily have significant minority populations. All three services had long waiting lists of colleges and universities that wanted to host an ROTC unit; in 1969, the army's list had 90 colleges, the navy's had 126, and the air force's had 116.[88] Until the AVF, however, enrollments had been high enough to permit the services to avoid trying something new; no new units had been added since the Korean War. The enrollment and financial pressures of the 1970s led ROTC headquarters in all three services to adopt a dual strategy of closing costly units (that is, those units producing too few officers) and opening a combined total of eighty new units at schools where they believed interest would be high enough to yield the contractual minimum of fifteen officers per year.

The new schools were decidedly different in character and specialization from those schools already in the program and those that were disestab-

lished. The closing of units at Ivy League schools received the most attention, but the services closed eighty-eight units in all during this era. To be
sure, the disestablished schools included Harvard, Yale, Columbia, Stanford,
and Dartmouth, where the services and the universities could not agree on
changes to the program, but much more numerous were small schools,
many of them liberal arts colleges like Franklin and Marshall, Grinnell, Davis and Elkins, and Denison, where the services initiated deactivation proceedings based on their inability to attract enough cadets without the coercion of the draft.

Thus ROTC units often closed for the undramatic reason of cost effectiveness. Historians Peter Karsten and Vance Mitchell agree that even without
the turmoil of the 1960s, the Ivy League schools "would probably have been
phased out within the next few years anyway" because they were "'self-
destructing' low producers," having accounted for less than 2 percent of
the total annual officer production for many years.[89] Harvard, Brown, and
Princeton each averaged fewer than seven AFROTC graduates per year in
the early 1960s.[90]

As long as the draft had existed, ROTC's "continued prolific production
was taken for granted."[91] Without the draft, the air force estimated that the
future viability of 40 percent of its ROTC units was in doubt. Many of those
schools, such as Case Western, Coe, and DePauw, had been low producers
for years; the AVF made them financially unsustainable.[92] Even large units
were suffering from the transition; in 1974, both the University of Michigan
and the University of Illinois AFROTC units dropped below the fifteen com-
missionees required by their contracts.[93] In such a climate, the services decided to finally disestablish chronic low producers and invest the money
saved into opening a new series of units based on hosts' "enrollment,
growth potential and student and faculty interest."[94]

Officials at one of the new schools, Columbus College, a public school in
Georgia first established as a junior college in 1958, saw the unit as a "wonderful opportunity" for the school and its students. The faculty committee
that investigated the acquisition of the unit noted the following benefits for
participating students: a monthly stipend; a paid six-week summer camp;
the availability of scholarships; and the opportunity to obtain an army commission. Columbus College thus agreed to pay the full cost of an 8,900-
square-foot building for the unit's classroom, storage, and office facilities.[95]
Columbus College was one of the new breed of ROTC hosts that was drasti-
cally changing the character of the program: it was public; it saw ROTC as a

point of pride; and its students supported the idea of having the program on campus.

The most immediately notable difference between the "old" units and the "new" ones was their location. As Table 6.2 indicates, the new units were disproportionately southern and midwestern, while the disestablished units were mostly eastern. The only significant variation among services occurred in the Midwest, where the army opened fifteen units and closed two; at the same time the air force closed seventeen while opening only one. This difference nicely illustrates the general tendency of the services to move away from private schools; the closed air force units were all at small, private institutions such as Otterbein, Grinnell, Kenyon, and St. Olaf. Conversely, the army opened four and five ROTC units on satellite campuses of the Oklahoma and Wisconsin systems, respectively.

It would be easy to argue that the services opened new units in the South and Midwest and at public schools because they could reliably expect that they would face much less of the student and faculty opposition that they had faced in the private schools of the East; this explanation alone, however, provides a rather limited view of the larger issue. Undoubtedly the expectation of more favorable treatment played a large role; all of the new units allowed academic credit for ROTC courses, for years a contentious issue on many campuses.[96] The services sought to establish units at schools that evinced a strong desire to become a host and where they believed student interest in the program would be high. As one navy observer noted, "Overall we wanted institutions who wanted us, irrespective of their program strengths."[97]

Table 6.2   Net gain or loss of ROTC units by region, 1968–1974

Region	Total units in 1968	Units closed	Units opened	Total units in 1974	Net change
East	123	43	13	93	−30
Midwest	115	19	16	112	−3
South	147	12	45	180	+33
West	88	14	6	80	−8
Total	473	88	80	465	−8

Source: Directory of ROTC/NDCC Units (Ft. Monroe, Va.: Headquarters, United States Continental Command, 1969 and 1974).

Not only were the new schools in the presumably more "promilitary" South and Midwest, many of these schools were also in or very near places with strong military communities and traditions: Old Dominion and Norfolk State are near both the Newport News naval complex and Ft. Monroe (home to AROTC headquarters); Fayetteville State is near Ft. Bragg; Alabama State is near Maxwell Air Force Base (home to AFROTC headquarters); and Benedict College is near Ft. Jackson, to name but a few. The director of development at Columbus College cited "close college ties with Fort Benning [also in Columbus, Georgia] and local interest in military affairs" when he announced that the unit would be "a great asset to the community as well as the college."[98]

Broadening the geographic focus of ROTC was consistent with a trend in DOD research funding as well. In an attempt to expand the base of scientific research in the nation's colleges and universities, the DOD awarded grants to 100 schools "well down the research university hierarchy."[99] These schools, too, were disproportionately in the South and Midwest. The shift in geographic representation of ROTC units therefore mirrored a larger trend of DOD cultivation of better relations with a larger number of schools beyond the traditional eastern colleges and universities. In large measure, the services hoped to compensate for the declining military presence on eastern campuses by substituting desire for institutional quality. In other words, the services sought new hosts based upon a logic analogous to that which informed the AVF: seek out motivated, eager volunteers.

Many of the new schools had specific technical emphases that the services found attractive; not surprisingly, some of these were military schools. The navy opened programs at the Citadel and Virginia Military Institute, which had long supported AROTC and AFROTC programs. These programs offered cadets at military colleges a faster path to the types of military training and jobs they desired. Similarly, the air force opened a unit at Norwich University, which in the nineteenth century had begun the tradition of training officers at the nation's civilian campuses (see Chapter 1). The services also instituted military training at schools that specialized in relevant civilian skills. In this vein, the navy opened units at Maine Maritime College and SUNY–Maritime College. The air force followed suit by establishing units at schools such as Embry-Riddle Aeronautical University in Florida.

The AVF sparked one other fundamental change to the nature of ROTC unit demographics. The 1964 Vitalization Act had authorized the establishment of so-called cross-enrollment agreements between ROTC host schools and nearby schools that did not host ROTC. These agreements permitted a student enrolled at a school without ROTC, or without the desired branch of ROTC, to commute to an ROTC host for his or her military training.[100] The cross-enrollment authorization had been used only sparingly before the AVF. In the era of the AVF, however, the services encouraged much wider use of cross-enrollment authority.[101]

Initially, ROTC hosts signed cross-enrollment agreements with schools of obvious qualitative value, such as Pittsburgh's AFROTC agreement with nearby Carnegie Mellon and Michigan's agreement with Western Michigan University, which had a degree program in aviation engineering.[102] Shortly thereafter, however, the services saw the advantages of rapidly expanding the cross-enrollment program for quantitative reasons, as it was inexpensive to do so and, especially in large cities, it dramatically increased the potential cadet pool. By 1975 the 156 Air Force ROTC hosts had signed a total of 316 cross-enrollment agreements, more than doubling the total number of campuses connected to AFROTC.[103]

Obviously, schools in areas with a high concentration of colleges and universities stood to benefit the most from cross-enrollments. The University of Pittsburgh signed seven such agreements with schools with a combined undergraduate enrollment of more than 16,000, and the University of Michigan signed three agreements with schools with a combined undergraduate enrollment of more than 27,000.[104] In 1976–77, cross-enrollees accounted for 32 percent of the University of Texas Army ROTC enrollments, including 75 percent of Texas's African American cadets. Cross-enrollments also had the advantage of allowing ROTC to target schools from specific categories, such as junior colleges or predominately female colleges; Smith, Wellesley, and Chatham all signed cross-enrollments agreements. Cross-enrollments also permitted students from recently disestablished host schools, such as Harvard and Amherst, to remain in the ROTC system.[105]

These changes in the nature of ROTC host schools and cadets mirrored geographic and other changes in the quality of academic institutions and their students more generally. Between 1960 and 1980 the number of public colleges and universities climbed from 700 to 1,500. Their total undergraduate populations rose from 2 million to 9.5 million, compared with the growth in private schools from 1.5 million undergraduates in 1960 to 2.5 million in 1980. ROTC, with "a move coincidental with the extension of college opportunities to this [southern and midwestern] segment of American youth," was going where the students were going.[106]

The integrations of women and African Americans into ROTC also reflected demographic changes in the American undergraduate population in the 1960s and the 1970s. Between 1960 and 1980 the percentage of all undergraduates who were female climbed from 37 percent to 51 percent. The percentage of all undergraduates who were African American rose from less than 4 percent to 10 percent.[107] ROTC units were therefore keeping pace with changes that affected their host schools.

The end of conscription thus forced the services to change the nature of their ROTC cadets and hosts. The AVF resulted in the addition of women and African Americans, as well as students from a much wider array of colleges and universities, both through the establishment of new units and through cross-enrollments. But widening the recruitment base alone could not save ROTC enrollments from continuing to fall. As was the case in the military more generally, conditions had to improve to attract men, and now women, to enlist voluntarily and remain in ROTC.

A More Humanized Approach

As noted, the architects of the AVF assumed that market incentives and a new, unforced patriotism would suffice to replace the draft as a major factor in enlistments. Chief among those incentives were higher pay and better conditions. For the American armed forces, better conditions meant a reduction in discipline and a change in many traditional features of military life, such as the disappearance of on-base, barracks-style housing. ROTC in the years immediately following the introduction of the AVF mirrored these changes. The "working conditions" of ROTC became less onerous as the services ameliorated many of the elements of ROTC training most distasteful to college students.

ROTC certainly benefited from renewed congressional attention in the early 1970s to improving military pay, benefits, and living conditions. To make the AVF work, Congress raised the average active-duty military salary 113 percent between fiscal years 1968 and 1974. In addition, Congress enriched the military health and pension systems, modernized military housing, and hired civilians for many of the more distasteful paperwork and clerical jobs formerly assigned to junior officers.[108] These changes benefited ROTC indirectly by improving the image of the military as an employer.

Increasing direct monetary compensation was one way for the services to quickly, if not cheaply, improve the recruiting environment for ROTC. As noted in Chapter 3, the army and the air force built up to their maximum authorization of 5,500 scholarships earlier than they had expected in an effort to curtail the falling enrollments of the late 1960s. Shortly thereafter, in anticipation of the end of the draft and with the expectation of further declines in enrollment, they pushed for an amendment to the Vitalization Act that would permit them to offer more scholarships and higher monthly stipends. In the early 1960s, the army and air force had responded to scholarship plans unenthusiastically; by the early 1970s, however, scholarships had become a critical part of their plan to save ROTC. The 1971 amendment to the Vitalization Act raised the scholarship authorization from 5,500 to 6,500 per service and increased stipends from $50 to $100 per month.

Pecuniary considerations were important, but changes in the daily life of the cadets were probably even more important. The services worked to introduce reforms that would permit college students to take ROTC without, in the words one Army ROTC instructor, making the cadet "walk around campus as a marked man."[109] ROTC instructors referred to these changes as "a more humanized approach" and "not much more than common sense."[110] They understood many of these changes to be only tangentially related to training issues. One PMS told an observer, "A lot of the meaningless things have been eliminated."[111]

Chief among these "meaningless things" were those elements of ROTC training that made the cadets visibly different from their non-ROTC peers. At most schools, hair regulations were substantially relaxed; African American students were allowed to wear Afros, and haircuts below the ears were tolerated as well.[112] "[W]e aren't so concerned about haircuts and that sort of thing," noted an army instructor. "It's not indicative of leadership."[113] The new hair policy was consistent with relaxations in hair regulations outside ROTC. The navy, prompted by a desire to raise reenlistment rates and convinced that "the conflict is not worth all the fuss," had already led the way in 1970, permitting beards, longer hair, and sideburns for its personnel.[114] While the service academies didn't go as far as ROTC, traditional crew cuts nevertheless gave way to "longer, thicker hair, with sideburns permitted down to midear."[115]

Uniform requirements were another target of reform. Some schools dropped uniform requirements altogether; students could attend ROTC classes in their civilian clothes if they wished.[116] The University of Pittsburgh ROTC staffs reduced time spent in uniform from three days per week to one. Other schools were also showing "less concern for the perfunctory" by permitting students to attend ROTC meetings (including one at Colorado with a major general) in civilian clothes and by becoming less exacting on the formal presentation of uniforms.[117] At Michigan, army cadets spent only one hour per week in uniform and NROTC students wore their uniforms only four times a year.[118] By the mid-1970s cadet yearbooks across the country began using candid photographs of students in civilian clothes instead of rigidly posed portraits taken in dress uniform. Compare these attitudes with those of 1963, when 97 percent of AFROTC cadets surveyed said that "care and wearing of the uniform" should be an important part of the precommissioning program and only 20 percent said that "students might be more interested in ROTC if there was [sic] no requirement for wearing the uniform on campus."[119]

The ROTC programs were now also characterized by significantly less drill, both because of its educational dissonance with civilian collegiate programs (as noted in Chapter 4) and because students themselves disliked it. After 1971 army cadets at Michigan spent just six hours per year in drill; Naval ROTC students spent only four hours marching in their entire ROTC career.[120] The reduction of the "spit and polish" elements of ROTC permitted substitution experiments to continue and appealed to undergraduates for the same reason that they were attracted to the new permission to keep longer hair: both changes made them less visibly distinct from their peers.

Similarly, ROTC instructors took great care to reduce the discipline that had marked ROTC in years past. They stopped issuing lengthy demerit lists and ceased using extra drill as punishment for misdemeanors. As a University of Texas PMS told an observer: "I consider my mission to balance the academia and the military. After all, we have students, not recruits. When a student rushes in late and out of breath after running over from the law school, we don't yell at him. And believe me, I've been in combat, so I know how to yell orders."[121]

Similar but less fundamental changes were also taking place at the service academies. While the academies retained "traditional military discipline" as a "basic ingredient," they nevertheless officially banned physical hazing and physical punishments such as "bracing" (standing rigidly at attention for long periods). They also broke down some barriers between first-year students and upperclassmen, as well as barriers between students and instructors.[122] Relative to civilian schools, the academies remained bastions of monastic dedication (Air Force Academy cadets were still not permitted to own a radio or watch television during their first semester), but they eliminated the "extremely childish and non-productive" harassments of years past.[123]

As with ROTC, changes at the academies were designed to increase the number of applications, reduce dropout rates, and improve the academic records of graduates. They were also designed to produce "a different breed of leaders for tomorrow's armed forces."[124] Those leaders took a curriculum that now included courses in Black studies, Roman classics, contemporary drama, music appreciation, and far eastern literature. As with ROTC, the changes reflected the military's general movement away from "crime and punishment" and toward the "development of leadership ability."[125]

Such reforms also kept pace with changes in the nature of the AVF-era officer candidate. Close observers of the ROTC program after 1972 identified a new "post-Vietnam generation" cadet who was much less concerned with the martial aspects of the program and much more concerned with the financial benefits and perceived advantages that ROTC and military service could provide for their postmilitary career. As a Pittsburgh reporter put it, "They think of the Reserve Officers' Training Corps as a door that will admit them into fields of their own choosing. Among the college students, the ROTC is no longer the symbol of a distant and despicable war."[126] ROTC had evolved from a mechanism for evading the draft to a pathway into the job market after an individual had fulfilled his or her service obligations. One cadet told a journalist, "I'm not in it [ROTC] for the war aspect, but for the growing up aspect." His interviewer noted that the cadet was

> one of those people who wouldn't have dared involve themselves in the military a decade ago, in the days of the anti-war movement when ROTC cadets were frequently objects of derision and hatred. He represents those students now joining ROTC for practical, calculated reasons—they like the idea of financial support and they like the idea of a job after college. These students sense a renewed respectability for ROTC on campus and want to take advantage of it . . . For most ROTC participants, the personal security motives are of such importance that the real purpose of ROTC—to prepare college-educated officers for military functions—is almost overlooked.[127]

In fact, the percentage of ROTC students desiring to make the military a career had always been small, and their propensity to leave the service after fulfilling their obligation had always been greater than that of academy graduates. What had changed was that the dominant definition of "calculated reasons" implied job market advantages in the 1970s, where it had meant draft evasion in the 1960s and the fulfillment of a moral obligation to serve the nation in the 1950s.

The ROTC advertisements of this era reflected this change. The ads of the 1950s that featured ROTC cadet Ted Wright had focused on the prestige in meeting one's contribution to the military, while the ads of the 1970s focused on job training and money. The students in the new ads explained why they had joined: "[ROTC] pays for all of my tuition, books and lab fees . . . it's really a good deal!" and "My reasons are basically selfish. Jobs are getting hard to get these days, and I know for a fact that a lot of employers think an ROTC guy's got a head start in management and things like that."[128] "Right now you may think Army ROTC will look small on your resume," read another ad, "but a lot of employers don't think so."[129] This line of recruitment reached full fruition in a 1985 army brochure, *The Margin of Difference: American Business and Industry Assess the Values of Army ROTC,* which featured testimonials on the value of ROTC training from the CEOs of thirty Fortune 500 corporations, including Xerox, Rockwell, Ford, and United States Steel.[130]

Ted Wright had been attracted by the chance to wear an army uniform and to participate in drill, ceremonies, and hours of physical and weapons training. The prospective cadets of the 1970s were told that "Army ROTC only takes up about three to five hours a week of your time while you're in college. No big thing."[131] Ted had also been drawn to ROTC as a way to fulfill his patriotic impulses and demonstrate his Americanism. By the 1970s, that mood had changed. "I've never considered myself especially patriotic," said one of the students in an ad. "With me, it all came down to one word," said another, "money. I needed a scholarship to go to college."[132] Little wonder then, with these being the advantages espoused by the military itself, that reenlistments of ROTC graduates beyond their obligation were so low. The services, looking for a quick fix for plunging enrollments, were selling ROTC as a temporary inconvenience, not a patriotic obligation as they had done with Ted Wright.

Many analysts have referred to military service as a trade-off of benefits and burdens; one gets benefits such as job training in return for the burden of potentially life-threatening service and time removed from the civilian job market. The ROTC ads of the Cold War era focused on the burdens; ROTC was arduous but necessary because of its centrality to the global struggle in which every American had a role. One's rewards came largely from the satisfaction of doing one's part. The same logic underscored ROTC's place on the Cold War campus. ROTC may have been a "burden" to collegiate faculties and administrators, but it was essential to national security and a sign that the campus, too, was doing its part. By the 1970s, ROTC ads stressed the financial and educational benefits of the program. ROTC became attractive because it made college possible for many and, for most, carried with it the presumption of a better place in the civilian job market after military service.

ROTC survived the AVF by reducing the ascriptive criteria for being an ROTC student and by making ROTC a less onerous course for students to take. Both of these steps had precedents in the era of the ROTC Vitalization Act, which expanded the pool of potential officers by including two-year cadets and transfers and also reduced the number of contact hours required in the ROTC curriculum. The changes brought about by the AVF followed similar goals but changed the quality and character of the program much more radically. With the incorporation of more African Americans and women, ROTC lost the white male focus that had characterized the life of Ted Wright. Furthermore, as one journalist put it, the AVF changed "the military's Spartan 'You will' doctrine on campus to an almost pleading 'Will you?' attitude," creating an ROTC program almost unrecognizable to those who had graduated from ROTC units in 1950 or 1964.[133]

These changes were indeed successful in bringing up enrollments, which began to rise by the middle of the 1970s (Table 6.3). All units did not share equally in the improvement, however; Michigan was on AFROTC probation from 1975 to 1978 due to low enrollment, and in 1978 it had the lowest Army ROTC enrollment of any of the state's eight units, despite being the

Table 6.3 ROTC enrollments 1976–1981, by service

Academic year	Army ROTC	Naval ROTC	Air Force ROTC
1975–76	44,363	7,016	14,589
1976–77	55,282	7,012	14,071
1977–78	57,910	7,095	14,660
1978–79	61,100	6,816	15,972
1979–80	66,212	6,685	18,387
1980–81	70,975	7,323	21,361

Source: Department of Defense Manpower Statistics, various years.

second largest university in the state. Still, even in Ann Arbor the picture was brighter from ROTC's point of view. The NROTC unit there reached its enrollment limit in 1978 for the first time in ten years, and student replies to the cards sent out to incoming freshman describing the ROTC program were up 25 percent from 1977.[134]

The dynamism that ROTC displayed in the 1970s was reflected in the fact that two schools that had disestablished their ROTC units, Princeton and Boston University, began negotiations for reinstatement and subsequently reopened their ROTC units. Indeed, even as ROTC demographics were changing, so was the ROTC curriculum. ROTC staffs answered the challenges laid out in faculty reports of 1970–71 to upgrade the quality of instruction as a precondition for reconsideration of academic credit. These curricular reforms set up new debates on much the same terms that had existed since the 1950s.

CHAPTER 7

A New Academic Program: ROTC, 1972–1980

> The question of reestablishing ROTC credit . . . should be quashed now. The issue was decided satisfactorily two years ago and attempts to push it through the back door won't wash.
>
> —Rutgers *Targum,* 1973

The war on the campuses, if not the ideological divisions, had conclusively ended by 1972; significant leftist elements remained after 1972, but they were much less confrontational than their predecessors had been.[1] As noted in Chapter 6, student demonstrations were by 1973 already being discussed as a quaint relic of an earlier time. The actions of student groups reflect this change. In 1974 the University of Michigan's Student Government Council rescinded its 1969 resolution calling for the abolition of ROTC, saying that the resolution "violated the rights of students desiring to be in ROTC."[2] Similarly, faculties had stopped assigning new ad hoc committees and faculty boards to study ROTC and recommend reforms. This changing climate led Assistant Secretary of Defense George Benson to announce in 1973 that "the troubled relationships [*sic*] between the military and academic world, which grew up during the university disturbances recently passed, is now pretty well resolved."[3]

ROTC's resurgence on some of the campuses that had earlier called for its abolition symbolized the change in climate and university attitudes. A 1972 survey at Princeton, whose trustees had voted two years earlier to sever all ties with ROTC, showed that 57 percent of the students and 73 percent of the faculty favored the return of ROTC.[4] Based on this evidence and pressure from the alumni, many of whom were proud ROTC graduates or military veterans, the trustees of Princeton voted to begin negotiations to reestablish its dormant ROTC program.[5] Boston University also reopened negotiations on ROTC after having requested discontinuance.

As had been the case at Michigan and other schools, ROTC gained support at Princeton from some of the same groups that had opposed it just a few years before. Furthermore, ROTC drew support at Princeton for many of the same reasons that schools like Georgia's Columbus College sought out new units.[6] The Council of the Princeton Community's Ad Hoc Committee on ROTC, comprised of students, faculty, and administrators, which in 1970 had voted to ban ROTC, argued three years later that ROTC courses were "pursued in an atmosphere conducive to open discussion and questioning." They further noted that ROTC was beneficial to the Princeton community because it permitted students a wider range of career choices, provided financial aid for select students, humanized the military, and supported the concept of national service.[7] Still, there was no consensus at Princeton for the return of the *status quo ante;* all the concerned groups at Princeton insisted that if ROTC were to return, it would have to do so without the sanction of academic credit. At Princeton and elsewhere, ROTC was experiencing a resurgence, but on terms heavily influenced by prewar and wartime concerns.

The resurgence of ROTC at Princeton occurred despite the notable absence of lobbying by service officials, who insisted that the decision of whether or not to keep ROTC was Princeton's alone.[8] Some army officials, including Professor of Military Science William Snyder, argued that it was not in the interests of the army to reestablish a unit at a school where the chances for meeting contractual enrollment minimums were slim; even before the Vietnam War, Princeton had been a low producer. Nevertheless, the army saw symbolic value in reestablishing a unit at a prestigious school that had so recently expressed a desire to sever relations with the military; it further hoped that "returning to Princeton would improve the image and status of ROTC at other institutions and with the public generally."[9] The army therefore agreed to the trustees' 1974 request to reopen the unit.

The return of ROTC to Princeton illustrates the prevailing compromises, directions, and terms of debate regarding ROTC in the post-Vietnam period. The unit returned, but not under the same conditions that had governed it before 1968. The reborn ROTC program included weapons and drill training (specifically banned by a 1970 Princeton report) alongside four classes, including military history, taught by regular Princeton faculty.[10] Only the civilian-taught courses received academic credit. These changes reflected the debates that had been a major feature of university-military relations since the 1950s and continued unabated into the 1970s.

As previous chapters have demonstrated, the significant changes to ROTC during the Vietnam era were more than a response to student, faculty, and administration dislike of the war. ROTC reform was much more than a way for university communities to "get" the military. Rather, they represented the fruition of years of study and concern about ROTC and its proper place on civilian campuses. Because all of these reforms had roots in an earlier period and because the reforms had many causes that were only indirectly connected to the war, they remained important for the shaping of ROTC even as the postwar era drew to a close in 1980.

The Changing ROTC Curriculum

As noted, ROTC courses had frequently been criticized as being intellectually bankrupt and devoid of contextual analysis or practice in decision-making skills. While most of these criticisms came from academics, several military officers had themselves come to question the academic value of much of the ROTC curriculum. Throughout the 1960s educators and military officers had worked together in a variety of ways, from sponsoring guest lectures to supporting the more elaborate National Security Information Center's New York Plan, in an effort to upgrade the quality of ROTC instruction and make the courses worthy of full admission into collegiate curricula. As a group, they understood that this would require the marginalization of some of the most martial of the ROTC courses. As one ROTC instructor noted, "Personally I do not believe that subjects we now teach, such as small unit tactics, tactical communications, and other fundamental military subjects, are college level courses. They are important and should be taught . . . but not [on campus] for academic credit."[11]

Much of the military and civilian motivation for improving the quality of the ROTC courses centered around making the nonmartial courses worthy of receiving academic credit on their own merit. Several military and civilian officials continued to hold to the position that without academic credit, ROTC programs would have a difficult time attracting quality students, especially if the all-volunteer force concept succeeded. Without quality students, they argued, the ROTC programs themselves were in jeopardy, and the services thereby ran the risk of being constituted of less than the best men and women available for the job.

To some civilian faculty, the continued denial of credit for ROTC in colleges of liberal arts ran the risk of isolating the military from sources of humanistic thought, undermining what for many was the most important justification for ROTC's existence: the university's ability to influence the military through the production of officers with a broad educational background. This debate, then, recalled issues that dated back to ROTC's creation and before. Academics remained on the whole committed to ROTC to assure that civilians would continue to influence the development of junior officers. To them, not having ROTC was a far greater danger than having it. A University of Michigan professor of astronomy argued:

> The . . . credit loss continues to pose a significant deterrent to students wishing to pursue ROTC, as such students are forced to carry effective overloads each term or add an additional semester to their undergraduate program to accommodate the non-credit military science courses. This imposes an undue financial and/or academic burden on those students formally pursuing ROTC and reinforces the general, if unfair, suspicion that ROTC courses are different from or less visible than standard elections in one of the undergraduate colleges of the university.
>
> The alternative to ROTC detachments on campuses such as the University of Michigan is the development of a professional military which does not have the sensitivity to the integrity of diverse ideas and various modes of thinking encouraged in the give and take of a liberal education. We . . . may have to face the concept of a professional military being developed apart from the intellectual and humane atmospheres of our great universities if steps are not taken to encourage the continuation of military officer training programs on campuses such as our own.[12]

By the post-Vietnam era, several civilian professors and military officers who were careful observers of the ROTC program were arguing that the courses had indeed been improved to the point where a discussion of the appropriateness of academic credit and other matters could begin anew. For others, the postwar period also offered a chance to discuss these issues more rationally than they believed had been the case during the war, when, according to the chair of the University of Pittsburgh's ROTC Study Committee, the academic issues had been "clouded over by anti-war sentiments." The clear message from these proponents was that the removal of ROTC credit had been "contrary to the wishes of the student body," the result of the administration's giving in to a vocal, but in their view misguided, minority.[13] With that minority no longer a force in campus politics, an opportunity existed to right the presumed wrong. This view contained some truth, but it completely ignored the long-standing debate over ROTC's place in the curriculum.

That debate had traditionally been centered around three interrelated concerns over ROTC: the quality of the courses; the quality of the instructors; and the degree to which their professional, military orientation (including their dependence on an outside agency for materials and guidance) conflicted with the overall mission of civilian colleges, especially liberal arts colleges. Still, to many professors and administrators the efforts of the military during the Vietnam War to upgrade ROTC courses had been successful. The dean of the University of Pittsburgh's College of Arts and Sciences, Jerome Schneewind, noted in 1972 that "The present ROTC program . . . is richer and more academically interesting" than it had been in 1968. This improvement, he believed, argued for a reexamination of the no-credit policy in place in the college.[14]

To judge from the changes in course descriptions and the proclamations of support from civilian faculty, the reforms of the Vietnam period had indeed produced ROTC courses that were less doctrinaire, that included more emphasis on the context within which military officers operated, and that involved much less rote memorization. ROTC course descriptions before 1970 reveal the dissonance of these courses from civilian counterparts. The description of the 1960 Military Science I course, taken by all AROTC freshmen, listed as some of its goals: "[To understand the] necessity for a large U.S. Army . . . To provide a thorough indoctrination in military discipline . . . [To instill a belief in the] necessity for discipline."[15] Similarly, a 1968 AFROTC course at the University of Illinois titled Freshman Theory Course was not focused on theory at all. Physical fitness and American citizenship were prerequisites for the course; half of the contact hours were devoted to drill.[16]

These nonintellectual, hyperpatriotic elements of ROTC courses were among the several features of the curriculum to which civilian faculty had objected in their numerous committee reports of the Vietnam era. As shown in previous chapters, steps taken by the services, including participating in the NSIC New York Plan, soliciting advice from civilian faculty in order to "incorporate recent research," and raising the academic qualifications of their instructors, yielded courses that were more like those offered by civilian faculty.[17] These courses dealt much more with problem solving and analysis of context, while still remaining focused on the military as an institution and an employer.

By 1973–74, course descriptions read less like those described above and more like this one for a University of Michigan AFROTC class called National Security Forces in Contemporary Society:

> Focusing on the Armed Forces as an integral element of society, this course provides an examination of the broad range of American civil-military relations and the environmental context in which defense policy is formulated. Special themes include: the role of the professional officer in a democratic society; socialization processes within the armed services; the requisites for maintaining adequate national security forces; political, economic, and social constraints upon the national defense structure; and the impact of technological and international developments upon strategic preparedness and the over-all defense policy-making process.[18]

To focus on one course's evolution as an example, Naval Science 101 had been known as late as 1968 by the title Naval Orientation and Sea Power and had drawn particular criticism for being anti-intellectual and narrow in scope. It was described in the 1968 University of Michigan undergraduate catalog as: "Introduction to basic Navy background, procedures, regulations, and organization, with emphasis on the junior officer['s] duties and responsibilities. The last third of the semester introduces Naval history and sea power."[19] By 1974 it had been redesigned and renamed Introduction to Naval Science and was described as "an introduction to structure and principles of naval organization and management. Practices and concepts lying behind naval organization and management are examined within the context of American social and industrial organization and practice."[20]

Courses had thus been redesigned and their emphasis changed in the direction that the faculty reports had suggested. They were now focusing on environment and context and had eliminated much of the memorization, drill, and corps activity. Furthermore, the services encouraged all students, even noncitizens, to take ROTC courses without an accompanying military obligation, to address ROTC's reputation as furtive and inaccessible to civilians; more than one hundred non-ROTC students at Duquesne University took advantage of that opportunity in 1976–77.[21] These changes reflected both the military's desire to become more acceptable to the students and administrators of civilian colleges and its own sense that military education after Vietnam had to be broadened.

Course descriptions provide only a limited sense of how a course has changed; authors can change the description without altering the substantive material of the course. However, as Jerome Schneewind's observation at Pittsburgh suggests, faculty and administrators who attended ROTC courses and examined the materials used were generally pleased with the new courses, with the notable exception of those courses that they understood to have no application outside a single profession.

In this vein, a 1974 faculty committee review of the ROTC courses at Michigan found that many courses could "stand on their own academic merit" and were "compatible with what we understand to be appropriate to the liberal arts curriculum." The committee recommended credit for all ROTC courses except Introduction to Small Arms, Conduct of Military Operations, Ship Systems II, Naval Operations, and Amphibious Warfare.[22] A separate subcommittee report recommended a reappraisal of the no-credit policy at Michigan, noting that "we found in the current course offerings none of those deficiencies that were found by the preceding ROTC sub-committee in the 1968–69 programs and which caused it to render the negative verdict leading to the withdrawal of all credit. The disparity between the earlier appraisal and the present one, we believe, is due not to different standards of evaluation or to a shift in academic values, but reflects a real change in the nature of ROTC courses."[23]

At several schools, many where the status of ROTC had survived the wartime period intact, the ROTC staffs redesigned curricula with the explicit intent of putting the ROTC courses up for review on the same standards as those obtaining for non-ROTC courses. The goal was "to provide a program compatible with the evolving environment of the academic community" and therefore fully capable of existing alongside other courses and making significant academic and intellectual contributions of their own.[24] At the University of Colorado, a Committee on Courses that investigated ROTC in 1976 found that "a serious review of the ROTC courses and of their conduct does not disclose an orientation in the direction of indoctrination or of the mastery of the mere techniques of military life." The committee was "favorably impressed by the willingness of the ROTC staffs to cooperate with [the College of Arts and Sciences] in modifying course content so as to make their curricula more acceptable to this College."[25]

These changes improved the standing of ROTC in the students' eyes as well. Although students lacked the perspective to compare ROTC courses to those of years past, cadets reported general satisfaction with the quality of

ROTC instruction. ROTC students and recent ROTC graduates testified at committee hearings at Michigan in 1975 that their courses were taught objectively and with critical presentations.[26] Three years later, an independent survey of AFROTC cadets found that four in five believed that the quality of instruction in their AFROTC courses compared favorably with the level of instruction in their civilian courses.[27]

Civilian faculties acknowledged that the ROTC instructors themselves were now better educated and more formally trained in educational methods. These qualifications, the schools believed, permitted the instructors to make substantive improvements in the courses and the presentation of material to cadets. After 1970, all military officers assigned to Kent State, Illinois, Michigan, and Pittsburgh had a master's degree, reflecting a trend nationwide, as shown in Table 7.1.[28]

The 1974 Army ROTC Advisory Panel noted that the new instructors were "one of the important factors in gaining faculty support" for reaccrediting ROTC courses.[29] The improvements in course quality and formal qualifications of the instructors thus created a paradox: there was a general sense that ROTC was of significantly higher quality than it had been before 1968, but despite these changes, it received less academic credit and status than it had previously enjoyed.

Furthermore, some changes to general university procedures made the sanctions imposed on ROTC look to some, in retrospect, more Draconian than was warranted. Several universities had introduced programs in the early 1970s through which undergraduates could teach their own courses in consultation with, but not under the supervision of, regular faculty. Such programs, military officers and some civilian faculty charged, undermined

Table 7.1 Highest degree attained by AFROTC officers, by year assigned

Year	Bachelor's	Master's	Ph.D.
1967–68	74%	25%	0%
1969–70	73%	26%	<1%
1971–72	26%	72%	1%
1977–78	1.5%	95%	3%

Source: Joseph Pearlman, "A Study Comparing and Contrasting Views of the Role of the Air Force ROTC in Relationship to the Role of the University, 1960–1978," Ph.D. diss., University of Denver, 1978, p. 83.

the faculties' demands that accredited courses be taught under the direct control of members of the faculty; accepting credit for these courses and denying credit for ROTC courses, they believed, amounted to a distinction that was certainly arbitrary, even if it was not directly aimed at the military. As Michigan president Robben Fleming told his Princeton counterpart, "The claim is made, probably with a good deal of justification, that the College is applying a double standard which is directed at the military."[30]

By 1975, then, a growing number of civilian faculty were arguing that ROTC was not what it had been in the Vietnam era and before, and that therefore it was time to revisit many of the sanctions imposed on ROTC during the war. For some, this reexamination was justified because the sanctions had been unwarranted even as they were being implemented. For most, the reexamination was needed because the program was qualitatively different from what it had been just a few years earlier.

"Under the Influence of an Outside Institution"

As noted in Chapter 5, the faculty reports of the Vietnam era did not mandate that ROTC courses be thereafter prohibited from receiving academic credit. Instead, they determined that to be accredited, ROTC would have to meet the same standards that civilian courses had to meet. At the University of Michigan's College of Literature, Science, and the Arts, this standard meant that ROTC courses would have to meet the following guidelines for accreditation: "Experiential courses involving work accompanying systematic learning under direct supervision of faculty of this College [or physical activities] accompanied by a conceptual framework furthering insights into concepts of culture within which performance is tested and interpreted."[31] The narrow professional courses that the 1974 faculty committee determined were unfit for credit failed to fit these guidelines because they lacked the conceptual framework that the guidelines described.

The efforts to reaccredit ROTC did not amount to a drive for a blanket restoration of academic status. Instead, ROTC staffs attempted to convince civilian faculty that many of their courses met the standards established by the colleges within which ROTC existed. The program's position in the national and international security apparatus no longer justified such concessions as blanket academic credit for causes that were, in the faculty's opinion, not always the intellectual equal of other programs.

In the 1970s, as a result of the growing sense that ROTC had indeed changed to become more academically respectable, civilian faculties again agreed to consider the issue of academic credit for ROTC courses. These reconsiderations took place in colleges of liberal arts, which had generally been quite critical of the services, and in engineering colleges, which had to this point largely avoided controversy over the issue of ROTC. The improvement of the courses notwithstanding, most of the liberal arts faculties of the postwar era upheld their bans against blanket ROTC credit. By contrast, engineering faculties, who for decades had seen ROTC as a dilution of the academic standards of their own curriculum, granted credit for ROTC courses, on some campuses for the first time.

The difference in the approaches of the liberal arts and engineering faculties can be only partially explained by a generally more hostile attitude among the former toward the military. As important as ideology was the long-standing aversion in liberal arts colleges to professional courses of all kinds. Faculty members in both engineering and liberal arts colleges agreed that the new ROTC courses were, by their standards, "better" and worthy of academic credit alongside civilian courses. However, the reforms were not enough for the liberal arts colleges, which continued to chafe at the outside control and professional emphasis that ROTC represented. In the engineering colleges, these issues were less urgent because of the professional orientation inherent in engineering curricula and the lack of a tradition of conflict with ROTC.[32] Therefore, by 1980 accreditation patterns on many campuses were the reverse of what they had been in 1950.

In the liberal arts colleges, faculties consistently either voted not to reconsider the issue of blanket ROTC credit or they voted against blanket restoration. Still, in some individual cases ROTC courses, with the support of a civilian department, were able to gain accreditation. The faculties continued to hold to the prohibitions on blanket credit, even while acknowledging the credit worthiness of several ROTC courses. Permitting blanket credit would, in the faculties' eyes, restore to ROTC the special privileges of the prewar era, which the faculties were loath to do.

The ROTC staffs themselves, while for the most part believing that some academic credit could be useful in bringing enrollments and cadet quality up, did not lobby civilian faculty for credit restoration. They understood, as their predecessors had, that if they pushed too hard they would risk producing ill will and antagonism. Instead civilian faculty who either saw ROTC as a means to civilianize the American military or believed that the ROTC courses were the intellectual equal of civilian courses introduced measures to reaccredit ROTC. ROTC instructors occasionally testified at faculty committee hearings, met privately with influential faculty members, and often opened their classes to faculty visitors (at Colorado, ROTC staffs invited the faculty to make unannounced visits whenever they wished[33]), but they did not press publicly for a reconsideration of academic credit.

Among the liberal arts colleges of the universities studied here, only the University of Illinois voted to restore substantial ROTC credit. In 1976 the Illinois College of Liberal Arts and Sciences, arguing that it was "educationally sound to enable our students to participate in [ROTC] programs," permitted students to count six ROTC credits toward graduation, far fewer than the fifteen credits of the prewar era but a clear change from the zero-credit policy passed in 1971. Illinois had, in effect, replaced the prewar blanket credit policy with a new policy that accredited only those courses, all above the freshman level, that the faculty believed merited consideration alongside civilian courses. Here, as elsewhere, the reconsideration of credit resulted from the faculty's belief in the genuine improvement in the quality of ROTC courses and the desire of the ROTC instructors to be a part of the campus community. As Illinois provost J. W. Peltason informed the army, "As important as the actual granting of credit, has been the *way* in which credit was granted—via a rigorous evaluation process. ROTC work is thus being viewed as it should be: a serious, academically legitimate program of pre-professional education."[34] At Illinois, ROTC's reaccreditation symbolized an acknowledgment of the improvement in the quality of ROTC and its appropriateness to the mission of the university.

Nevertheless, liberal arts faculties continued to express deep concerns over the wisdom of permitting an outside agency to determine the course content of an accredited offering. Most faculty members could agree that at least some ROTC courses were intellectually equal to accredited civilian courses, but ROTC's anomalous position and character argued against a reconsideration of blanket credit.[35] In 1972 a Pittsburgh College of Arts and Sciences faculty cabinet voted thirty-seven to nine to reject a proposal to reconsider the issue of academic credit for ROTC, arguing that ROTC materials were "under the influence of an outside institution and cannot be controlled by the University."[36]

Michigan's College of Literature, Science, and the Arts (LSA) faculty debated the issue of academic credit in 1975 and again in 1979; both times, ROTC came away without credit. In 1975 the faculty "overwhelmingly" rejected a proposal to reaccredit ROTC despite an executive committee report that argued for ROTC credit because military instructors "now teach courses our way."[37] The committee members had divided ROTC courses into four groups: history/political science, management, technical, and military. They argued that courses in the first three groups were professional but analogous to regular university courses in content and quality and therefore worthy of credit after a faculty review of the course materials and the instructor's qualifications. Those in the last category, however, were deemed to have no academic equivalent.[38] "Armies must salute, of course," said the executive committee's chairman, "but we don't want anything to do with that."[39]

Of course, the military itself was not asking for credit for courses like drill. The significance of the Michigan committee's report was its recognition that "technical" courses, like Navigation, and "management" courses like Principles of Leadership were on the same professional level as other vocational courses, which were themselves becoming a larger part of liberal arts curricula. As economics professor W. H. Anderson, a strong ROTC critic in 1969, argued, "LSA is getting more professionalized, and there isn't that great a distinction between these LSA courses and the ROTC courses which train for a different profession."[40]

Nevertheless, ROTC most clearly symbolized the sole-employer model that was anathema to many faculty members in colleges of liberal arts. As such, the Michigan executive committee added the stipulation that credit would need to be awarded anew every year after a faculty review of relevant materials. Thus it implicitly acknowledged the anomaly inherent in ROTC. Even if ROTC were the intellectual equal of civilian courses, it was different in ways important enough to warrant special supervision. Such supervision was necessary because without it an outside agency would have unchecked authority over accredited course offerings, a condition that did not exist anywhere in the university. The 1975 faculty vote to deny ROTC credit was based on these issues, not on the propriety of military training per se. The LSA dean observed that

> it was my sense of the meeting, confirmed by discussions since the meeting with a considerable number of faculty members, that the vote was not based primarily on political views or an effort to strike out at the Military Services. Rather, I think it was predominately based on broader academic issues, including unnecessary course duplication, methods of selection and certification of instructors in contrast to the selection of our own faculty, and *particularly* the propriety of permitting an outside agency to enjoy the

privilege of exercising special influence over any portion of the curriculum.[41]

The fact that the outside agency was the military did not help the case of accrediting ROTC, but neither did it make the negative votes a certainty. No outside agency had the special privileges that ROTC was requesting, and in the absence of a global crisis such as the Cold War, faculties could find no compelling reason to reinstitute them.

When the issue arose again at Michigan in 1979, the situation had changed only slightly. By then, some civilian professors were still arguing that the no-credit situation impaired the overall success of ROTC, but the officers themselves, while hoping for a restoration of credit, were emphatically stating that regardless of the outcome, ROTC was at Michigan to stay. They were also willing to consider further changes to their program to satisfy civilians. "We would appreciate your telling us what standards you have or want," one officer told a faculty subcommittee. "You name it; we'll do it."[42] ROTC looked in 1979 decidedly less threatened and less threatening than it had a decade earlier. Still, the faculty rejected by a large margin the request to repeal the no-credit policy. Again participants, such as LSA associate dean John Knott, observed that they were "satisfied that the discussion focused on academic questions":

> Two of the issues in particular strike me as likely to come up at [future] faculty meetings on the issue. The first argument is based upon credentials. The officers who teach the ROTC courses, although screened by a faculty committee, are likely to have a masters degree at best and this is not always in the subject that they are teaching . . . The second argument has to do with the fact that the officers owe their primary allegiance to an organization other than the University.[43]

The contested issues of 1979 were thus little different from those of 1969 or even 1959.

At the same time, engineering colleges were increasing academic credit for ROTC. As early as 1973, some schools began to anticipate a change in policy from the Engineers Council for Professional Development (ECPD), which accredits engineering programs. Illinois raised credit for ROTC classes from six to twelve hours in its College of Engineering, anticipating no resistance from the ECPD and anxious to acknowledge what it saw as the improved ROTC curriculum.[44] In 1977 the ECPD formally changed its policies to permit ROTC credit to count toward the sixteen hours of social science and humanities credits it required of all engineering students. Michigan initially responded by permitting four ROTC hours to count toward graduation, but within a year it had voted to award credit "as earned" for all courses except drill, meaning that Michigan engineering students could earn up to sixteen credits for ROTC.[45]

The change in engineering school policy was a reflection of three factors. The most important was an understanding, mirrored in the liberal arts colleges, that the ROTC courses themselves no longer diluted the curriculum. The second was an awareness that ROTC, especially Naval ROTC, was seeking to have more of its scholarship students enter colleges of engineering; given that the courses were no longer evidently inferior, it made sense to encourage the navy's efforts in this direction. Last, ROTC had fewer vocal opponents in engineering colleges. While this factor alone made little difference, when combined with the rise in course quality and military's desire to produce more engineers, it yielded a decidedly more friendly atmosphere among engineering faculty.[46]

The efforts to reaccredit ROTC by restoring the program's prewar blanket credit privileges failed at most of the campuses where the issue was contested. Civilian faculties in the colleges of liberal arts were simply unwilling to return ROTC to a status with which many had always been uncomfortable.

Having been denied its status quo ante, ROTC sought to restore its prewar curricular status through avenues opened after the implementation of the post-Tet faculty reports. Cross-listings (officially listing an ROTC course with the offerings of a civilian department) and joint appointments (gaining an adjunct appointment in a civilian department) offered guaranteed paths to accreditation without formal approval from a college's assembled faculty. But here, too, the ROTC units had little success. Civilian departments recognized only those ROTC courses that filled an obvious gap in that department's undergraduate offerings, such as when the NROTC executive officer at Michigan succeeded in securing a joint appointment in the department of naval architecture and marine engineering and cross-listings for aeronautical engineering and navigation courses.[47] Where the proposed ROTC course filled no departmental need, the departments rejected requests for both cross-listings and joint appointments. Engineering and liberal arts colleges rejected these requests with equal regularity, arguing that ROTC courses had little overlap with their own offerings except in such areas as political science, management, and military history, where the courses were taught satisfactorily by regular faculty. Furthermore, they argued, ROTC instructors were not interested in relevant research, a common (though not necessary) qualification for adjunct and visiting professorships.

Civilian faculties, with few exceptions, rejected formal associations with ROTC because the instructors were employed by an outside agency and the programs offered no courses that filled obvious gaps in regular civilian offerings. For both of these reasons, Michigan's history department rejected a proposal to use military officers as teaching assistants in a military history survey course run by a member of the history faculty.[48] The department argued that its graduate students, under the department's direct supervision, were sufficient for the job. Using the same logic, the College of Engineering at Illinois consistently rejected ROTC requests for cross-listings.[49]

The faculty reports of 1969 and 1970 represented more than a vehicle for some faculty members to lash out at what they perceived as an immoral and corrupting military establishment. They represented a prevailing belief among civilian faculty members, especially in colleges of liberal arts, that ROTC programs were not the intellectual and academic equal of regular civilian offerings. After 1972, when campus tensions had eased and some student groups were rescinding anti-ROTC proclamations, liberal arts faculties had the opportunity to restore academic credit and status to the ROTC programs. On most campuses they did not; in upholding the decisions they had made a few years earlier, they used many of the same arguments that their predecessors had used. ROTC, they contended, while beneficial in many important ways, was different enough from civilian academic programs to warrant special distinctions.

The Military and ROTC

Despite its inability to achieve a satisfactory conclusion to the question of academic credit, the military remained generally pleased with ROTC, especially as enrollments began to climb in the mid-1970s (see Chapter 6). Qualitatively, ROTC students were at least the equivalent of their non-ROTC peers, even at competitive schools such as Michigan (see Table 7.2). Nationally, the mean composite SAT score of entering college freshmen fell from 924 in 1974 to 878 in 1979. The mean composite score of ROTC scholarship students, however, rose by at least 100 points in all four services in the same period.[50]

Table 7.2   Mean composite SAT scores

Students	Score
AROTC scholarship students, 1978	1,285
NROTC scholarship students, 1978	1,246
AFROTC scholarship students, 1978	1,220
U.S. Naval Academy, 1976	1,220
College average, 1976	930

Sources: Rear Admiral Robert McNitt, Dean of Admissions, "Naval Academy Admissions" (1978), University of Michigan Archives, Bentley Historical Library, Vice-President for Academic Affairs Papers, Box 141, Navy Curriculum 1974–1980 Folder; Department of Defense, *Report on the Reserve Officers' Training Corps* (Washington, D.C.: Government Printing Office, 1980).

Even at some of the schools where ROTC-university relations were most tumultuous, the quality of cadet produced remained high. Furthermore, those schools were among the most popular choices for scholarship winners, because of their prestige and because the scholarship made the university affordable in an era of rapidly rising education costs.[51] During the 1970s, in-state tuition rose by 415 percent at the University of Illinois and 220 percent at the University of Michigan. Out-of-state tuition, usually three to four times more expensive, rose 298 percent and 188 percent at those schools, respectively.[52] ROTC thus became all the more appealing to students. Public schools commonly had half or more of their cadets come from out of state (in 1971, thirty-two of Georgia Tech's fifty-eight NROTC seniors were from out of state[53]). In-state students used ROTC to make their state's flagship institutions more affordable. In 1974, 40 percent of the Army ROTC scholarship winners from the state of Michigan used their scholarship to attend the University of Michigan. No other school accounted for more than 10 percent.[54]

The services were willing to accept the no-credit status in place at several schools because those schools continued to supply high-quality students. As cadet quality and enrollments reached acceptable levels, arguments that the no-credit situation impaired ROTC's mission became less germane. Nevertheless, the accreditation debates of the late 1960s and 1970s created an impression among some military officials that the actions of liberal arts colleges were "discriminatory," "demeaning," and "unfair" to the military.[55] As engineering colleges concurrently increased academic credit, some officials began to argue that creating formal links between engineering colleges and ROTC units might be an appropriate way to improve relations significantly between the universities and ROTC. In this vein, the University of Michigan PNS proposed having his unit "co-opted" by the College of Engineering.[56]

A general impression that liberal arts faculties were antimilitary coincided in the middle of the 1970s with a shortage of junior naval officers qualified to serve in the rapidly expanding and technologically complex nuclear fleet. Admiral Hyman G. Rickover led a navywide effort to see that virtually all officers were qualified to serve in the nuclear fleet that, in the late 1970s, was quickly replacing the diesel and electric fleet as a result of Title 8 of the 1975 Defense Appropriations Act.[57] That act mandated that all major combat ships be nuclear powered, except by a special written directive of the president.

In 1976, as a result of Title 8, the United States planned to build 41 new nuclear-powered ships to complement the 114 already in the fleet. Ironically, the navy's reputation for quality nuclear training made it difficult to staff the new ships. By the navy's own estimate, former naval personnel operated 60 percent of the nation's civilian nuclear industry. That industry could offer significantly higher salaries than the navy. As a result, retention problems compounded recruitment problems for the nuclear fleet.[58]

Consistent with these problems, the navy announced that beginning in the fall of 1977, 80 percent of all NROTC scholarship students would be required to have an engineering or "hard science" major. The navy had always been the most engineering-intensive service, but to some naval officers, what became known as the 80-20 requirement seemed unnecessary.[59] The NROTC curriculum, originally designed in 1947, had traditionally emphasized the accession of "outstanding young college men of diverse and superior educational background representing a wide and catholic range of interest, imposing and introducing a critical sense of values, frankly unregimented in a professional sense."[60] As late as 1973 the chief of naval education and training had informed a conference of professors of naval science that all academic majors were acceptable to the navy.[61] The new plan thus represented a sharp break from NROTC tradition.

Additionally, the navy designed a new NROTC curriculum that more closely resembled that of the engineering-intensive U.S. Naval Academy. All NROTC students were now required to take two semesters of calculus and physics and one semester each of math, chemistry, and computer science, in addition to their NROTC courses and the courses required for the completion of their degree. In recognition of "the overload situation" created by the new curriculum, American Military History and National Security Affairs became optional courses for engineers.[62] Most engineering students would take the science and math courses whether or not they were also enrolled in NROTC, so the real effect of the new requirements was to discourage humanities and social science students from taking an NROTC scholarship. The navy's shift to engineers caused rapid changes. Whereas in 1974 only 41 percent of NROTC graduates nationwide had completed calculus and physics, by 1978, 79 percent had done so.[63]

While not intended as a snub to liberal arts colleges, the 80-20 requirement moved the NROTC program almost entirely into the presumably more friendly environment of the engineering colleges. Administrators and faculty in the liberal arts colleges were not, however, willing to surrender the principle that junior officers should come from a wide variety of educational backgrounds. The best example of such a viewpoint came from Adam Yarmolinsky, a former Pentagon official and professor at the University of Massachusetts, who argued that the post-Vietnam military's

> primary mission [will be] deterrence, rather than warmaking . . . A [military] that will probably spend all its time preparing for wars it may never fight needs highly sophisticated leadership, [with the] capability of resisting the tendency of entrenched bureaucracy toward either rot or rigidity and [the] ability to draw on inner resources to combat boredom and inertia. If this is the definition of a liberally educated person, perhaps a liberal education is necessary to produce him—or her.[64]

Yarmolinsky reflected the concerns of many academics who believed that a liberal education was critical to creating an officer corps that would be responsive to American society and to the many conditions that officers might have to face in as yet undefined missions.[65] Many educators thus believed that while the 80-20 requirement fulfilled a short-term, bureaucratic goal of producing more engineers, it threatened long-term harm to the military by creating a more narrowly educated officer corps. The Association of NROTC Colleges and Universities noted:

> In view of the historical role of the NROTC in the staff[ing] of the officer corps of the United States Navy with officers of equal abilities, but different academic traditions from graduates of the United States Naval Academy, the

members of this Association respectfully express their deep concern over the unilateral decision to state as a goal that 80 percent of NROTC scholarship students graduate from technical and/or scientific areas.[66]

The move to recruit more engineers also threatened to impair navy attempts to recruit more minorities and women, because those two groups remained underrepresented in colleges of engineering. Still, the top leaders of the navy saw the production of personnel qualified to serve in the nuclear fleet as critical to national security. Therefore, they told the association that "the 80-20 hard science requirement stands, and is not debatable."[67]

When placed within the context of university-ROTC relations since 1916, the ANROTCCU's defense of the place of liberal arts graduates in the NROTC program reveals the universities' fundamental desire to participate in ROTC training. Their "deep concern" over the 80-20 requirement stemmed from a genuine belief that the participation of men and women from "different academic traditions" improved the military and gave the universities an opportunity to influence—positively, they contended—the quality and character of the armed forces. As University of Minnesota president C. Peter Magrath told the navy, "We believe that [this policy] is not in the best interests of the Navy. Certainly it is not in the best interests of the nation to have most officers of the future educated in technical/scientific areas to the detriment of the liberal arts or humanities . . . I can only contemplate with alarm any proposal that would provide us with a single-minded, inflexible Navy. Like the nation, the Navy needs a variety of points of view."[68]

As such, the 80-20 discussions recalled debates in 1962 between universities and the army over the question of enrollment limits (see Chapter 2). In both cases, administrators were willing to fight for their own views about national security and the role of the educational system in producing junior officers. In neither case did university administrators seek disestablishment from ROTC; to the contrary, they actively sought the opportunity to participate in officer training, but they fought for their own vision of how such training should be conducted.

The universities tried to continue a policy, dating back to the 1950s, of actively participating in the determination of the ROTC curriculum. They paid careful attention to the evolution of the military curriculum and protested those changes that threatened a denigration of their basic principles. Thus their goal was not to keep the military out of the university but to ensure that the university would continue to exercise influence over the military through the production of officers on terms amenable to civilian educators.

In 1974 Michigan AFROTC professor of air science Colonel Marvin Grunzke failed to obtain credit for two air science classes, Concepts of Leadership and Principles of Management, despite the significant improvements made in them. The university also denied him a joint appointment in the department of psychology, despite his Ph.D. in psychology from Yale. Frustrated, he told the air force that "it must be concluded that there is insufficient interest within the University of Michigan representative structure to support a viable Air Force Officer Education Program as an integral part of the total educational complex encompassed by the University of Michigan."[69] The colonel was perhaps more astute than he knew; he had hit on exactly the point of faculty actions in the 1960s and 1970s. Similarly, when in the following year the Princeton trustees voted to readmit ROTC, they also voted in favor of a change in the wording of the part of the contract regarding ROTC's place on campus, from "an integral academic and administrative department" to "an integral element."[70] These changes and observations reveal a critical point: the faculties of the liberal arts colleges under study here were not at all interested in having ROTC as "an integral part of the total educational complex" on their campus. They were willing to accept or tolerate ROTC because of the benefits it provided to students, the university, and the nation, but they were unwilling to give it the same status, privileges, and rights as regular civilian departments.

The debates over abiding matters in the postwar era demonstrate that ROTC reform has to be seen through a much wider lens than one that encompasses only the turbulence of Vietnam. The refusal of liberal arts colleges to reaccredit ROTC after the Vietnam era—despite improvements in the quality of the courses and the people who taught them—argues for looking at the issue over a longer period of time. Faculty and administration opposition to ROTC had been consistently focused since the 1950s on the ways in which ROTC differed from civilian academic programs. The universities, as a body, could accept the logic that the ROTC programs served the public good and fit in with the service role of American universities, especially those supported with public money. They drew a line, however, at including these anomalous programs as regular intellectual and academic offerings on a par with their own.

Epilogue

Having taught navy and marine NROTC students at Carnegie Mellon as well as Air Force Academy cadets, I know the stereotypes that exist about both. To many Americans generally unfamiliar with the military, the service academies immediately call to mind an image of a hyperpatriotic automaton ready to subvert Congress if so ordered. As I prepared to leave Pittsburgh for Colorado Springs, one of my fellow historians told me to "watch out for the Oliver Norths" that were sure to be my students and colleagues at the Air Force Academy. North personified for many a problem seen by Moderate and Radical Whigs alike: as an academy-educated agent for the executive branch, he found a way around the "constitutional safeguards" established to prevent the military professional from acting without the legislature's knowledge.

ROTC, on the other hand, calls to mind a much more comfortable image, that of a competent and less threatening military officer entirely content with civilian oversight. As with all stereotypes, these images do not correspond exactly to reality; nevertheless, they exist. The citizen-soldier iconography is no less profound now than it was in the days of Paul Revere. Americans still prefer having soldiers who are not totally military, as the nightly "Joe in the field" interviews during the Persian Gulf War attest.

The survival of ROTC, even in the face of some serious crises, stands as a testimony to American values regarding its military officers. Even during the Vietnam War few Americans (influenced as they were by Moderate Whig ideology) were willing to surrender the idea that civilian education and influence served a critical role in preparing officers. As this book has shown, resistance to the American military and the wars it has fought has often had the ironic effect of *increasing* support for ROTC.

That support has never been in serious doubt in the minds of the faculties, students, and administrators of the nation's public universities. Almost since ROTC's inception, university communities and the military have debated details, but public universities have never wanted to turn the training of military officers exclusively over to the military itself. Neither has the military wanted (or been able to afford) to do that job itself. For all of its faults, ROTC fit almost everyone's idea of how to commission officers.

That fit, of course, has never stopped the push for important reforms. ROTC has had to change as American higher education and the military have changed. ROTC simply was not the same institution in 1933 (when none of the presidents from the nation's twenty-five largest public schools had served in the military or the State Department) as it was in 1950, when 40 percent of those presidents (including the presidents of six of the ten schools under study here) had a background of such service. Similarly, the end of the war in Vietnam and the concurrent end of the draft forced more changes. By 1980 ROTC no longer claimed that it stood on the line between freedom and a total communist takeover. It had become a part of campus life that was no longer so easy to distinguish. As the University of Washington's professor of naval science said in a *Washington Daily* article on October 14, 1980, "We're not saviors of democracy. We're just here."

Abbreviations

AALGCSU	American Association of Land-Grant Colleges and State Universities
AAUP	American Association of University Professors
AFB	air force base
AFROTC	Air Force Reserve Officers' Training Corps
ANROTCCU	Association of Naval Reserve Officers' Training Corps Colleges and Universities
AROTC	Army Reserve Officers' Training Corps
AVF	all-volunteer force
DOD	Department of Defense
ECPD	Engineers Council for Professional Development
GMS	general military science
JROTC	Junior Reserve Officers' Training Corps
MOEP	Military Officer Education Program
NASULGC	National Association of State Universities and Land-Grant Colleges
NDA	National Defense Act (of 1916)
NROTC	Naval Reserve Officers' Training Corps
NSIC	National Security Information Center
OCS	Officer Candidate School
PAS	professor of air science
PMS	professor of military science
PNS	professor of naval science
ROTC	Reserve Officers' Training Corps
SDS	Students for a Democratic Society
SNCC	Student Nonviolent Coordinating Committee
UMT	universal military training
USAF	United States Air Force
WAC	Women's Army Corps
WAF	Women in the Air Force
WAFROTC	Women in the Air Force Reserve Officers' Training Corps
WAVES	Women Accepted for Volunteer Emergency Service

Notes

Introduction

1. "ROTC Officer Transferred amid Charges of Coercion," *Chronicle of Higher Education,* July 12, 1996, p. A6.
2. Colleen Cordes, "MIT Tries a New Approach in the Battle over ROTC," *Chronicle of Higher Education,* May 31, 1996, p. A23. MIT's case is just one example; virtually all ROTC host universities have expressed some degree of discomfort with the "don't ask, don't tell" policy. Most have worked out a truce with the Department of Defense to open all on-campus ROTC classes to all students, regardless of sexual orientation. Some schools, like MIT, have pledged financial aid to any gay or lesbian ROTC cadet who loses his or her scholarship.
3. James L. Morrison, "Military Education and Strategic Thought, 1846–1861," in Kenneth J. Hagan and William R. Roberts, eds., *Against All Enemies: Interpretations of American Military History from Colonial Times to the Present* (New York: Greenwood Press, 1986), pp. 113–131, quotations from pp. 117, 121, and 120.
4. Lawrence Cress, *Citizens in Arms: The Army and Militia in American Society to the War of 1812* (Chapel Hill: University of North Carolina Press, 1982). See also William B. Skelton, "Samuel P. Huntington and the Roots of the American Military Tradition," *Journal of Military History* 60 (April 1996): 325–338.
5. Skelton, "Samuel P. Huntington," p. 328.
6. Cress, *Citizens in Arms,* p. 22.
7. Ibid., p. 60.
8. Ibid.
9. Ibid., p. 26.
10. There have, of course, been several military champions of the ROTC program, such as Admiral James Holloway in the navy and Brigadier General William Lindley in the air force.
11. I could cite several important studies here, but the best examples are found in the introduction and several essays in Peter Karsten, ed., *The Military in America from Colonial Times to the Present* (New York: Free Press, 1986).
12. John Keegan, *The Mask of Command* (New York: Viking Press, 1988), p. 2.

13. See Roger Geiger's *Research and Relevant Knowledge: American Research Universities since World War II* (New York: Oxford University Press, 1993) and *To Advance Knowledge: The Growth of American Research Universities, 1900–1940* (New York: Oxford University Press, 1986). Julie Reuben's *The Making of the Modern University: Intellectual Transformation and the Marginalization of Morality* (Chicago: University of Chicago Press, 1996) provides a wonderful analysis of the development of nineteenth- and early twentieth-century American universities.

14. Adam Garfinkle, *Telltale Hearts: The Origins and Impact of the Vietnam Antiwar Movement* (New York: St. Martin's Press, 1995); Kenneth Heineman, *Campus Wars: The Peace Movement at American State Universities in the Vietnam Era* (New York: New York University Press, 1993).

15. Christian Appy, *Working-Class War: American Combat Soldiers in Vietnam* (Chapel Hill: University of North Carolina Press, 1993).

16. They are: Maxwell J. Richards, "A Ten-Year History of Air Force ROTC, 1946–1956," master's thesis, University of Maryland, 1957; Gene Lyons and John Masland, *Education and Military Leadership: A Study of the ROTC* (Princeton, N.J.: Princeton University Press, 1959); Victor Hirshauer, "The History of the Army ROTC," (Ph.D. diss., Johns Hopkins University, 1975; Joseph Pearlman, "A Study Comparing and Contrasting Views of the Role of Air Force ROTC in Relationship to the University, 1960–1978," Ph.D. diss., University of Denver, 1978; Donald Cummings, "Army ROTC: A Study of the Army's Primary Officer Procurement Program," Ph.D. diss., University of California at Santa Barbara, 1982.

17. Hirshauer used ROTC institutional files that he obtained at Ft. Meade in Maryland. I was unable to locate these records.

18. Pearlman, "A Study Comparing and Contrasting," p. 87.

19. Hirshauer, "The History of the Army ROTC," p. 383. A focus on the Pentagon is all the more misleading because the key military agencies in charge of ROTC were not in Washington at all, but in Annapolis, Montgomery, Pensacola, and Ft. Monroe.

20. The Cold War, obviously, extended past 1964. I use the phrase "Cold War period" and focus on 1950 to 1964 to underscore the importance that the developing Cold War had for the concurrent development of an active-duty ROTC program.

21. To a lesser extent, I have also included Columbus College, Duquesne University, and Princeton. Their stories are interesting, but extant archival material limited the attention that I could devote to them.

22. Cress, *Citizens in Arms*, p. 39.

1. ROTC and the American Military Tradition

1. Contrast these officers with General Dwight D. Eisenhower, who successfully used his military career to attain the presidency. Unlike North and MacArthur, Eisenhower projected a distinctly unaristocratic image. As Paul Fussell noted,

"General Eisenhower [was] popular with the troops because [he was] in so many ways the typical Second World War American serviceman and thus sympathetic with their needs." See Paul Fussell, *Wartime: Understanding and Behavior in the Second World War* (New York: Oxford University Press, 1989), p. 145.

2. Samuel Huntington, *The Soldier and the State: The Theory and Politics of Civil-Military Relations* (Cambridge, Mass.: Harvard University Press, 1959), p. 159.

3. Lawrence Cress, *Citizens in Arms: The Army and Militia in American Society to the War of 1812* (Chapel Hill: University of North Carolina Press, 1982). Please see the introduction for a fuller discussion of Cress's arguments.

4. *Company grade* and *field grade* are army terms that divide the nongeneral officer corps into two groups. In the army, air force, and marines, the lieutenants and captains constitute the company grades, while the majors, lieutenant colonels, and colonels constitute the field grades. Equivalent navy ranks are ensign, lieutenant (junior grade), and lieutenant; and lieutenant commander, commander, and captain.

5. Ira D. Gruber, "The Anglo-American Military Tradition and the War for American Independence," in Kenneth J. Hagan and William R. Roberts, eds., *Against All Enemies: Interpretations of American Military History from Colonial Times to the Present* (New York: Greenwood Press, 1986), pp. 21–47, quotation from p. 29.

6. Richard H. Kohn, "The Inside History of the Newburgh Conspiracy," in Peter Karsten, ed., *The Military in America from Colonial Times to the Present* (New York: Free Press, 1986), pp. 79–91, quotation from p. 81. Kohn was talking here about New England, but his comments are equally relevant for other sections of the new United States.

7. Kohn, "The Inside History," pp. 80 and 89.

8. Richard Kohn, "Out of Control: The Crisis in Civil-Military Relations," *The National Interest* 35 (Spring 1994): 3–17, quotation from p. 15.

9. Kohn, "The Inside History," p. 90.

10. Russell Weigley, *The American Way of War* (Bloomington: Indiana University Press, 1973), p. 41.

11. Arthur Coumbe and Lee S. Harford, *U.S. Army Cadet Command: The Ten-Year History* (Ft. Monroe, Va.: Office of the Command Historian, U.S. Army Cadet Command, 1996), p. 7.

12. James Madison, "Federalist Number Forty-One," in Roy Fairfield, ed., *The Federalist Papers* (Garden City, N.Y.: Doubleday Anchor Press, 1966), pp. 118–126, quotations from p. 120.

13. Harry Coles, "From Peaceable Coercion to Balanced Forces," in Kenneth J. Hagan and William R. Roberts, eds., *Against All Enemies: Interpretations of American Military History from Colonial Times to the Present* (New York: Greenwood Press, 1986), pp. 71–89, quotation from p. 79.

14. Quoted in R. Ernest Dupuy and Trevor Dupuy, *Military Heritage of America* (New York: McGraw-Hill, 1956), p. 121.

15. Huntington, *The Soldier and the State*, p. 198.

16. Dupuy and Dupuy, *Military Heritage*, p. 139.

17. William B. Skelton, "The Army in the Age of the Common Man, 1815–1845," in Kenneth J. Hagan and William R. Roberts, eds., *Against All Enemies: Interpretations of American Military History from Colonial Times to the Present* (New York: Greenwood Press, 1986), pp. 91–112.

18. Alden Partridge quoted in Coumbe and Harford, *Cadet Command*, p. 8.

19. Gene Lyons and John Masland, *Education and Military Leadership: A Study of the ROTC* (Princeton, N.J.: Princeton University Press, 1959), p. 28.

20. Coumbe and Harford, *Cadet Command*, p. 8. This was also the period when southern military colleges like VMI and the Citadel were formed. While created partly to support the citizen-soldier model, they also owe their creation to the southern belief that military training was important to character development. As these schools were almost exclusively military, they do not fit the overall pattern being discussed here.

21. Skelton, "The Army in the Age of the Common Man," p. 97.

22. Ibid., p. 98.

23. James L. Morrison, "Military Education and Strategic Thought, 1846–1861," in Kenneth J. Hagan and William R. Roberts, eds., *Against All Enemies: Interpretations of American Military History from Colonial Times to the Present* (New York: Greenwood Press, 1986), pp. 113–131, quotation from p. 121.

24. Skelton, "The Army in the Age of the Common Man," p. 105.

25. Peter Karsten, *The Naval Aristocracy: The Golden Age of Annapolis and the Emergence of Modern Navalism* (New York: Free Press, 1972), chap. 1.

26. Coumbe and Harford, *Cadet Command*, p. 8.

27. Shaw and Chamberlain were educated at Harvard and Bowdoin, respectively. The classic study of nonprofessionals in the American Civil War is Gerald Linderman's *Embattled Courage: The Experience of Combat in the American Civil War* (New York: Free Press, 1987). See also Joseph T. Glatthaar, *Forged in Battle: The Civil War Alliance of Black Soldiers and White Officers* (New York: Free Press, 1990).

28. Jomini was the most widely read military historian and theorist at West Point in the antebellum years. In 1862, West Point curriculum developers wrote that "General Jomini is admitted by all competent judges to be one of the ablest military critics and historians of this or any other day." See Baron de Jomini, *The Art of War* (Philadelphia: J. P. Lippincott, 1862), p. 5. Jomini's studies of Napoleon and Frederick the Great led him to believe that successful strategy prescribed "offensive action to mass forces against weaker enemy forces at some decisive point." Between the time of Jomini's writings and the Civil War, however, rifled guns had replaced muskets, vastly increasing the range and lethality of defenders against massed forces. See John Shy, "Jomini," in Peter Paret, ed., *Makers of Modern Strategy from Machiavelli to the Nuclear Age* (Princeton, N.J.: Princeton University Press, 1986), pp. 143–185, quotation from p. 146.

29. The Morrill Bill, without the provision for military tactics, had been vetoed by President Buchanan in 1857.

30. Lyons and Masland, *Education and Military Leadership*, p. 30.

31. Coumbe and Harford, *Cadet Command,* p. 11. It should be noted that the "bottleneck" of officers who entered the army between 1861 and 1864 meant that some lieutenants had twelve or more years of service. Junior officers were often much more experienced than their ranks might indicate. See Peter Karsten, "Armed Progressives," in Peter Karsten, ed., *The Military in America from Colonial Times to the Present* (New York: Free Press, 1986), pp. 239–274.

32. Arthur Russell La Belle, "Kansas State Agricultural College Military Science and Tactics Department, 1863–1918," unpublished student paper, Kansas State University, May 1987, pp. 10–11.

33. Karsten, "Armed Progressives," p. 239.

34. Gerald Linderman, "The Spanish-American War and the Small-Town Community," in Peter Karsten, ed., *The Military in America from Colonial Times to the Present* (New York: Free Press, 1986), pp. 275–294, quotation from p. 278. See also the book from which this article was excerpted, *The Mirror of War: American Society and the Spanish-American War* (Ann Arbor: University of Michigan Press, 1974).

35. Of course, Roosevelt wielded a great deal of influence over the military, but he did so *as a civilian.* He served as assistant secretary of the navy until he joined the Rough Riders, but he was a product of civilian upbringing and education, not a graduate of West Point or Annapolis.

36. For more, see Russell Weigley, *A History of the United States Army* (New York: Mac Millan, 1967), pp. 347–349.

37. Lyons and Masland, *Education and Military Leadership,* p. 37.

38. Coumbe and Harford, *Cadet Command,* p. 13.

39. Lyons and Masland, *Education and Military Leadership,* pp. 42–43.

40. Barrow, *Universities and the Capitalist State,* pp. 135–136.

41. Procedure Preliminary to Inauguration of Military Training at the University of Pittsburgh [May 1916], University of Pittsburgh Archives, Hillman Library, Classification Number 2/10/1904–20, File Folder 40.

42. Chancellor McCormick to Adjutant General, U.S. Army, Dec. 12, 1917, ibid.

43. Chancellor McCormick to Senator Philander Knox, Jan. 8, 1918, ibid.

44. Robert McMath, *Engineering the New South: Georgia Tech, 1885–1985* (Athens: University of Georgia Press), p. 147.

45. Ronald Schaffer, *America in the Great War: The Rise of the War Welfare State* (New York: Oxford University Press, 1991), p. 127.

46. Quotation from ibid., p. 128.

47. Ibid., p. 146.

48. La Belle, "Kansas State Agricultural College," p. 15.

49. Charles Gates, *The First Century at the University of Washington: 1861–1961* (Seattle: University of Washington Press, 1961), p. 154.

50. Louis Marley, "The Civil Administration of the University of Pittsburgh as a Student's Army Training Corps Unit," Feb. 17, 1919, University of Pittsburgh Archives, Hillman Library, Classification Number 2/10/1904–20, File Folder 41.

51. *Kansas State Collegian,* Feb. 7, 1919, cited in Kansas State University Historical Index, Kansas State University Archives.

52. Ibid., pp. 148–149.

53. President Suzzallo to Commandant, 13th Naval District, Sept. 8, 1917, University of Washington Archives, Allen Library, W. U. President's Papers, 71–34, Box 129, Naval ROTC, 1917–1926 Folder.

54. McMath, *Engineering the New South,* p. 149.

55. Julie Reuben, *The Making of the Modern University: Intellectual Transformation and the Marginalization of Morality* (Chicago: University of Chicago Press, 1996), p. 5.

56. William H. S. Demarest, *A History of Rutgers College, 1766–1924* (New Brunswick, N.J.: Rutgers University Press, 1924), p. 520.

57. Coumbe and Harford, *Cadet Command,* p. 16.

58. Lyons and Masland, *Education and Military Leadership,* p. 44.

59. Morris Janowitz, *The Professional Soldier* (Glencoe, Ill.: Free Press, 1960), p. 106.

60. LeMay received an ROTC commission (to the reserves) that year from Ohio State, but he did not receive his degree, due to, in his words, "my own private course in 'Advanced Slumbering.'" See General Curtis E. LeMay with MacKinley Kantor, *Mission with LeMay: My Story* (Garden City, N.Y.: Doubleday and Company, 1965), p. 42.

61. It is also unlikely that the $9 monthly stipend given to advanced cadets made a significant difference in their decision making. But for some men, especially those outside of the prestigious eastern universities, the money played a small role. One future Marine Corps commandant, General David M. Shoup, noted that the money made his stay at DePauw College in the mid-1920s possible: "in all truth [the money] was the only reason I signed up for the senior ROTC." Shoup came from a poor farming family in Indiana. For more on Shoup, see Howard Jablon, "General David M. Shoup, USMC: Warrior and War Protester," *Journal of Military History* 60 (July 1996): 513–538, quotation from p. 514.

62. Coumbe and Harford, *Cadet Command,* p. 14.

63. Ibid.

64. Ronald Schaffer, "The War Department's Defense of ROTC, 1920–1940," *Wisconsin Magazine of History* 53 (Winter 1969–70): 108–120, quotation from p. 110.

65. See James Hawkes, "Antimilitarism at State Universities: The Campaign against Compulsory ROTC, 1920–1940," *Wisconsin History* 49 (Autumn 1965): 41–54.

66. Kathryn McKay, "The Debate over ROTC at the University of Delaware, 1920–1940," *Delaware History* 23 (Spring–Summer 1989): 232.

67. *Hamilton et al. vs. the Regents of the University of California,* 239 U.S. 245 (1934).

68. See Lyons and Masland, *Education and Military Leadership,* chap. 2.

69. Schaffer, "The War Department's Defense," pp. 110. The military itself had just 134,024 men and officers in 1932, a number significantly below the 280,000

authorized by Congress. Given the low number of men in uniform, many War Department officials argued that mandatory training simply had no understood purpose in an army that was already overpopulated with World War I veterans.

70. Lyons and Masland, *Education and Military Leadership*, p. 51.

71. F. D. Farrell to C. M. Harger, Jan. 17, 1935, Kansas State University Archives, President's Papers, 1934–1935, File Folder 43.

72. Robert McNamara, *In Retrospect* (New York: Random House, 1995), p. 6.

73. Ross Parmenter quoted in Paul Fussell, *Wartime: Understanding and Behavior in the Second World War* (New York: Oxford University Press, 1989), p. 61.

74. Clem Work, "ROTC Has Long History on CU Campus," *Rocky Mountain News*, April 21, 1969, p. 5. University of Colorado at Boulder Library, Archives, CU History (Departments), ROTC Folder.

75. Fussell, *Wartime*, p. 60.

76. Quoted in Peter Schrijvers, *The Crash of Ruin: American Combat Soldiers in Europe during World War II* (New York: New York University Press, 1998), p. 63.

77. Quoted in Danforth Eddy, *Colleges for Our Land and Time* (New York: Harper and Bros., 1957), p. 224.

78. Rear Admiral J. Cary Jones, Commander Ninth Naval District, to President Robert Stearns, Sept. 5, 1950, Archives, University of Colorado at Boulder Libraries, Central Administration, President's Office, Series I, Box 331, ROTC—Navy 1940–1977 Folder.

79. "ROTC Halves Tech Induction," *Atlanta Journal*, Jan. 11, 1951.

80. Nathan M. Pusey, *American Higher Education, 1945–1970* (Cambridge, Mass.: Harvard University Press, 1978), p. 9.

81. Coumbe and Harford, *U.S. Army Cadet*, p. 22. Emphasis mine.

2. A Favored Position on Campus

1. See Paul Boyer, *By the Bomb's Early Light: American Thought and Culture at the Dawn of the Atomic Age* (New York: Pantheon Books, 1985), and the film *The Atomic Café* (1982).

2. For more on the Holloway Plan please see James Holloway, "The Holloway Plan," *Proceedings of the U.S. Naval Institute* (Nov. 1947): 1299.

3. Nathan Pusey, *American Higher Education, 1945–1970: A Personal Report* (Cambridge, Mass.: Harvard University Press, 1978), p. 151.

4. Ibid., p. 152.

5. Russell Weigley, *The History of the United States Army* (New York: Macmillan, 1967), p. 508.

6. Pusey, *American Higher Education*, p. 45.

7. See Roger Geiger, *Research and Relevant Knowledge: American Research Universities since World War II* (New York: Oxford University Press, 1993), chap. 1.

8. See Vincent Davis, *The Admiral's Lobby* (Chapel Hill: University of North Carolina Press, 1967), chap. 2.

9. M. K. Deichelman to Logan Wilson, Apr. 12, 1955, University of Texas President's Office Records, VF 30/A.b, Air Science and Tactics 1954–55 Folder.

10. Nathan Pusey included a lengthy and detailed discussion of the finances of higher education in his book, but there is no mention of ROTC. Between 1940 and 1970 the operating costs of American higher education rose from $600 million to $24 billion. In this large picture, ROTC finances appear minuscule. See Pusey, *American Higher Education*, p. 7 and chap. 3.

11. Seymour Harris, ed., *A Statistical Portrait of Higher Education* (New York: McGraw-Hill, 1972), pp. 790–791.

12. For schools like Pittsburgh, Illinois, and Michigan, ROTC was important enough for the uniformed men at headquarters to merit access to that most prized of big-school perks—an invitation to a football game in the president's box.

13. Russell Thackrey, "Some Current ROTC Problems," in *Current Issues in Higher Education: Proceedings of the Ninth Annual Conference on Higher Education,* Chicago, 1954 (n.p.), pp. 294–296.

14. Army ROTC pamphlet, *Quality Is the Answer,* 1960.

15. Mark Grandstaff, "Making the Military American: Advertising, Reform, and the Demise of an Antistanding Military Tradition, 1945–1955," *Journal of Military History* 60 (Apr. 1996): 299–324; quotation from p. 315.

16. Quoted in ibid., p. 315.

17. Ibid., p. 316.

18. Enock Dyrness, "Recorder's Report, Group 37," in *Proceedings of the Ninth Annual Conference on Higher Education*, p. 301.

19. Pusey, *American Higher Education*, pp. 131–133.

20. Geiger, *Research and Relevant Knowledge*, p. 315.

21. John Monro, "Strengthening the ROTC Curriculum," in *Role of the Colleges and Universities in ROTC Programs* (Columbus: Ohio State University Press, 1960), p. 13.

22. George Flynn, *The Draft* (Lawrence: University of Kansas Press, 1993), pp. 135–137.

23. Davis, *The Admiral's Lobby*, p. 5.

24. Vance Mitchell, *Air Force Officers: Personnel Policy Development, 1944–1974* (Washington, D.C.: Air Force History and Museums Program, 1996), p. 59.

25. Mays was drafted in 1952, the year after he won the National League Rookie of the Year award.

26. "Colleges See Lean Pickings in the Fall as Draft Gains Force," *Atlanta Journal,* Jan. 5, 1951.

27. Quoted in Flynn, *The Draft,* p. 150. PFC stands for private first class, a low army enlisted rank.

28. Colonel Eugene Lee to Secretary of the Army, Jan. 27, 1958, Suitland Federal Records Center, Record Group 335, Box 798.

29. Army ROTC, *Quality Is the Answer.*

30. Janowitz, *The Professional Soldier*, p. 45. The "tooth-to-tail" ratio refers to the number of men in combat to the number of men in support. According to Janowitz, the percentage of army enlisted personnel in the tooth went from 93.2 percent in the Civil War to 36.2 percent in World War II to 28.8 percent in 1954. See Janowitz, *The Professional Soldier*, p. 65. This percentage continued to decline well into the Vietnam War era.

31. Report of the Ad Hoc Committee to Study ROTC Programs, Apr. 21, 1961, University of Washington Archives, Allen Library, W. U. Presidents Papers, 71–34, Box 52, Folder 18.

32. Samuel Huntington, "Power, Expertise, and the Military Profession" *Daedalus* 92 (Fall 1963): 785–807, quotation from p. 793.

33. Mitchell, *Air Force Officers*, pp. 50–51.

34. Huntington, "Power, Expertise, and the Military Profession," p. 805 n. 7.

35. Quoted in Maxwell J. Richards, "A Ten-Year History of Air Force ROTC, 1946–1956," M.A. thesis, University of Maryland, 1957, p. 55.

36. Ibid., p. 9.

37. J. Robert Moskin, "Our Military Manpower Scandal," *Look* 22 (Mar. 18, 1958): 27–33.

38. The head of an ROTC unit was usually a colonel (in the navy, a captain).

39. Russell Thackrey, Executive Secretary of AALGCSU, to David Henry, Jan. 23, 1957, University of Illinois Archives, President David Henry Papers, Box 26, ROTC–Air Science Folder. See also Russell Thackrey, "Financing ROTC Programs," in *Role of Colleges*, pp. 37–42, where he discusses the loyalty oath further. The American Association of Land-Grant Colleges and State Universities changed its name to the National Association of State Universities and Land-Grant Colleges in 1962.

40. David Henry to Russell Thackrey, Executive Secretary of AALGCSU, Feb. 8, 1957, University of Illinois Archives, President David Henry Papers, Box 26, ROTC–Air Science Folder.

41. Geiger, *Research and Relevant Knowledge*, p. 53.

42. John Hannah, Statement before the Armed Forces Policy Board, Oct. 1, 1957, University of Illinois Archives, President David Henry Papers, Box 26, ROTC Folder.

43. Monro, "Strengthening the ROTC Curriculum," p. 16.

44. University of Texas, *College of Engineering Catalogue*, 1954–1956; University of Texas, *General Information*, Main University, 1955–56.

45. Frank G. Dickey, President, University of Kentucky, to Major General Frederick Warren, Apr. 28, 1962, Suitland Federal Records Center, Record Group 335, Box 1227.

46. Paul Miller, President, West Virginia University, to Major General Frederick Warren, May 2, 1962, ibid.

47. Right Reverend Wilfrid Nash, President, Gannon College to Major General Frederick Warren, May 2, 1962, ibid.

48. R. H. Woods, President, Murray State College, to Major General Frederick Warren, May 1, 1962, ibid.

49. David Guerrieri, "Open Forum: Unreason at Duquesne," *The Duke,* May 11, 1962.

50. Henry McAnulty to David Guerrieri, May 18, 1962, Duquesne University Archives, ROTC Box 1, ROTC–Army Correspondence 1953–1965.

51. Elvis Stahr, Secretary of the Army to the Secretary of Defense, May 11, 1962, Suitland Federal Records Center, Record Group 335, Box 1227.

52. Major General Frederick Warren to University Presidents, n.d., ibid.

53. Christian Arnold, ed., *Proceedings of the National Association of State Universities and Land-Grant Colleges Seventy-sixth Annual Convention* (Washington, D.C.: NASULGC, 1962), p. 46.

54. As noted earlier, the NASULGC was known as the American Association of Land-Grant Colleges and State Universities until 1962. I am going to take the liberty of using NASULGC exclusively in this section to avoid confusion.

55. Colonel Josef Prall, Assistant Executive, General Staff, to Assistant Secretary of the Army (Manpower, Personnel, and Reserve Forces), Mar. 26, 1957, Suitland Federal Records Center, Record Group 335, Box 798.

56. Frank Millard, General Counsel, to Assistant Secretary of the Army (Manpower, Personnel, and Reserve Forces), Dec. 19, 1957, ibid.

57. As early as 1953, the Air Force Bureau of the Budget had internally proposed a switch to voluntary ROTC in the interests of economy. "A Study Leading to the Development of a Long Range AFROTC Program," unpublished Air University Study [1968], ROTC History Office, Building 78, Maxwell AFB, Montgomery, Alabama.

58. Mitchell, *Air Force Officers,* p. 161.

59. *History of the Air Force Reserve Officers' Training Corps,* Twentieth Anniversary Command Edition, 1966, Air University, Maxwell AFB, Montgomery, Alabama. These arguments proved valid in the end. Although basic enrollments did fall, AFROTC advance enrollments did not immediately fall. "The earlier fear of losing the selection base with the loss of compulsory ROTC was groundless since no appreciable decrease occurred in advance course enrollments due to the wholesale change from compulsory to elective ROTC," p. 33.

60. "ROTC Is Voluntary," *Targum* extra edition, Apr. 26, 1960, p. 1.

61. "Army Recommendations" [1958], University of Illinois Archives, National Association of State Universities and Land-Grant Colleges Papers, Series Number 10/3/57, Box 14, 1958 Folder.

62. Major General J. W. Bowen quoted in *Role of Colleges,* p. 50.

63. Eliot Cohen, *Citizens and Soldiers* (Ithaca, N.Y.: Cornell University Press, 1985), p. 159.

64. "The Battle Is Over," *Targum* extra edition, Apr. 26, 1960, p. 1.

65. "A Word about ROTC," *Targum,* Sept. 11, 1960, p. 1.

66. *History of the AFROTC,* Jan. 1, to June 30, 1964, vol. 8, appendix H, Air Force Historical Research Agency, Maxwell AFB, Montgomery, Alabama.

67. Charles Finucane to C. M. Hardin, President of AALGCSU, Feb. 15, 1960, University of Illinois Archives, Series Number 27/3/5, Box 1.
68. John Hannah, Statement before the Armed Forces Policy Board.
69. Russell Thackrey to Robert Thurston, July 24, 1959, University of Illinois Archives, National Association of State Universities and Land-Grant Colleges Papers, Series Number 10/3/57, Box 14.
70. Russell Thackrey, Executive Secretary, NASULGC, to Jack Raymond, Feb. 17, 1960, ibid.
71. Russell Thackrey to Colonel L. D. Farnsworthy, Apr. 25, 1960, ibid.
72. "Significant Elements in U.S. Army ROTC Program," Dec. 17, 1963, University of Illinois Archives, Series Number 4/2/14, Box 3.
73. David Henry to Carlyle Runge, Assistant Secretary of Defense for Manpower, Mar. 31, 1961, University of Illinois Archives, National Association of State Universities and Land-Grant Colleges Papers, Series Number 10/3/57, Box 14.
74. Richard Harvill, President of University of Arizona, to Major General Frederick Warren, Chief RROTC, Apr. 28, 1962, Suitland Federal Records Center, Record Group 335, Secretary of the Army General Correspondence, Box 1227.
75. Captain John Sibbald, "A History of the Military Department at the University of Illinois, 1868–1964," unpublished paper, 1965, Army ROTC Historical Files, University of Illinois Department of Military Science Library, 0.432.
76. "Army and Air Force ROTC," University of Illinois Archives, National Association of State Universities and Land-Grant Colleges Papers, Series Number 10/3/57, Box 15.
77. Transcript of Meeting of AFROTC Advisory Panel, Dec. 9, 1963, ibid.; *History of the AFROTC.* Uniform cost savings represent the period from 1960 to 1964.
78. "The Battle Is Over."
79. *The Army ROTC at the University of Illinois,* 1965, Army ROTC Historical Files, University of Illinois Department of Military Science, 0.432.

3. The Origins of Postwar Dissatisfaction

1. Mark Grandstaff, "Making the Military American: Advertising, Reform, and the Demise of an Antistanding Military Tradition, 1945–1955." *Journal of Military History* 60 (Apr. 1996): 299–324, quotation from p. 301 n. 7.
2. Samuel Huntington, *The Soldier and the State: The Theory and Politics of Civil-Military Relations* (Cambridge, Mass.: Harvard University Press, 1959), p. 351.
3. Grant Advertising, Chicago, Research Studies for ROTC, September–November 1950, Chief of Army Reserve General Correspondence 1948–1954, National Archives, Record Group 319, Box 50.
4. For Ted, the uniform served as an important identifier. He is shown wearing the uniform to all of his classes, civilian and military. As we will see, Ted's attitude toward his uniform would not be shared by later cadets and midshipmen.
5. "You and the Army ROTC" [1960], University of Illinois Archives, National As-

sociation of State Universities and Land-Grant Colleges Papers, Series Number 10/3/57, Box 15.

6. Leo Bogart's *Social Research and the Desegregation of the United States Army* (Chicago: Markham Publishing, 1969) convincingly argues that the experience of combat for integrated units in the Korean War was crucial to a general acceptance among military personnel of the idea of integration. See also Sherie Mershon and Steven Schlossman, *Foxholes and Color Lines: Desegregating the U.S. Armed Forces* (Baltimore: Johns Hopkins University Press, 1998); Bernard Nalty, *Strength for the Fight* (New York: Free Press, 1986); and Richard Dalfiume, *The Desegregation of the U.S. Armed Forces* (Columbia: University of Missouri Press, 1969).

7. Peter Braestrup, "Rights Unit Asks Congress to End Union Race Bars," *New York Times,* Oct. 14, 1961, p. 1. Recall that the National Guard units were legally under the control of state governors but subject to federal authority. Therefore the Guard units did not necessarily integrate as the rest of the military did. The Hannah Commission wanted the president to use his authority to force integration under threat of federalization.

8. Transcript of Meeting of AFROTC Advisory Panel, Dec. 9, 1963, University of Illinois Archives, National Association of State Universities and Land-Grant Colleges Papers, Series Number 10/3/57, Box 15.

9. Colonel R. W. Koontz, "Equal Opportunity and the AFROTC," presented to the AFROTC Advisory Panel, Dec. 9, 1963, ibid.

10. It should be noted that significant variation existed by region. The highest percentage of students who intended to continue on to advanced ROTC (94.3 percent) came from the Fourth Army area (Texas, Oklahoma, and Arkansas), followed by the Second Army area (including Pennsylvania, Ohio, Virginia, and Maryland) at 75 percent, the First Army area (New England and New York) at 61.8 percent, and the Third Army area (the Southeast) at 57.7 percent. The lowest percentages (39.7 percent and 49.1 percent) came from the Sixth Army area (California, Oregon, and Washington) and the Fifth Army area (Midwest), respectively.

11. Grant Advertising, Research Studies for ROTC. The schools from which students were sampled were: Yale, Fordham, Vermont, NYU, Carnegie Tech, University of Cincinnati, Ohio State, VMI, Howard, Emory, Alabama, Florida, North Carolina State, Oklahoma A & M, Henderson State, Texas A & M, Knox College, Kansas, Nebraska, North Dakota Agricultural, Iowa State, Wyoming, San Jose State, California, and Oregon. The survey can be found in Chief of Army Reserve General Correspondence 1948–1954, National Archives, Record Group 319, Box 50.

12. Associated Students of the University of Washington, "Compulsory ROTC at Washington," Feb. 1, 1961, University of Washington Archives, Allen Library, W. U. Presidents Papers, 71–34, Box 52, Folder 18.

13. Grandstaff, "Making the Military American," pp. 306 and 304.

14. Morris Janowitz, *The Professional Soldier* (Glencoe, Ill.: Free Press, 1960), p. 227.

This survey was conducted by Public Opinion Surveys, Inc. The four professions more highly esteemed by male teenagers than military officer were: physician, scientist, lawyer, and college professor. The national adult sample rated military officer seventh behind physician, scientist, college professor, lawyer, minister or priest, and public school teacher.

15. Grandstaff, "Making the Military American," p. 310.
16. Vance Mitchell, *Air Force Officers: Personnel Policy Development, 1944–1974* (Washington, D.C.: Air Force History and Museums Program, 1996), p. 159.
17. Ibid., pp. 182–183.
18. Ibid., p. 182.
19. Samuel Huntington, "Power, Expertise, and the Military Profession," *Daedalus* 92 (Fall 1963): 785–807, quotation from p. 792.
20. Quoted in Richard Abrams, "The U.S. Military and Higher Education: A Brief History," *Annals of the American Academy of Political and Social Science* 502 (Mar. 1989): 15–28, quotation from p. 24.
21. J. W. Bowles and Donald Torr, *An Attitude Survey of AFROTC Cadets*, Nov. 1955, Air Force Historical Research Agency, Maxwell AFB, Montgomery, Alabama.
22. "Report of the Institutional-USAF Conference on Air Force ROTC Affairs, 9–10 December, 1959, Maxwell AFB, Montgomery, Alabama, p. 16.
23. Russell Thackrey, "Some Current ROTC Problems," in *Current Issues in Higher Education: Proceedings of the Ninth Annual Conference on Higher Education*, Chicago, 1954 (n.p.), p. 299.
24. University of Pittsburgh Military Science Department, *Standing Operating Procedure for Cadets*, Sept. 1, 1954, University of Pittsburgh Archives, Hillman Library, Classification Number 35/2-B, File Folder 1. Recall the pledge pin from the film *Animal House*.
25. *Duquesne University Cadet Handbook: Learn Today, Lead Tomorrow*, 1956, Duquesne University Archives, ROTC Box 1, ROTC 1958–65 Folder. Emphasis in original.
26. *History of the Air University*, Aug. to Dec. 1952, Air Force Historical Research Agency, Maxwell AFB, Montgomery, Alabama, appendix 74, letter from Brigadier General M. K. Deichelmann, AFROTC Commandant, to all PAS, n.d.
27. University of Texas, Department of Military Science, *Army ROTC Cadet Regulations, 1962*. Emphasis in original.
28. Paul Fussell, *Wartime: Understanding and Behavior in the Second World War* (New York: Oxford University Press, 1989), p. 80. The possibilities for abuse were made more rampant by the practice of allowing advanced cadets to drill the basic cadets.
29. *Flight 56* (Texas AFROTC Yearbook), University of Texas Archives, UG 638.8 F5553 TXC 1955/56.
30. University of Texas Center of American History, Department of Military Science Papers, *Army ROTC Cadet Regulations*.
31. *History of the Air Force Reserve Officers' Training Corps*, July 1 to Dec. 31, 1963, Air Force Historical Research Agency, Maxwell AFB, Montgomery, Alabama.

32. The closest analogy in academic settings was engineering, where curricula were set by engineering societies, though those societies certainly had more faculty input than did ROTC curricula. As noted earlier, the professional orientation of engineering colleges helped to reduce levels of dissonance between engineering faculty and the military.

33. The same logic underlay the joint university-military creation of permanent research labs in the Cold War era. See Roger Geiger, *Research and Relevant Knowledge: American Research Universities Since World War II* (New York: Oxford University Press, 1993), p. 14.

34. Maxwell J. Richards, "A Ten-Year History of Air Force ROTC, 1946–1956," M.A. thesis, University of Maryland, 1957, p. 11.

35. "For Wider ROTC Plan," *New York Times,* Nov. 4, 1953, p. 25, col. 3.

36. Gene Lyons and John Masland, *Education and Military Leadership: A Study of the ROTC* (Princeton, N.J.: Princeton University Press, 1959), p. 12. This study was funded by the Carnegie Corporation as part of a large grant given to several schools to study international affairs. The authors were in Dartmouth's School of Government. The impact of Korea is noted in "A Study Leading to the Development of a Long Range AFROTC Program," unpublished Air University Study [1968], ROTC History Office, Building 78, Maxwell AFB, Montgomery, Alabama, pp. 52–53.

37. The number of specializations themselves grew from just 24 in the World War II–era Army Air Corps to more than 300 by the beginning of the 1960s. See Mitchell, *Air Force Officers,* chap. 11.

38. Lyons and Masland, *Education and Military Leadership,* p. 13

39. Quoted in Benjamin Fine, "Army Will Spread Change in ROTC," *New York Times,* May 10, 1953, p. 26, col. 3.

40. Lyons and Masland, *Education and Military Leadership,* p. 183.

41. [W. H. S. Wright], Headquarters, U.S. Continental Command, Ft. Monroe, Virginia, Senior Division Army ROTC Program, Jan. 27, 1964, Suitland Federal Records Center, Secretary of the Army General Correspondence, Record Group 335, Box 1228.

42. University of Colorado NROTC, *Knots and Fathoms,* 1953, University of Colorado at Boulder Library, Archives, 378.788 Un3PK 1953.

43. *History of the Air University,* Aug. to Dec. 1952, p. 48.

44. Quoted in Lyons and Masland, *Education and Military Leadership,* p. 180.

45. Grant Advertising, Research Studies for ROTC. The ad certainly seems patronizing and even insulting in retrospect, but Grant Advertising's research indicated that Ted was a hit. Their survey of 1,500 college men (half of whom were not in ROTC) from twenty-six schools nationwide showed that only 6.6 percent remembered not liking the ad.

46. *Kent State University Bulletin: The Reserve Officer Training Corps Program,* Aug. 1952, Kent State University Archives, Series Number 33.13.3.

47. Paul Wolff, Army PMS, to Alan Rankin, Oct. 10, 1960, University of Pittsburgh Archives, Hillman Library, Classification Number 55/1, File Folder 188.

48. "Transfer of Air Force ROTC Responsibilities," supporting document 33.

49. *The University of Pittsburgh School of Liberal Arts Bulletin,* 1961–1962, p. 1.

50. H. Malcolm Macdonald to Vice Admiral H. P. Smith, Oct. 27, 1958, University of Texas President's Office Records, VF 30/A.b, Naval Science 1958–59 Folder.

51. *The University of Pittsburgh College Bulletin, 1950–1951,* p. 81.

52. *Kent State University Bulletin,* 1952.

53. Agreement regarding Credit Applicable towards Graduation, Feb. 16, 1954, University of Texas President's Office Records, VF 20/A.b, ROTC General, 1953 Folder.

54. *The University of Pittsburgh School of Liberal Arts Bulletin,* 1961–1962, pp. 4–5; *The University of Pittsburgh School of Engineering and Mines Bulletin,* 1964–66, p. 32. By way of comparison, the freshman English composition course was worth 6 credits.

55. Gordon Ray to Colonel Howder, Aug. 27, 1957, University of Illinois Archives, President David Henry Papers, Box 26, ROTC—Air Science Folder.

56. "Rot-Cee Ranks," *Newsweek,* Feb. 24, 1964.

57. Report of the Executive Committee Meeting of the Association of NROTC Colleges, Oct. 30, 1950, University of Texas President's Office Records, VF 17/C.a, Association of NROTC Colleges Folder.

58. Hanson Baldwin, "The ROTC—III," *New York Times,* Aug. 27, 1960, p. 8, col. 2.

59. Royen Dangerfeld to Colonel L. J. Rohrs, Jan. 4, 1960, University of Illinois Archives, President David Henry Papers, Box 51, ROTC—Air Science Folder.

60. Colonel J. D. Howder to President David Henry, Jan. 30, 1958, ibid., Box 26, ROTC—Air Science Folder.

61. John Lisack, "Qualitative Educational Requirements for Air Force Officers," n.d., American Society of Mechanical Engineers Paper Number 63-AHGT-83, located in the James Shelburne Papers, Maxwell AFB, Montgomery, Alabama, 168.7036–32, vol. 5.

62. *History of the Air University,* Jan. 1, to June 30, 1964, vol. 8, appendix H.

63. O. Meredith Wilson, President, University of Minnesota, to Elvis Stahr, Secretary of the Army, June 15, 1962, Suitland Federal Records Center, Record Group 335, Box 1227.

64. E. R. Durgin, Secretary-Treasurer, Association of NROTC Colleges, to K. L. Nutting, Assistant, Director, Center for Naval Education and Training, Jan. 29, 1957, University of Illinois Archives, President David Henry Papers, Box 26, ROTC—Naval Science Folder.

65. Lewis Jones to H. F. Harding, June 9, 1958, Rutgers University Archives, Office of the President (Lewis W. Jones), Box 10, Air Force ROTC Folder.

66. H. F. Harding, Chairman, Air Science Department, Ohio State University, to President Henry, Apr. 10, 1958, University of Illinois Archives, President David Henry Papers, Box 26, ROTC Folder.

67. Major General T. C. Rogers, USAF ROTC Commandant, to President Henry, May 5, 1958, ibid.

68. Ray Hawk, "A New Program for the AFROTC," *Journal of Higher Education* 31 (Feb. 1960): 103–106.

69. Jerome Rosenberg, Secretary, Senate Educational Policies Committee, to Dr.

Edward Litchfield, Chancellor, Apr. 30, 1959, University of Pittsburgh Archives, Hillman Library, Classification Number 55/1, File Folder 186.

70. Alan Rankin, "Report on Progress in Implementing the Recommendations of the Educational Policies Committee of the University Senate with Regard to the ROTC Programs," Nov. 13, 1959, ibid.

71. "The Revolution at Service Academies," *U.S. News and World Report,* Dec. 2, 1963, pp. 75–77.

72. "Updating the Academies," *Time,* Sept. 7, 1959, p. 61.

73. Alan Rankin to Edward Litchfield, Dec. 18, 1959, University of Pittsburgh Archives, Hillman Library, Classification Number 55/1, File Folder 190.

74. Major General Frederick Warren to Russell Thackrey, Feb. 12, 1960, University of Illinois Archives, National Association of State Universities and Land-Grant Colleges Papers, Series Number 10/3/57, Box 14.

75. Telegram from Army ROTC Adjutant General [Major General Frederick Warren] to David Henry, Feb. 15, 1960, University of Illinois Archives, President David Henry Papers, Box 51, ROTC—Miscellaneous Folder.

76. Funari to Alan Rankin, May 12, 1960. University of Pittsburgh Archives, Hillman Library, Classification Number 55/1, File Folder 186.

77. Captain J. A. Lark, quoted in *The Role of Colleges and Universities in ROTC Programs* (Columbus: Ohio State University Press, 1960), p. 57.

78. Grant Advertising, Research Studies for ROTC.

79. Report of the Meeting of the Army Advisory Panel on ROTC Affairs, Apr. 25, 1961, University of Pittsburgh Archives, Hillman Library, Classification Number 55/1, File Folder 188.

80. "ROTC Proposals," *New York Times,* July 17, 1960, sec. 4, p. 7, col. 6.

81. "ROTC Presents New Curriculum," *The Technique,* Feb. 19, 1960, p. 1, col. 4; "Army, Air Force ROTC Reduce Hours to Afford More Academic Study Time," *The Technique,* Oct. 20, 1961, p. 6, col. 3. The Army ROTC followed the AFROTC's lead, reducing time in the freshman year by one-third. See "Army ROTC Unit Submits Proposed Major Change," *The Technique,* Nov. 18, 1960, p. 1, col. 1.

4. The ROTC Vitalization Act, 1964–1968

1. C. Wright Mills, *The Power Elite* (New York: Oxford University Press, 1956), p. 217.

2. Ibid., pp. 218–219.

3. Dwight D. Eisenhower, Farewell Address, Jan. 17, 1961.

4. SDS's early activities focused more on civil rights than on the Vietnam War, but many members quickly came to argue that American prosecution of the war overseas and racism at home were linked. For more on New Left origins, see Todd Gitlin's *The Sixties: Years of Hope, Days of Rage* (New York: Bantam Books, 1987).

5. Roger Geiger argues that the consensus of the 1950s was that government

influence did *not* greatly affect research and education missions. It should also be noted that the DOD's relative share of the federal dollars flowing to universities was declining due to the enlarging support coming from the National Science Foundation and NASA. See Geiger's *Research and Relevant Knowledge: American Research Universities since World War II* (New York: Oxford University Press, 1993).

6. *History of the Air Force Reserve Officers' Training Corps*, July 1 to Dec. 31, 1962, Air Force Historical Research Agency, Maxwell AFB, Montgomery, Alabama; Lieutenant General W. H. S. Wright, Chief Officer of Reserve Components, U.S. Army, to Harlan Hatcher, Nov. 18, 1963, University of Michigan Archives, Bentley Historical Library, Harlan Hatcher Papers, Box 37, Folder 11.

7. Mershon National Security Program, *Role of the Colleges and Universities in ROTC Programs* (Columbus: Ohio State University Press, 1960), statement of Colonel William Lindley.

8. Background Information to ROTC Information Plan, [1964], Suitland Federal Records Center, Secretary of the Army General Correspondence, Record Group 335, Box 1228. In 1949 the services and the DOD agreed not to merge the three ROTC programs into one large officer-training program. At the same time, they set compatibility as a goal to reduce competition among the programs.

9. *History of the Air University*, Jan. 1 to June 30, 1964. Air Force Historical Research Agency, Maxwell AFB, Montgomery, Alabama, Call Number K239.01, vol. 8, appendix H.

10. Lieutenant General W. H. S. Wright to Harlan Hatcher.

11. "Significant Elements in U.S. Army ROTC Program," Dec. 17, 1963, University of Illinois Archives, Series Number 4/2/14, Box 3.

12. Gordon Moon, "ROTC on the Rebound," *Army* (Aug. 1967): 46–55.

13. *History of the Air University.*

14. Lieutenant General W. H. S. Wright to Harlan Hatcher.

15. Robert Williams to Dean James Wallace, Nov. 6, 1962, University of Michigan Archives, Bentley Historical Library, Vice-President for Academic Affairs Papers, Box 39, ROTC General, 1957–1962 Folder.

16. "Proceedings of the 26 October 1962 Meeting of the Army Advisory Panel on ROTC Affairs," Duquesne University Archives, ROTC Box 1, ROTC—Army Correspondence 1953–1965.

17. George Flynn, *The Draft* (Lawrence: University of Kansas Press, 1993), p. 168.

18. Philip Caputo, *A Rumor of War* (New York: Ballantine Books, 1977), p. 7.

19. Ebert's lens on student life is located in "Rot-Cee Ranks," *Newsweek*, Feb. 24, 1964, p. 84.

20. *History of the Air University.*

21. "A Study Leading to the Development of a Long Range AFROTC Program," unpublished Air University study, ROTC History Office, Building 78, Maxwell AFB, Montgomery, Alabama. Benjamin Fridge, Special Assistant to the Secretary of the Air Force for Manpower, Personnel, and Reserve Forces, *Statement*

before Subcommittee no. 3, Committee on Armed Services, House of Representatives, September 1963, University of Illinois Archives, National Association of State Universities and Land-Grant Colleges Papers, Series Number 10/3/57, Box 15.

22. *History of the Air University.*
23. "Conclusions of the Army Advisory Panel on ROTC Affairs, 25 April 1961," Duquesne University Archives, ROTC Box 1, ROTC—Army Correspondence 1953–1965.
24. "Proceedings of the 26 October 1962 Meeting of the Army Advisory Panel on ROTC Affairs," ibid.
25. *History of the Air University.*
26. Association of State Universities and Land-Grant Colleges Circular Letter #5, Feb. 27, 1963, University of Illinois Archives, Series Number 4/6/26, Box 1.
27. "Report of the Military Affairs Committee," Oct. 1, 1963, ibid., Series Number 4/2/14, Box 3.
28. *History of AFROTC,* July 1 to Dec. 31, 1964.
29. Quotation from "Rot-Cee Ranks." In 1963, 23 percent of AFROTC cadets graduated from engineering programs. Shortly afterward, the air force set a goal of having 60 percent of its graduates come from engineering. *History of the Air University,* Jan. 1 to June 30, 1964, vol. 6.
30. *History of the AFROTC,* July 1 to Dec. 31, 1962.
31. Russell Thackrey to Oliver Meadows, Dec. 13, 1963, University of Illinois Archives, National Association of State Universities and Land-Grant Colleges Papers, Series Number 10/3/57, Box 15. Emphasis in original.
32. Christian Arnold, ed., *Proceedings of the Association of State Universities and Land-Grant Colleges Seventy-seventh Annual Convention,* Chicago, 1963 (n.p.), p. 60.
33. Christian Arnold, ed., *Proceedings of the Association of State Universities and Land-Grant Colleges Seventy-sixth Annual Convention,* Washington, D.C., 1962 (n.p.), p. 72.
34. Congressman Hébert forced the defeat of the bill in the 1963 session when he blocked the "Powell Amendment" from being added. The Powell Amendment would have denied federal funds to any ROTC host school that practiced segregation. By the time the bill came up in the 1964 session, Congress had already passed the Civil Rights Act, making the Powell Amendment superfluous.
35. Hébert was particularly interested in the development of the Junior ROTC program (for high school). He devoted much of his time on the bill to expanding the JROTC program nationwide. The Senate authorized fewer JROTC units than Hébert wanted, but the total program was nonetheless expanded dramatically. James D. Hittle, interview with the author, Aug. 5, 1997.
36. *Congressional Record* (June 23, 1964) vol. 110, p. 14686.
37. "The New Air Force Curriculum," May 29, 1964, Kent State University Archives, President Robert White Papers, Folder 14, Army and Air Force ROTC Correspondence, 1962–1964.
38. Morris Janowitz, *The Professional Soldier,* (Glencoe, Ill.: Free Press, 1960), p. 41.
39. Lieutenant Colonel G. A. Payne, Assistant Adjutant General to Chief of Office

of Reserve Components, Feb. 28, 1964, Suitland Federal Records Center, Secretary of the Army General Correspondence, Record Group 335, Box 1228.

40. [W. H. S. Wright], Headquarters, U.S. Continental Command, Ft. Monroe, Virginia, Senior Division Army ROTC Program, Jan. 27, 1964, Suitland Federal Records Center, Secretary of the Army General Correspondence, Record Group 335, Box 1228.

41. *History of the AFROTC,* July 1 to Dec. 31, 1964; U.S. Army Command Information Unit, *Army ROTC Newsletter,* June 1965, Duquesne University Archives, ROTC Box 1, ROTC 1958–65 Folder. Ninety-four air force and 213 army units chose to open two-year programs, maintaining their four-year programs as well.

42. *United States Army Command Information Fact Sheet #53,* May 25, 1966, United States Army Center of Military History, Washington, D.C., Decimal Number 326.6.

43. [W. H. S. Wright], Senior Division Army ROTC Program.

44. David Henry to Brigadier General William Lindley, May 8, 1964, University of Illinois Archives, President David Henry Papers, Box 123, ROTC—Air Science; Robert White to Ohio Senators, Sept. 18, 1964, Kent State University Archives, President Robert White Papers, Folder 19, Army ROTC Correspondence, 1964–1965.

45. "Rot-Cee Ranks," p. 84.

46. *Congressional Record* (June 23, 1964), vol. 110, pp. 14685–6.

47. "Rot-Cee Ranks," p. 84.

48. Clair Worthy, University of Illinois Professor of Military Science, to Royen Dangerfeld, Aug. 13, 1964, University of Illinois Archives, President David Henry Papers, Box 123, ROTC—Military Science.

49. [W. H. S. Wright], Senior Division Army ROTC Program.

50. Robert Williams to the Committee on ROTC Affairs, March 31, 1969, University of Michigan Archives, Bentley Historical Library, Vice-President for Academic Affairs Papers, Box 39, Advisory Committee on ROTC Affairs Folder.

51. Robert Clifford to Stephen Ailes, Secretary of the Army, Dec. 27, 1964, Suitland Federal Records Center, Record Group 335, Box 1228.

52. Robert Williams to Arthur Stone, Dec. 8, 1964, University of Michigan Archives, Bentley Historical Library, University of Michigan Vice-President for Academic Affairs Papers, Box 39, ROTC—Air Force 1964 Folder.

53. "Ford Grants to Liberal Arts Colleges," *School and Society* (Nov. 18, 1961): 388–389. The five grant recipients with ROTC programs were Brown, Johns Hopkins, Notre Dame, Stanford, and Vanderbilt.

54. *NASULGC Circular Letter #38,* Nov. 4, 1965, University of Michigan Archives, Bentley Historical Library, Vice-President for Academic Affairs Papers, Box 39, ROTC General, 1965 Folder.

55. Robert Williams to ROTC Staff, Nov. 19, 1965, ibid.

56. Moon, "ROTC on the Rebound."

57. *History of the AFROTC,* Twentieth Anniversary Command Edition, 1966.

58. *History of the AFROTC,* Jan. 1 to June 30, 1966. The percentage of transfers from junior colleges was lower than the air force had hoped despite several programs, including the assignment of ROTC units to recruit and publicize the two-year option at nearby junior colleges. This trend mirrored larger trend in American higher education: junior college students did not transfer to four-year schools in the numbers educators had anticipated.

59. Major John Rogers, Acting Professor of Military Science, to Harold Roskens, Dec. 13, 1965, Kent State University Archives, Robert White Papers, Folder 29, Army ROTC Correspondence 1965–1966.

60. Army ROTC Unit, University of Pittsburgh, to David Kurtzman, Mar. 1, 1966, University of Pittsburgh Archives 2/10 1966/67 Box 26, File Folder 243. The University of Pittsburgh system then included campuses in Bradford, Greensburg, Johnstown, and Titusville. See Robert Alberts, *Pitt: The Story of the University of Pittsburgh, 1787–1987* (Pittsburgh: University of Pittsburgh Press, 1986), p. 343.

61. *Annual Report,* Department of Military Science, Academic Year 1968–1969, University of Washington Archives, Allen Library, W. U. Reserve Officers Training Corps Program, Military Science, 95–289, V.F. 2457.

62. *History of the AFROTC,* July 1 to June 30, 1967.

63. "Rot-Cee Ranks," p. 84.

64. Colonel Rashid to Mary Helen Pendel, Mar. 6, 1964, Duquesne University Archives, ROTC Box 1, ROTC History Folder.

65. "Significant Elements in U.S. Army ROTC Program."

66. Lupe Zamarripa, "Commission Possible from ROTC Program," *Daily Texan,* Aug. 19, 1966.

67. "Significant Elements in U.S. Army ROTC Program."

68. Flynn, *The Draft,* p. 197.

69. Ibid., p. 199.

70. Quoted in Dan Booker, "ROTC Enrollment Up 70 Percent," *Pitt News,* Sept. 12, 1966, p. 1.

71. Booker, "ROTC Enrollment Up 70 Percent."

72. Interestingly, membership in female auxiliary societies was at even higher levels than those of the male honor societies. This subject is covered more fully in Chapter 6.

73. "Worcester Polytech Institute Conducts Mock Invasion of Middleboro, Mass." *New York Times,* May 2, 1966, p. 40, col. 6.

74. Frank Fischer, PMS, to President Odegaard, Feb. 1, 1967, University of Washington Archives, Allen Library, W. U. Presidents Papers, 71–34, Box 39, Folder 3.

75. Julie Emery, "Cadets Trained to 'Spy' on Left-Wing Groups," *Seattle Times,* Jan. 25, 1967, ibid., "Statement of George Smith, AROTC Senior," n.d., ibid; President Odegaard to Lieutenant General James Richardson, Nov. 3, 1966, ibid.

76. During the briefing, cadets had been shown a slide explaining how to identify

subversive groups. The slide read: "If it walks like a duck, talks like a duck, and lays eggs like a duck, then it is a duck." See "Army Makes Spies Out of Students; Cadets Snoop on SNCC, SDS," *Sunday Ramparts* [1966], ibid; "ROTC Topic for Program," *The Washington Daily,* Feb. 16, 1967, p. 5.

77. "ROTC Invited," *The Washington Daily,* Feb. 17, 1967, p. 2.

78. Clair Worthy to Royen Dangerfield, August 13, 1964.

79. "Working Paper from the Report from the Subcommittee on the Navy," Committee on Officer Education, July 1, 1965, University of Washington Archives, Allen Library, W. U. Presidents Papers, 71–34, Box 53, Folder 2.

80. *History of the Air University,* Jan. 1 to June 30, 1964.

81. Association of NROTC Colleges Minutes, Dec. 13, 1965, University of Illinois Archives, President David Henry Papers, Box 154, ROTC—Naval Science.

82. *History of the AFROTC,* July 1 to Dec. 31, 1965.

83. Clair Worthy to Royen Dangerfield, Aug. 13, 1964.

84. [Colonel C. E. Curran], "Recommendations of the PMS, 1965," University of Illinois Army ROTC Historical Files, Military Science Department Library, 0.432.

85. *History of the AFROTC,* Twentieth Anniversary Command Edition.

86. "Officer Training and Education," *Naval Training Bulletin* (Fall 1965), Air Force Historical Research Agency, J. C. Shelburne Papers, Call Number 168.7036–32, vol. 5.

87. Association of NROTC Colleges Minutes, Dec. 13, 1965. In some cases, the universities accepted advanced degrees from a service school, such as one of the war colleges, as a substitute for a Masters degree, but they did not wish to do so as a matter of policy.

88. J. W. Briscoe, Associate Provost, to Brigadier General Joseph Jones, Apr. 8, 1966, University of Illinois Archives, President David Henry Papers, Box 154, ROTC—Military Science.

89. *History of the AFROTC,* Twentieth Anniversary Command Edition.

90. Lieutenant General J. H. Michaels to David Henry, April 14, 1967, University of Illinois Archives, President David Henry Papers, Box 176, ROTC—Military Science.

91. "Working Paper from the Report From the Subcommittee on the Navy," and "Working Paper from the Report from the Subcommittee on the Air Force," Committee on Officer Education, July 1, 1965, University of Washington Archives, Allen Library, W. U. Presidents Papers, 71–34, Box 53, Folder 2.

92. *History of the AFROTC,* Jan. 1 to June 30, 1966. Emphasis in original.

93. "Awarding Academic Credit for ROTC Courses," Army Advisory Panel on ROTC Affairs, Oct. 26, 1967, University of Illinois Archives, National Association of State Universities and Land-Grant Colleges Papers, Series Number 10/3/57, Box 15.

94. "Credit for AFROTC Courses," Air University presentation to the AFROTC Advisory Panel, Dec. 5, 1966, ibid.

95. H. Malcolm Macdonald to Brigadier General William Lindley, Mar. 23, 1965, University of Texas President's Office Records, VF37/C.b, Air Force Science 1960–1968 Folder.

96. Leslie Gelb and Richard Betts, *The Irony of Vietnam: The System Worked* (Washington, D.C.: Brookings Institute, 1979), p. 130.

97. George Herring, *America's Longest War: The United States and Vietnam, 1950–1975* (New York: McGraw-Hill, 1986), p. 146.

98. "ROTC History: University of Illinois at Urbana-Champaign" [1965], University of Illinois Military Science Department Library, Army ROTC Historical Files, 0.432.

99. Benjamin Hollis to Dr. Crawford, Acting Chancellor, "Possible Subversive Activity," Sept. 27, 1965, University of Pittsburgh Archives 2/10 1966/67, Box 26, File Folder 243.

100. "Students Protest against ROTC," *Pitt News*, Nov. 3, 1967, p. 7.

101. Don Marbury, "University Professor Argues ROTC Should Be Abolished," *Pitt News*, Nov. 15, 1967, p. 3, col. 1.

102. "Korona Evaluates ROTC Course," *Targum*, Sept. 12, 1967.

103. Gelb and Betts, *The Irony of Vietnam*, p. 162.

104. "Korona Evaluates ROTC Course."

105. Colonel R. J. Jackson to Robert White, Oct. 26, 1967, Kent State University Archives, Robert White Papers, Folder 30, Army ROTC Correspondence, 1967–1968.

106. "Officer Says Sit-In Will Help ROTC," *Targum*, Nov. 13, 1967.

107. Janowitz, *The Professional Soldier*, p. 429.

5. ROTC from Tet to the All-Volunteer Force

1. Quoted in George Herring, *America's Longest War: The United States and Vietnam, 1950–1975* (New York: McGraw-Hill, 1979), p. 91.

2. Quoted in Todd Gitlin, *The Sixties: Years of Hope, Days of Rage* (New York: Bantam Books, 1987), p. 300.

3. Neil Sheehan, *A Bright Shining Lie: John Paul Vann and America in Vietnam* (New York: Random House, 1988), p. 717.

4. Gitlin, *The Sixties,* p. 301.

5. Leslie Gelb and Richard Betts, *The Irony of Vietnam: The System Worked* (Washington, D.C.: Brookings Institute, 1979), p. 163.

6. This wonderful phrase belongs to Roger Geiger. See *Research and Relevant Knowledge: American Research Universities since World War II* (New York: Oxford University Press, 1993), chap. 8.

7. Gitlin, *The Sixties,* p. 300.

8. Sheehan, *A Bright Shining Lie,* pp. 717–718.

9. "ROTC under Fire," *Wall Street Journal,* Mar. 22, 1968.

10. Quoted in Gitlin, *The Sixties,* p. 285.

11. Ileana Brown, *History of the Air Force Reserve Officers Training Corps,* July 1, 1967

to June 30, 1968, Air Force Historical Research Agency, Maxwell Air Force Base, Montgomery, Alabama. Call Number K239.07 K.

12. *History of the AFROTC,* July 1, 1968 to June 30, 1969, AFROTC History Office, Maxwell AFB, Montgomery, Alabama.

13. David Rosenblum, "Today's Next Court Case: ROTC versus 'Democracy,'" *Pitt News,* Oct. 25, 1968, p. 5.

14. Ed Moss, "ROTC: Controversial Comment, Official Facts and Apology," *Pitt News,* Nov. 1 1968, p. 4. Emphasis added.

15. Noel Schutz, "Understanding Student Dissent," *Air University Air Force ROTC Education Bulletin* (Feb. 1969), p. 6.

16. Department of Defense, *Selected Manpower Statistics,* May 1978, p. 109.

17. Andrew Malcom, "New Enrollment in College ROTC Shows Sharp Dip," *New York Times,* Oct. 20, 1969, p. 1, col. 1.

18. "Statement regarding ROTC Programs from National Association of State Universities and Land-Grant Colleges," Mar. 18, 1970, University of Illinois Archives, Chancellor's Office Papers, Series Number 24/1/1, Box 42, Armed Forces Folder.

19. *Summary Report: Status of Reserve Officer Training Corps Programs at AAU Member Institutions* [1969], University of Illinois Archives, National Association of State Universities and Land-Grant Colleges Papers, Series Number 10/3/57, Box 16.

20. M. R. Rose to Joy Klieger, Sept. 19, 1969, University of Pittsburgh Archives, Hillman Library, Classification Number 3/1/1, File Folder 232.

21. "ROTC Enrollments and Number of Commissioned Officers," n.d., University of Illinois Archives, President David Henry Papers, Box 235, ROTC Folder.

22. *Air Force ROTC Bulletin,* Dec. 1970, p. 22.

23. "ROTC under Fire."

24. Robert C. McMath et al., *Engineering the New South: Georgia Tech, 1885–1985* (Athens: University of Georgia Press, 1985), p. 388; Wayne Bridges to President Hansen, May 28, 1970, Georgia Institute of Technology Library and Information Center, 86–05–01, Office of the President Records, 1961–1972, Box 14, Folder 33.

25. Herring, *America's Longest War,* p. 243.

26. Sheehan, *A Bright Shining Lie,* p. 741. Lieutenant General Harold (Hal) Moore, USA (Ret.), was an American field commander at the first large-scale battle between American ground troops and North Vietnamese soldiers. His account of the 1965 battle in the Ia Drang Valley can be found in Harold Moore and Joseph Galloway, *We Were Soldiers Once—And Young: Ia Drang, the Battle That Changed the War in Vietnam* (New York: Random House, 1992).

27. This is, of course, not to deny the brutality of the war before Tet. For more on the nature of the war following Tet, see Ronald Spector, *After Tet: The Bloodiest Year in Vietnam* (New York: Free Press, 1993).

28. For more on the origins and controversies of the lottery system, see George Q. Flynn, *The Draft* (Lawrence: University of Kansas Press, 1993), chap. 9.

29. Robert Goldrich, "The Senior Reserve Officer Training Corps: Recent Trends

and Current Status," Apr. 19, 1974, Library of Congress Congressional Research Service, p. 24.

30. B. B. Cassiday, "Report to the AFROTC Advisory Panel," Sept. 18, 1972, University of Illinois Archives, President John Corbally Papers, Box 33, ROTC—Air Force.

31. *Air Force ROTC Bulletin,* Dec. 1970, p. 23. Only 9 percent said they had joined because of a "desire to make the Air Force a career."

32. Cassiday, "Report to the AFROTC Advisory Panel."

33. Lawrence Baskir and William Strauss, *Chance and Circumstance: The Draft, the War, and the Vietnam Generation* (New York: Alfred A. Knopf, 1978), p. 54.

34. University of Pittsburgh ROTC Departments, recruiting poster, 1969, University of Pittsburgh Archives, Hillman Library, Classification Number 35-A, File Folder 3.

35. "Join the Army and See the World," *The Technique,* Feb. 13 1970, p. 3, col. 1.

36. Arthur Hansen to Joseph Spitler, Dec. 1, 1970, Georgia Institute of Technology Library and Information Center, 86–05–01, Office of the President Records, 1961–1972, Box 14, Folder 33.

37. Goldrich, "The Senior Reserve Officer Training Corps," p. 26.

38. Compare these findings to the responses of AFROTC graduates in 1963. When asked, "What one factor was most influential in causing you to seek an Air Force commission?" the draft appeared fourth, after the opportunity to fly, prestige, and career opportunities. See "Summary of Precommissioning Questionnaire," in *History of the AFROTC,* July 1 to Dec. 31, 1963, Air Force Historical Research Agency. Call Number K239.07 K.

39. Kingman Brewster, President, Yale University, Text of Special Report to Alumni, Feb. 22, 1969, University of Pittsburgh Archives, Hillman Library, Classification Number 3/1/1, File Folder 238.

40. Michael Duto quoted in Peter Karsten, "Anti-ROTC: Response to Vietnam or 'Consciousness III'?" in John Lovell and Philip Kronenberg, eds., *New Civil-Military Relations: The Agonies of Adjustment to Post-Vietnam Realities* (New Brunswick, N.J.: Transaction Books, 1974): 111–127. Quotation from p. 113.

41. Andrew H. Malcom, "New Enrollment in College ROTC Shows Sharp Dip," *New York Times,* Oct. 20, 1969, p. 1, col. 1.

42. Michael Kaufman, "Two Students Challenge ROTC Regulations on Hair," ibid., May 28, 1970, p. 41, col. 1.

43. Quoted in Karsten, "Anti-ROTC," pp. 113–114.

44. "End Credit, Faculty Status for ROTC" (editorial), *Daily Illini,* Feb. 27, 1970.

45. Quoted in "ROTC under Fire."

46. Students for a Democratic Society, "ROTC Marches On" [Oct. 1970], University of Michigan Archives, Bentley Historical Library, President's Papers, Box 23, ROTC Folder.

47. "SDS Ejects United Fruit Rep.," *The Washington Daily,* Feb. 25, 1969, p. 1.

48. Bruce Drake, "The Battle over ROTC," *Johns Hopkins Magazine* (Spring 1969): 3–4.

49. *History of the AFROTC,* July 1, 1968 to June 30, 1969.

50. *History of the Air University,* Fiscal Year 1970, Air Force Historical Research Agency, Maxwell AFB, Montgomery, Alabama. Call Number K239.01.

51. Ibid., "Windows Smashed in Protest," *New York Times,* Feb. 2 1970, p. 10.

52. "Report of the Department of Military Science, Academic Year 1969–70," University of Illinois Army ROTC Historical Files, Military Science Department Library, 0.432.

53. Fleming also believed that at Michigan the student radicals "didn't play into [the decision-making on ROTC] very much." Robben Fleming, interview with the author, Ann Arbor, Mich., Dec. 12, 1995.

54. Paul Stoller, "Students Appeal for Vietnam Negotiations in Referendum," ibid., Jan. 25, 1968, p. 1; "SG Referendum," *Pitt News,* Nov. 20 1968, p. 1. The January referendum attracted 2,422 voters. The November referendum attracted 3,869 voters.

55. Kent State University News Service, Aug. 14, 1970, Kent State University Archives, Charles Kegley May 4th Materials 34.13, Box 102, Folder 44.

56. National Association of State Universities and Land-Grant Colleges, Circular Number 154, June 30, 1970; Kent State University Archives, Charles Kegley May 4th Materials 34.13, Box 102, Folder 42.

57. James Foley and Robert Foley, *The College Scene: Students Tell It Like It Is* (New York: Cowles Books, 1969), p. 126.

58. Ibid., pp. 31 and 130–131.

59. Brigadier General Donald Blake to AFROTC Advisory Panel, Aug. 13, 1969, University of Illinois Archives, President David Henry Papers, Box 235, ROTC—Air Science.

60. National Association of State Universities and Land-Grant Colleges, Circular Number 154.

61. "Notes from the Thirty-First Meeting of the Faculty of Rutgers College," May 18, 1970, Rutgers University Archives, President Gross Papers, Box 28, File ROTC 1969–1971. Emphasis mine.

62. Yale University News Bureau, Feb. 22, 1969, Historical Society of Western Pennsylvania, Robert McConnell Papers, Box 1 Folder 8.

63. Damaine Martin, "ROTC Open Forum: The Good Guys vs. The Bad Guys?" *Pitt News,* Nov. 25, 1968, p. 1.

64. "Statement of M. J. Sinnott before the Academic Affairs Committee" [June 25, 1969], University of Michigan Archives, Bentley Historical Library, Vice-President for Academic Affairs Papers, Box 18, ROTC 1968–69 Folder. Despite the ECPD's oversight, a limited number of engineering schools, such as that at the University of Illinois, allowed ROTC credit to count toward elective credit.

65. James Gindin, Carl Cohen, John LaPrelle and Locke Anderson, "Report from the Curriculum Committee on the Issue of Accreditation for ROTC," Mar. 25, 1969, University of Michigan Navy ROTC Accreditation/Relations File 1969, North Hall.

66. "Student Affairs Committee of the University Senate Recommendation," Apr.

4, 1968, University of Pittsburgh Archives, Hillman Library, Provost Office Files 1965–1970, Classification Number 3/1/1, File Folder 239.

67. Princeton University, "Report of the Ad Hoc Committee on ROTC to the University Faculty," Mar. 3, 1969, Historical Society of Western Pennsylvania, Robert McConnell Papers, Box 1, Folder 8.

68. "Report to [Urbana-Champaign] Senate on ROTC Matters," May 7, 1970, University of Illinois Archives, Chancellor's Office Papers, Series Number 24/1/1, Box 42, Armed Forces Folder.

69. J. W. Briscoe to Colonel Frank Bexfield [Maxwell AFB], Dec. 30, 1968, University of Illinois Archives, President David Henry Papers, Box 213, ROTC—Air Force.

70. Quoted in Dave Kuhns, "ROTC 'Dis-Credited,'" *Pitt News,* Dec. 4, 1968, p. 1.

71. H. Malcolm Macdonald to Theodore Marrs, Oct. 1, 1968, University of Texas President's Office Records, VF 20/A.b, ROTC Air Science 1968–1969 Folder.

72. "Notes from the Thirty-First Meeting of the Faculty of Rutgers College," May 18, 1970, Rutgers University Archives, President Gross Papers, Box 28, ROTC 1969–1971 File.

73. Cornell University, "Report of the Special Faculty Committee on Military Training," Nov. 14, 1969, University of Pittsburgh Archives, Hillman Library, Provost Office Files 1965–1970, Classification Number 3/1/1, File Folder 233.

74. Colonel Arthur Wade to Colonel David Clagett, Feb. 24, 1969, Robert McConnell Papers, Historical Society of Western Pennsylvania, Box 1, Folder 8.

75. "Student Affairs Committee of the University Senate Recommendation"; Princeton University, "Report of the Ad Hoc Committee on ROTC to the University Faculty."

76. "Recommendations of the Advisory Committee on Educational Policies," July 22, 1969, University of Michigan Archives, Bentley Historical Library, Vice-President for Academic Affairs Papers, Box 26, ROTC 1969–70 Folder.

77. "Yale 'Busts' the ROTC," *New York Times,* Feb. 2, 1969, sec. 4, p. 9, col. 2.

78. Princeton University, "Report of the Ad Hoc Committee on ROTC to the University Faculty."

79. Gindin, Cohen, LaPrelle, and Anderson, Report from the Curriculum Committee on the Issue of Accreditation for ROTC.

80. David Smith to David Clagett and Reuben Chandler, Sept. 5, 1968, University of Pittsburgh Archives, Hillman Library, Provost Office Files 1965–1970, Classification Number 3/1/1, File Folder 235.

81. Task Force on ROTC to [Kegley] Commission to Implement a Commitment to Non-Violence, July 23 and 31, 1970, Kent State University Archives, Charles Kegley May 4th Materials 34.13, Box 102, Folder 41. Emphasis in original.

82. Princeton University, "Report of the Ad Hoc Committee on ROTC to the University Faculty"; Norman Parker, Chancellor, University of Illinois at Chicago Circle, to David Henry, Nov. 19, 1970, University of Illinois Archives, President David Henry Papers, Box 255, ROTC—Military Science.

83. "The Battle over ROTC," p. 2.

84. "NASULGC Special Subcommittee on ROTC Policy Report," June 1968, University of Illinois Archives, National Association of State Universities and Land-Grant Colleges Papers, Series Number 10/3/57, Box 15.

85. University of Colorado Minutes of the Faculty Meeting, Apr. 16, 1970, Archives, University of Colorado at Boulder Libraries, Central Administration, Faculty Council General Files, Series IV, Box 4, Folder 16; Dean W. E. Briggs to President Thieme, Oct. 28, 1970, ibid. President's Office, Series I, Box 330, ROTC General Information, 1973–1976 Folder. This faculty vote recommended faculty review of ROTC courses, a restriction of weapons training (although the faculty approved drill without weapons), and more use of substitution.

86. Richard Jessor, telephone interview with the author, Sept. 5, 1997.

87. Arval Morris, "ROTC: A Definitive Policy Statement," *Washington Daily,* Feb. 26, 1969, p. 1.

88. Bruce Chalmers to Robert McConnell, Mar. 12, 1969, Robert McConnell Papers, Historical Society of Western Pennsylvania, Box 1, Folder 8.

89. Archibald MacLeish, editorial, *Shannonigans* 13 (1969): 2, ibid.

90. Robert Williams to Robben Fleming and Allan Smith, Oct. 8, 1969, University of Michigan Archives, Bentley Historical Library, Vice-President for Academic Affairs Papers, Box 26, ROTC 1969–70 Folder.

91. Laird articulated his belief in the importance of personnel issues in his book *People, Not Hardware: The Highest Defense Priority* (Washington, D.C.: American Enterprise Institute, 1980).

92. *Report of the Special Subcommittee on ROTC to the Secretary of Defense* (Washington, D.C.: Government Printing Office, 1969).

93. Ibid., p. 2.

94. Ibid., pp. 25–26

95. Ibid., p. 27.

96. Christian Arnold, ed., "Report of the Senate," *Proceedings of the National Association of State Universities and Land-Grant Colleges Eighty-third Annual Convention,* Chicago, 1969 (n.p.), p. 100.

97. Christian Arnold, ed., "Report of the Senate," *Proceedings of the National Association of State Universities and Land-Grant Colleges Eighty-fourth Annual Convention,* Washington, 1970 (n.p.), p. 73.

98. *Report of the Special Subcommittee on ROTC,* p. 4.

99. Maurice Hartle, "A Comparative Study of the Professional Performance of Selected Naval Educational Programs, 1962–1972," Ph.D diss., 1973, Miami University, Ohio, p. 63.

100. National Security Information Center, "Summary of Activities," June 1969, University of Michigan Archives, Bentley Historical Library, Vice-President for Academic Affairs Papers, Box 40, ROTC—Air Force 1972 Folder.

101. "Army ROTC Establishes Curriculum Review Board," *The Technique,* Oct. 31, 1969, p. 1.

102. A 1971 survey of Annapolis students and ROTC students at Ohio State and

Pittsburgh provided some justification for the fear of an academy elite. One in three of the Annapolis students "could conceive of circumstances in which a takeover of the U.S. government by the military would be justified." To be sure, an alarming one in five ROTC students felt the same say, but the point here is that academy students were significantly more inclined to agree. Similarly, three in four Annapolis students found the adage "my country right or wrong" to be attractive, compared with only 40 percent of ROTC students. For more, see Ed Berger et al., "ROTC, My Lai, and the Volunteer Army," *Foreign Policy* 2 (Spring 1971): 135–160, quotation from p. 142.

103. Ralph K. Huitt, Executive Director NASULGC, to John Bitner, Apr. 29, 1970, University of Illinois Archives, National Association of State Universities and Land-Grant Colleges Papers, Series Number 10/3/57, Box 16.

104. Recall that the universities were responsible for overhead costs and the salaries of secretarial and janitorial services.

105. The University of Illinois, "Report of the Board of Trustees," 1966–1968, p. 182.

106. "Expenditures in Support of ROTC Units at the University of Michigan by the Department of Defense, 1968–69," University of Michigan Archives, Bentley Historical Library, Vice-President for Academic Affairs Papers, Box 18, ROTC 1968–69 Folder.

107. This issue took on renewed importance in 1969, when the House Armed Services Committee considered a bill to ban federal funds to schools that dropped ROTC.

108. Christian Arnold, ed., *Proceedings of the National Association of State Universities and Land-Grant Colleges Seventy-ninth Annual Convention*, Minneapolis, 1965 (n.p.), p. 60.

109. "Statement regarding ROTC Programs from National Association of State Universities and Land-Grant Colleges," Mar. 18, 1970, University of Illinois Archives, Chancellor's Office Papers, Series Number 24/1/1, Box 42, Armed Forces Folder.

110. When Nixon was inaugurated in January 1969, the United States had 540,000 men in Vietnam. That June Nixon instituted a policy of withdrawal of American forces. By December 1969 the United States had 480,000 men in Vietnam. By December 1970 troop levels were down to 280,000. See Stanley Karnow, *Vietnam* (New York: King, 1983), pp. 684–685.

111. George Benson, "Academic World and Military Education," *Air Force ROTC Education Bulletin* (Feb. 1971): 6.

112. The figure cited here is from the Criminal Investigation Division of the DOD. Seymour Hersh, who won a Pulitzer Prize for his exposure of the massacre, put the figure closer to five hundred. See his *My Lai 4: A Report on the Massacre and Its Aftermath* (New York: Random House, 1970).

113. Quoted in Berger et al., "ROTC, My Lai and the Volunteer Army," p. 143.

114. Natalie Meisler, "ASUC Senate Backs Five SMC Demands," *Colorado Daily,* Apr. 3, 1970.

115. Quoted in Christian Appy, *Working-Class War: American Combat Soldiers in Vietnam* (Chapel Hill: University of North Carolina Press, 1993), p. 269.

116. Arnold, ed., "Report of the Senate," *Proceedings of the National Association of State Universities and Land-Grant Colleges Eighty-fourth Annual Convention*, p. 15.

117. Christian Arnold, ed., "Report of the Senate," *Proceedings of the National Association of State Universities and Land-Grant Colleges Eighty-fifth Annual Convention*, New Orleans, 1971 (n.p.), p. 43.

118. Robben Fleming to John Pemberton, Executive Director, American Civil Liberties Union, Mar. 19, 1969, University of Michigan Archives, Bentley Historical Library, President's Papers, Box 10, ROTC Folder.

119. William Deibler, "Posvar Backs Faculty's Right to Nix ROTC," *Pittsburgh Post-Gazette*, Mar. 5, 1969, p. 1.

120. Robben Fleming, personal correspondence to the author, Oct. 26, 1995.

121. William Beecher, "Pentagon Is Willing to Alter ROTC but Not 'Degrade' It," *New York Times*, Apr. 30, 1969, p. 27, col. 1.

122. *Air University Air Force ROTC Education Bulletin* (May 1969), Air University Library, Maxwell AFB, Montgomery, Alabama.

123. In 1968 only 11 percent of AFROTC junior and senior cadets agreed with the statement that "most [freshman and sophomore] cadets look forward to and enjoy participating in military drill periods." Only 40 percent of senior cadets agreed with the statement: "Cadets marching in the Ranks learn discipline, respect for authority, and *esprit-de-corps*." Five percent agreed that "the campus respects and encourages drill." The author of the article concluded that these data argued for a "reconsideration [of AFROTC's] position on drill." See "Drill and Corps Training," *Air Force ROTC Bulletin* (Dec. 1970): 23.

124. William F. Muhlenfeld, "Our Embattled ROTC," *Army* (Feb. 1969): 21.

125. Quoted in David Rosenbaum, "Campus Attacks on ROTC Stir Pentagon," *New York Times*, Apr. 19, 1969, p. 19, col. 3.

126. F. Edward Hébert to Mendel Rivers, Aug. 7, 1969, University of Pittsburgh Archives, Hillman Library, Provost Office Files 1965–1970, Classification Number 3/1/1, File Folder 237.

127. Brigadier General C. P. Hannum, Memo for the File, "ROTC Briefing—Congressman Hébert," Mar. 11, 1970, United States Army Center of Military History, Washington, D.C., HRC 326.6.

128. Robert Williams, Meeting with the Bureau of Naval Personnel, Aug. 21, 1969, University of Michigan Archives, Bentley Historical Library, Vice-President for Academic Affairs Papers, Box 39, Advisory Committee on ROTC Affairs Folder.

129. Dayton Pickett to Joseph Spitler, Dec. 18, 1970, University of Illinois Archives, Chancellor's Office Papers, Series Number 24/1/1, Box 70, Armed Forces Folder.

130. Gerald Perselay and Raymond Grenier, "New Directions in Corps Training," *Air University Air Force ROTC Education Bulletin* (April 1971).

131. "Senior Division Army ROTC Program of Instruction," Aug. 7, 1969, University of Illinois Archives, National Association of State Universities and Land-Grant Colleges Papers, 10/3/57, Box 15.

132. Robert Williams to Robben Fleming, May 23, 1969, University of Michigan Archives, Bentley Historical Library, President's Papers, Box 10, ROTC Folder.

133. Donald Blake to Robben Fleming, Mar. 26, 1969, ibid.

134. Robben Fleming to the Regents, June 9, 1970, University of Michigan Archives, Bentley Historical Library, President's Papers, Box 15, ROTC Folder.

135. "Supplementary Memorandum of Understanding," Nov. 15, 1971, University of Michigan Archives, Bentley Historical Library, Vice-President for Academic Affairs Papers, Box 40, ROTC—Air Force 1971 Folder.

136. "University of Pittsburgh Department of Military Science (Army ROTC): An Overview," Jan. 1969, University of Pittsburgh Archives, Hillman Library, Classification Number 90/6-B.

137. "Subcommittee of the Military Education Council for the Review of the Army ROTC Curriculum," Mar. 29, 1971, University of Illinois Archives, Series Number 27/3/1, Box 1.

138. Liaison Officer for ROTC to PMS, PNS, and PAS, Oct. 14, 1969, University of Texas President's Office Records, AR 80–50, Liaison Officer, ROTC, 1969–1970 Folder. Texas began to require a master's degree for all senior officers and a bachelor's degree and a minimum of four years of military service for junior officers. The university also informed the services that preference would go to junior officers with master's degrees and that it would reject candidates for whom it believed ROTC duty would be a terminal assignment.

139. National Security Information Center, Inc., "Summary Report: 1968–1973," New York University/National Security Information Center, Inc., May 1973.

140. Ibid.

141. National Security Information Center, "Summary Report," appendix A.

142. "AFNIA: Atlanta Forum on National and International Affairs" [Nov. 1971], Georgia Institute of Technology Library and Information Center, 86–05–01, Office of the President Records, 1961–1972, Box 14, Folder 33.

143. "AFNIA: Dean Rusk Speaks Thursday," *The Technique*, Nov. 7, 1972, p. 1, col. 1.

144. "Annual Report," Department of Military Science, Academic Year 1968–69, University of Washington Archives, Allen Library, W. U. Reserve Officers' Training Corps Program, Military Science, 95–289, V.F. 2457.

145. Oral History of Major General Stanley Beck, Dec. 12–14, 1988, United States Air Force Historical Research Agency, Maxwell AFB, Montgomery, Alabama, pp. 88–89.

146. Virginia Joyce, "ROTC Head Watkins Analyzes Role," *Pitt News*, Sept. 4, 1969, p. 3.

147. Robert Williams to Robben Fleming and Allan Smith, Apr. 20, 1971, University of Michigan Archives, Bentley Historical Library, President's Papers, Box 23, ROTC Folder.

148. W. L. Rigot, "Status and Future Prospects of Navy Officer Education Program," University of Michigan, n.d., Navy ROTC Accreditation/Relations File 1973–1974, North Hall.

149. Robert Williams to Colonel M. D. Schiller, Apr. 20, 1971, University of Michigan Archives, Bentley Historical Library, Vice-President for Academic Affairs Papers, Box 40, ROTC—Army, 1971 Folder.

150. *History of the Air University*, Fiscal Year 1970.

151. Freeman Miller to Senator George Kuhn, Oct. 15, 1969, University of Michigan Archives, Bentley Historical Library, Vice-President for Academic Affairs Papers, Box 39, ROTC General, 1969 Folder.
152. Senate Appropriations Committee Hearings, June 10, 1969, ibid., Box 26, ROTC 1969–70 Folder.
153. Ben Cassiday to Wesley Posvar, Oct. 17, 1969, University of Pittsburgh Archives, Hillman Library, Classification Number 3/1/1, FF 232.
154. "Curricular and Other Changes Introduced into ROTC Programs, January 1, 1969, to June 1, 1969," June 1969, University of Michigan Navy ROTC Accreditation/Relations File 1969, North Hall.
155. Supplemental agreements between the schools and the DOD provided a way around the statutory provisions of the Vitalization Act.
156. Dayton Pickett to Barry Munitz, Associate Provost, University of Illinois at Chicago Circle, Sept. 24, 1971, University of Illinois Archives, Chancellor's Office Papers, Series Number 24/1/1, Box 90, Armed Forces Folder.
157. Freeman Miller to Senator George Kuhn.
158. Ben Cassiday, Memorandum for the Record, Apr. 24, 1970, University of Michigan Archives, Bentley Historical Library, Vice-President for Academic Affairs Papers, Box 40, ROTC—Air Force 1970 Folder.
159. "Final Report of the Ad Hoc Committee on ROTC Credit," Sept. 8, 1971, University of Illinois Archives, President John Corbally Papers, Box 15, ROTC.
160. This incident is recounted in Arthur Coumbe and Lee S. Harford, *U.S. Army Cadet Command: The Ten-Year History* (Ft. Monroe, Va.: Office of the Command Historian, U.S. Army Cadet Command, 1996), p. 77.
161. Isadore Shrensky, "Pitt Battle May Be Lost, ROTC Chief Says," *Pittsburgh Press,* Aug. 17, 1969, p. 8.
162. Robert Williams to Robben Fleming, Mar. 16, 1971, University of Michigan Archives, Bentley Historical Library, President's Papers, Box 23, ROTC Folder.
163. Muhlenfeld, "Our Embattled ROTC."
164. Senate Appropriations Committee Hearings, June 10, 1969. University of Pittsburgh Archives, Hillman Library, Provost Office Files 1965–1970, Classification Number 3/1/1, File Folder 238.
165. Peter Karsten, "Statement on ROTC," Nov. 29, 1968, ibid., File Folder 239.
166. Provost Charles Peake to Henry Avery, Group Vice President, USS Chemicals, May 7, 1969, ibid., File Folder 238.
167. Robert Williams, Notes for Visit with Admiral Kinney—May 12, 1970, University of Michigan Archives, Bentley Historical Library, Vice-President for Academic Affairs Papers, Box 40, ROTC—1970 Folder.
168. Robert Williams to Robben Fleming and Allan Smith, Nov. 5, 1970, ibid., President's Papers, Box 23, ROTC Folder.
169. John Corbally to Lieutenant Colonel Edward Crum, Oct. 19, 1971, University of Illinois Archives, President John Corbally Papers, Box 15, ROTC.
170. J. W. Peltason, Chancellor, to Lieutenant Colonel Edward Crum, USAF (ret.), Nov. 3, 1971, ibid.
171. Rear Admiral J. L. Abbot, Director of Educational Development, to Captain

William Rigot, July 22, 1973, University of Michigan Navy ROTC Accreditation/Relations File 1973–1974, North Hall.

172. Robert Williams, Memo to the Files, May 14, 1970, University of Michigan Archives, Bentley Historical Library, President's Papers, Box 15, ROTC Folder.

173. "1819–1969: The 150th Year of Officer Training on the College Campus," United States Army Center of Military History, Washington, D.C., HRC 326.6.

174. Freeman Miller to Robben Fleming, Jan. 28, 1974, University of Michigan Archives, Bentley Historical Library, Vice-President for Academic Affairs Papers, Box 45, Military Officer Education Programs (ROTC) Folder.

175. "AFROTC 1973 Commandant's Annual Report to the AFROTC Advisory Panel," University of Illinois Archives, President John Corbally Papers, Box 33, ROTC.

6. ROTC in the Era of the All-Volunteer Force

1. David R. Segal, *Recruiting for Uncle Sam: Citizenship and Military Manpower Policy* (Lawrence: University of Kansas Press, 1989), p. 35.

2. Of course draft resistance and antidraft sentiment in this country were not new to the Vietnam years. They date back to the American Revolution and also inspired riots in New York City during the Civil War.

3. *The Report of the President's Commission on an All-Volunteer Armed Force* (New York: Collier's, 1970), pp. 5–6. The Gates Commission included economists Milton Friedman and Alan Greenspan as well as Notre Dame president Theodore Hesburgh and NAACP director Roy Wilkins. The commission was formed in March 1969 with former Secretary of Defense Thomas Gates as chairman.

4. See, for example, Larry H. Ingraham, *The Boys in the Barracks: Observations on American Military Life* (Philadelphia: Institute for the Study of Human Issues, 1984), and Sar Levitan and K. C. Alderman, *Warriors at Work: The Volunteer Armed Force* (Beverly Hills, Calif.: Sage Publications, 1977).

5. Quoted in James Pullen, "A Comparative Study of Personality Factors and Certain Other Variables of Army ROTC Cadets Terminating with the Basic Program and Those Electing to Continue in the Advanced Program," Ed.D. thesis, University of South Dakota, 1971.

6. These included gaining weight, losing weight, moving to Canada or Sweden, and noncompliance. For some specific examples and a discussion of draft evasion, see Lawrence Baskir and William Strauss, *Chance and Circumstance: The Draft, the War, and the Vietnam Generation* (New York: Alfred A. Knopf, 1978).

7. Lee Sherman Dreyfus, Chancellor, University of Wisconsin at Stevens Point and Chairman of the ROTC Advisory Panel, to Howard Callaway, Secretary of the Army, Mar. 20, 1974, University of Michigan Archives, Bentley Historical Library, Vice-President for Academic Affairs Papers, Box 55, ROTC 1973–74 Folder.

8. Thomas Woodley to Assistant and Associate Deans, Jan. 28, 1974, University of Illinois Archives 27/3/1 Box 1; "ROTC Enrollments and Commissioned

Officers," University of Texas President's Office Papers AR 80–50, Liaison Officer 1969–1970 and 1973–1974 Folders. Total Illinois ROTC enrollments were 1,518 in 1966 and 270 in 1974; total Texas ROTC enrollments were 877 in 1966 and 295 in 1974.

9. Quoted in "ROTC Marches Back," *Princeton Alumni Weekly* (Feb. 1, 1972).

10. Roger Geiger, *Research and Relevant Knowledge: American Research Universities since World War II* (New York: Oxford University Press, 1993), p. 260.

11. The major issues of concern for the architects of Title 9 were equal pay for female faculty and equal access for women to graduate schools.

12. Geiger, *Research and Relevant Knowledge*, p. 260.

13. Ibid., chap. 8.

14. Floris Wood, ed., *An American Profile: Opinions and Behavior, 1972–1989* (Detroit: Gale Research, 1990), pp. 641 and 652.

15. Ibid., pp. 642 and 654.

16. For one example, see Stephen Hersh, "Students Organize ROTC Protest," *Michigan Daily*, Jan. 30, 1975. Hersh noted that "organizers attempting to muster anti-ROTC sentiment at the University found their stock in short supply: they could only attract 40 students and members of local left groups to their meeting at East Quad last night."

17. "Upward Trend for ROTC," *Army ROTC in Review, 1972–73*, p. 11, University of Pittsburgh Archives, Hillman Library, Classification Number 35/2-B, Folder 1.

18. Quoted in William Treml, "Departing ROTC Chief Optimistic," *Ann Arbor News*, June 29, 1975.

19. *The Report of the President's Commission on an All Volunteer Armed Force*, p. 74.

20. "ROTC: A Silent Retreat from Campus?" *University Record*, Apr. 1, 1974.

21. These auxiliaries were created in the World War II era with the goal of keeping women administratively and functionally separate from men.

22. Kansas State *Industrialist*, Feb. 16, 1927, Kansas State University Archives, Kansas State University Historical Index, Military Training, 1927.

23. "Angels in Blue Brighten Cadet Corps," *Flight Lines: University of Illinois Cadet AFROTC Newsletter*, May 1964, p. 1.

24. *History of the Air Force Reserve Officers' Training Corps*, Jan. 1 to June 30, 1966, Air Force Historical Research Agency, Maxwell AFB, Montgomery, Alabama.

25. "Military Ball Queen Contestants Plan Tea," *Pitt News*, Feb. 15, 1961, p. 5.

26. *Cadet News* [AFROTC newsletter], Oct. 22, 1959, Archives, University of Colorado at Boulder Libraries, V. C. for Academic Affairs, ROTC Box, Cadet News Folder.

27. Army ROTC, *Quality Is the Answer: The Role of the ROTC in the Supreme Contest of Our Times* [1960], University of Illinois Archives, National Association of State Universities and Land-Grant Colleges Papers, Series Number 10/3/57, Box 14. Emphasis in original.

28. *Cadet News* [AFROTC newsletter], Nov. 5, 1959, University of Colorado at Boulder Library, Archives, V. C. for Academic Affairs, ROTC Box, Cadet News Folder.

29. Vance Mitchell, *Air Force Officers: Personnel Policy Development, 1944–1974* (Washington, D.C.: Air Force History and Museums Program, 1996), p. 314.

30. "Women to Train for the Air Force," *New York Times,* June 24, 1956, p. 40, col. 1.

31. Captain Levy Morrow, USAF to All Professors of Air Science, Apr. 12, 1957, University of Illinois Archives, President David Henry Papers, Box 26, ROTC—Air Science Folder.

32. "Women in AFROTC," *Precommissioning Education Review* (Spring 1980): 3–7.

33. Captain John Sibbald, "A History of the Military Department at the University of Illinois, 1868–1964," history term paper, 1965, University of Illinois Army ROTC Historical Files, Military Science Department Library, 0.432.

34. "Report of the Department of Military Science, Academic Year 1959–60," ibid.

35. "Angels in Blue Brighten Cadet Corps"; *Brigade Review,* University of Texas Army ROTC, 1966, University of Texas Archives, U 428.5 B7532 TXC.

36. Military Science Department to Robert White, Mar. 31, 1967, Kent State University Archives, President Robert White Papers, Box 33, Folder 29, Army ROTC Correspondence, 1966–1967.

37. Quoted in Mary Beth Norton, ed., *Major Problems in American Women's History* (Lexington, Mass.: D. C. Heath Company, 1989), p. 397.

38. Lynda Van Devanter, *Home before Morning: The True Story of an Army Nurse in Vietnam* (New York: Beaufort Books, 1983), p. 21.

39. Quoted in Jeanne Holm, *Women in the Military: An Unfinished Revolution* (Novato, Calif.: Presidio Press, 1992), p. 191.

40. In the WAC in 1966 there were 77 female lieutenant colonels and 237 female majors but, by law, only one female colonel. Thirty-nine of the lieutenant colonels were in the "promotion zone for colonel, but, because they were women, could not even be considered." Holm, *Women in the Military,* p. 193. The female officer hierarchy remained pyramidal, while the male hierarchy was at the same time assuming a diamond shape due to the increased presence of mid-level officers. This process, also to be found in other Western militaries, such as that of France, was the result of the increasing level of technological competence the military professional needed.

41. Ileana Brown, *History of the AFROTC,* July 1, 1967 to June 30, 1968, p. 26.

42. *History of AFROTC,* July 1, 1968 to June 30, 1969, Supporting Document 6, "Report of the Air Force ROTC Advisory Panel, 13 January 1969."

43. Holm, *Women in the Military,* p. 267. Holm, then a major, had been involved in the gender-integration experiment of AFROTC in the 1950s.

44. Quoted in *History of Women in the Air Force,* July 1 to Dec. 31, 1968, Air Force Historical Research Agency, Maxwell AFB, Montgomery, Alabama.

45. The Air Force's OCS program is technically called Officer Training School (OTS). For the sake of convenience, I have taken the liberty of referring to the postgraduation commissioning programs of all three services as OCS.

46. Jon Nordheimer, "Lipstick Is Part of the Uniform," *New York Times,* Dec. 17, 1969, p. 37, col. 1.

47. "Eight Coeds Keep in Step—With 537 Male Cadets," *New York Times,* Apr. 8, 1969, p. 22, col. 5.
48. Nordheimer, "Lipstick Is Part of the Uniform."
49. Harvard researchers did find that women had a warmer "feeling thermometer" toward the military than did men. In 1974, for example, women's feelings for the military registered 72.0, compared with 68.7 among men. Women still felt nearly four "degrees" warmer toward the military in 1976. See Philip Converse, et al., *American Social Attitudes Data Sourcebook, 1947–1978* (Cambridge, Mass.: Harvard University Press, 1980), p. 43.
50. "Navy to Keep Its Academy All-Male," *New York Times,* Feb. 9, 1972, p. 43, col. 5.
51. Robert Goldrich, "The Senior Reserve Officer Training Corps: Recent Trends and Current Status," Apr. 19, 1974, Library of Congress Congressional Research Service.
52. Andrew Malcolm, "Coeds Finding a Welcome in ROTC," *New York Times,* Dec. 4 1972, p. 1, col. 1.
53. "Will You Please Be My Angel?" *The Flying Flak,* Oct. 4 1971, University of Illinois Archives, Series Number 27/2/0/6, Box 1.
54. Michael Farrell, "Women's Army ROTC Program at the University of Hawaii," *Army ROTC Education Commentary,* September–October 1973. The contrast between the initial reactions of the Illinois and Hawaii units lends credence to the "contact hypothesis," which argues that the more integrated a unit, the more successful the minority members of that unit will perform.
55. "ROTC Opens for More Women," Ibid.
56. "Recommendations of the Air Force ROTC Advisory Panel and Air Staff Comments," Jan. 22, 1973, University of Illinois Archives, President John Corbally Papers, Box 33, ROTC—Air Force.
57. Air Force ROTC, "Capsule Facts for Advisors," June 3, 1974, University of Pittsburgh Archives, Hillman Library, Classification Number 35-A, File Folder 3.
58. Brigadier General Sinclair Melner to Acting CU President Roland Rautenstraus, Aug. 11, 1975, University of Colorado at Boulder Library, Archives, Central Administration, President's Office, Series I, Box 330, ROTC General Information, 1973–1976 Folder.
59. "Coed Leads ROTC Unit," *New York Times,* Jan. 21, 1971, p. 20, col. 1.
60. "Arnold Activities," *The Flying Flak,* Dec. 8, 1976, University of Illinois Archives 27/2/0/6, Box 1; C. Russell Geigon, "The Woman Soldier," *Daily Texan,* Jan. 14, 1976.
61. University of Illinois at Urbana-Champaign Office of Public Information, Aug. 25, 1978, University of Illinois Archives, President John Corbally Papers, Box 120, ROTC—Military Science.
62. Nordheimer, "Lipstick Is Part of the Uniform."
63. "Women in AFROTC," pp. 3–7.
64. Office of the Assistant Secretary of Defense, Manpower and Reserve Affairs,

Central All-Volunteer Force Task Force: Utilization of Military Women (Washington, D.C.: Government Printing Office, 1972), p. 30. Emphasis added.

65. *Central All-Volunteer Force Task Force,* p. ix. In 1973 the Supreme Court, in *Frontiero v. Richardson* 411 U.S. 677 [1973], ruled that the services had to provide the same benefits to military husbands that they provided to military wives. In the same year, the DOD changed "wife" and "husband" to "spouse" in its directives. In several other cases in the early 1970s, the courts forced the services to modify, then abandon, the automatic dismissal of pregnant women.

66. Quoted in Malcolm, "Coeds Finding a Welcome in ROTC."

67. Department of Defense, *Report on the Reserve Officers Training Corps* (Washington, D.C.: Government Printing Office, 1980).

68. "Women in AFROTC," p. 3.

69. U.S. Department of Commerce, *Statistical Abstracts of the United States* (Washington, D.C.: Government Printing Office, 1980), pp. 417–418.

70. In 1966 more than one in five fatalities in Southeast Asia was an African American. The DOD took active steps to reduce that percentage, but throughout the course of the war a perception existed that African Americans were given the most dangerous military jobs and therefore were more likely to suffer casualties. African Americans comprised 10.3 percent of the American military force in Vietnam, but suffered 13 percent of its fatalities. See Bernard Nalty, *Strength for the Fight: A History of Black Americans in the Military* (New York: Free Press, 1986), 298.

71. Bernard Nalty and Morris MacGregor, eds., *Blacks in the Military: Essential Documents* (Wilmington, Del.: Scholarly Resources, 1981), p. 344.

72. Nalty, *Strength for the Fight,* p. 328.

73. Dana Adams Schmidt, "Navy Opens a Recruiting Drive to Increase Black Enlistments," *New York Times,* Apr. 1, 1971, p. 29, col. 1.

74. Ben Cassiday, "Report to the AFROTC Advisory Panel," Sept. 18, 1972, University of Illinois Archives, President John Corbally Papers, Box 33, ROTC.

75. Alvin Schexnider, "Expectations from the Ranks: Representativeness and Value Systems" *American Behavioral Scientist* 15 (May/June 1976): 523–542.

76. Joseph Lelyveld, "Navy ROTC at Negro School Graduates Its First Thirteen Officers," *New York Times,* May 18, 1970, p. 1, col. 7.

77. Nalty, *Strength for the Fight,* p. 341.

78. Quoted in Christian Appy, *Working-Class War: American Combat Soldiers in Vietnam* (Chapel Hill: University of North Carolina Press, 1993), p. 21.

79. Nalty, *Strength for the Fight,* p. 328.

80. Lelyveld, "Navy ROTC at Negro School Graduates Its First Thirteen Officers."

81. Charles Peake to Wesley Posvar, Apr. 27, 1970, University of Pittsburgh Archives, Hillman Library, Classification Number 3/1/1, File Folder 232.

82. Wavie Sharp, "Record Number of Blacks Attend Knox Basic Camp," *Army ROTC Education Commentary,* September–October 1973.

83. Department of Defense, *A Primer on ROTC* (Washington, D.C.: Government

Printing Office, 1982). The University of Alabama was the only unit with a higher total enrollment.

84. "Fact Sheet," Conference of Presidents/Chancellors, of Historically Black Colleges, Tuskegee Institute, Mar. 4–6 1980, pp. 33–35, William Snyder Papers, in the author's possession.

85. "1971 Grand Military Ball (Program)" 1971 Duquesne University Archives, ROTC Box 1, Military Balls and Awards Folder.

86. Geiger, *Research and Relevant Knowledge*, p. 249.

87. Ibid., p. 262.

88. David Halliday to Alan Anderson, Feb. 27, 1969, University of Pittsburgh Archives, Hillman Library, Classification Number 3/1/1, File Folder 235.

89. Peter Karsten, "Anti-ROTC: Response to Vietnam or 'Consciousness III'?" in John Lovell and Philip Kronenberg, eds., *New Civil-Military Relations: The Agonies of Adjustment to Post-Vietnam Realities* (New Brunswick: Transaction Books, 1974): 111–127, quotation from p. 115.

90. Mitchell, *Air Force Officers*, p. 455 n. 78.

91. William Calhoun, "Bullish on ROTC," *Army* 24 (May 1974): 36–38.

92. *History of the Air University, Fiscal Year 1973*, vol. 1. Air Force Historical Research Agency, Maxwell AFB, Montgomery, Alabama.

93. *Report of the Department of Aerospace Studies, Academic Year 1972–1973*, July 27, 1973, University of Illinois Archives, President John Corbally Papers, Box 33, ROTC—Air Force. In 1967 the AFROTC unit at Illinois produced eighty-three officers. Illinois officials predicted that only twelve officers would be produced in 1974.

94. "College to Get ROTC Unit," *Columbus*, (Ga.) *Ledger*, Jan. 27, 1972, p. 15.

95. "ROTC Approved for CC," Columbus College *Saber*, Jan. 31, 1972, p. 2.

96. Columbus College also agreed to include a rifle range in the new ROTC building, at a time when weapons bans existed on some established ROTC host campuses. See "College to Get ROTC Unit."

97. William Maloy, "The Education and Training of Naval Officers: An Investment in the Future," *Naval Review* 101 (1975): 134–149.

98. "College to Get ROTC Unit." Compare this statement to one made by Michigan vice president Robert Williams to General Wagstaff in the same year: "Ann Arbor is like Berkeley, an anti-military town and has always been so . . . [I] admit that Ann Arbor is a tough town for any military related activity." Robert Williams, Notes for Meeting with General Wagstaff on July 24, 1972, n.d., University of Michigan Archives, Bentley Historical Library, Vice-President for Academic Affairs Papers, Box 40, ROTC—Army, 1972 Folder.

99. Geiger, *Research and Relevant Knowledge*, p. 192.

100. If, for example, a student desired a navy commission but her school offered only Air Force ROTC, she could commute to a nearby school with an NROTC unit for her training.

101. In 1972 the services authorized military officers to travel to cross-enrolled

schools instead of putting the burden of travel on the student. Mitchell, *Air Force Officers,* p. 268.

102. Marvin Grunzke to Robert Williams, Nov. 14, 1972, University of Michigan Archives, Bentley Historical Library, Vice-President for Academic Affairs Papers, Box 40, ROTC—Air Force 1973–1974 Folder.

103. *Air University Air Force ROTC Bulletin,* May 1, 1975, Air University Library, Maxwell AFB, Montgomery, Alabama.

104. Ibid. Michigan's agreements were with Eastern Michigan, Western Michigan, and the University of Michigan at Dearborn. Pittsburgh's agreements were with Carlow College, Carnegie Mellon, Chatham College, the Community College of Allegheny County, Duquesne University, Point Park College, and Robert Morris College. Enrollment figures are from 1980.

105. Harvard's agreeing to cross-enrollment for its students suggests that the university administration and faculty supported the concept of ROTC and the right of Harvard students to choose a military career. The problem at Harvard and elsewhere was the special privileges that ROTC had acquired, such as academic credit, professorial titles, and so on. Allowing Harvard students to take ROTC at nearby MIT allowed Harvard to remain a part of a system it supported without making distasteful compromises on its own campus. Harvard officials had tried once before to remove military training from the campus while still remaining a part of the ROTC system. In 1954 the army rejected the university's request that it conduct all of its military training at summer camps. See Arthur Coumbe and Lee S. Harford, *U.S. Army Cadet Command: The Ten-Year History.* (Ft. Monroe, Va.: Office of the Command Historian, U.S. Army Cadet Command, 1996), p. 308 n. 43.

106. Karsten, "Anti-ROTC," p. 123.

107. *Statistical Abstracts of the United States* (Washington, D.C.: Government Printing Office, 1985), p. 152.

108. Martin Binkin and John Johnson, *All-Volunteer Armed Forces: Progress, Problems, and Prospects* (Washington, D.C.: Brookings Institute, 1973), p. 24.

109. Quoted in Jim Kentch, "ROTC: Aiming at Freshmen," *Michigan Daily,* July 21, 1972, p. 3.

110. Quoted in Roy McHugh, "ROTC in Step with Career Plans, Pitt Students Find," *Pittsburgh Press,* Sept. 20, 1973, p. 2; Lawrence Walsh, "ROTC Here on March Again; New Approach, Viet Cuts Help," *Pittsburgh Press,* Jan. 16, 1972, p. G-1.

111. Quoted in Walsh, "ROTC Here on March Again."

112. McHugh, "ROTC in Step with Career Plans."

113. Quoted in Richard Berke, "ROTC: New Role, Old Conflicts," *The Michigan Daily,* Feb. 19, 1978, p. 4, col. 1.

114. R. E. Stivers, "The Long and Short," *Navy* 13 (Oct. 1970): 30–34, quotation from p. 30.

115. "Military Academies Changing Their Ways," *U.S. News and World Report* 69 (Nov. 9, 1970): 47.

116. Walsh, "ROTC Here on March Again."

117. Berke, "ROTC: New Role, Old Conflicts"; Colonel Warren Spaulding to All Concerned, Jan. 30, 1974, Archives, University of Colorado at Boulder Libraries, Central Administration, President's Office, Series I, Box 331, ROTC—Army 1940–1977 Folder.

118. Minutes of the LSA Curriculum Committee Meeting, Mar. 27, 1979, University of Michigan Archives, Bentley Historical Library, University of Michigan Vice-President for Academic Affairs, Box 116, ROTC—Military Officer Education Programs Folder.

119. "Summary of Precommissioning Questionnaire," in *History of the AFROTC,* July 1 to Dec. 31, 1963, Call Number K239.07 K.

120. Minutes of the LSA Curriculum Committee Meeting, Mar. 27, 1979.

121. Rick Codina, "Veteran Soldiers Become Educators to Command University Curriculum," *Daily Texan,* Mar. 28, 1971.

122. "Military Academies Changing Their Ways," p. 47.

123. Air Force Academy commandant Brigadier General Robin Olds quoted in ibid., p. 49. In another example of the continued strict discipline, in 1970 the entire Annapolis student body had its weekend leave privileges cut in half when "a few plebes overindulged at beer parties after an academy football game." See ibid., p. 48. West Point superintendent Lieutenant General William Knowlton told a reporter: "We're always going to be leaner, meaner, tougher and more conservative than civilian schools." See "Braced for Reform," *Newsweek* 82 (Sept. 24, 1973): 36.

124. "Military Academies Changing Their Ways," p. 46.

125. "Braced for Reform," p. 36.

126. McHugh, "ROTC in Step with Career Plans."

127. Berke, "ROTC: New Role, Old Conflicts."

128. "Why Would Anybody Take ROTC?," advertisement, *Ebony* 27 (Nov. 1971): 99.

129. "Army ROTC: It's No Big Thing," advertisement, *Ebony* 27 (Sept. 1972): 67. Only one of the ads in this campaign seemed to be aimed specifically at African Americans. That ad showed an African American family standing on the steps of an obviously run-down ghetto apartment building. Above the photo the text read, "Save your family $11,280.00." *Ebony* 27 (Oct. 1972): 47.

130. *ROTC: The Margin of Difference: American Business and Industry Assess the Values of Army ROTC* [1985], Duquesne University Archives, ROTC Box 1, ROTC 1958–65 Folder.

131. "Army ROTC: It's No Big Thing."

132. "Why Would Anybody Take ROTC?"

133. Thomas Hritz, "The New ROTC: You'd Hardly Recognize It," *Pittsburgh Post-Gazette,* Nov. 27, 1979.

134. Minutes of the Committee for Military Officer Education Programs, May 4, 1978, University of Michigan Archives, Bentley Historical Library, Vice-President for Academic Affairs Papers, Box 94, Military Officer Education Programs (ROTC) Folder.

7. A New Academic Program

1. See, for example, Roger Geiger, *Research and Relevant Knowledge: American Research Universities since World War II* (New York: Oxford University Press, 1994), chap. 8.
2. University of Michigan Student Government Council, "ROTC Resolution," May 13, 1974, University of Michigan Navy ROTC Accreditation/Relations File 1973–1974, North Hall.
3. Quoted in "Upward Trend for ROTC," *Army ROTC in Review* (1972–73): 11, University of Pittsburgh Archives, Hillman Library, Classification Number 35/2-B, File Folder 1.
4. William Snyder to Commanding General, First U.S. Army, May 24, 1972, William Snyder Papers, Princeton University Folder, in author's possession. The referendum involved 2,176 students. Between June 1971 and June 1972, the Princeton ROTC program existed on paper only; for that year no students were enrolled (a few Princeton students took ROTC training at nearby Rider University), and no military officers were assigned to the campus.
5. William Snyder, personal correspondence, May 18, 1995, in author's possession.
6. See Chapter 6 for a discussion of this issue.
7. "Report of the Council of the Princeton Community Ad Hoc Committee on ROTC," August 1973, William Snyder Papers, Princeton University Folder, in author's possession.
8. "Memorandum for the Record, Meeting with Brigadier General Tackaberry," June 15, 1972, ibid.
9. William Snyder to Jack Bitner, Nov. 30, 1973, ibid.
10. "The ROTC Curriculum at Princeton University," Sept. 5, 1974, ibid.
11. Colonel I. J. Irvin to Geza Grosschmid, Academic Vice President, Aug. 9, 1972, Duquesne University Archives, ROTC Box 1, ROTC 1972–1976 Folder.
12. Freeman Miller to College of Literature, Science, and the Arts (LSA) associate dean Jean Carduner, Sept. 27, 1974, University of Michigan Archives, Bentley Historical Library, President's Papers, Box 52, ROTC Folder.
13. Quoted in Cindy Morgan, "FASC Ponders Re-opening ROTC Credit Issue," *Pitt News*, Jan. 28, 1972, p. 1.
14. Ibid.
15. Headquarters, Department of the Army, Army Training Program, "General Military Science Curriculum for Civilian and Military Colleges," Dec. 22, 1960, Duquesne University Archives, ROTC Box 1, ROTC 1958–1965 Folder.
16. Martin L. Zeigler to J. W. Briscoe, Apr. 18, 1968, University of Illinois Archives, Chancellor's Office Papers, Series Number 24/1/1, Box 113, Armed Forces Folder.
17. Colonel Marvin Grunzke to J. E. Keith Smith, Psychology, Sept. 18, 1972, University of Michigan Navy ROTC Accreditation/Relations File 1973–1974, North Hall.

18. "Tentative Grouping of 1975–1976 ROTC Courses by Subject Matter" [1974], ibid.

19. The undergraduate catalog was excerpted in "A Review of the University of Michigan Departments of Military Science, Naval Science, and Air Science," Sept. 1968, University of Michigan Navy ROTC Accreditation/Relations File, 1968 and earlier.

20. "Tentative Grouping of 1975–1976 ROTC Courses by Subject Matter."

21. [Colonel James Bambery], "Department of Military Science Annual Report," SY 76–77, Aug. 30, 1977, Duquesne University Archives, ROTC Box 1, Annual Report 1973–76 Folder.

22. Freeman Miller to LSA Associate Dean Charles Witke, Feb. 22, 1974, University of Michigan Navy ROTC Accreditation/Relations File 1973–1974, North Hall.

23. "Report of the Subcommittee on Military Officer Education Programs to the LSA Committee on Curriculum," Jan. 14, 1975, ibid.

24. [Colonel I. J. Irvin], "Department of Military Science Annual Report," SY 72–73, Aug. 23, 1973, Duquesne University Archives, ROTC Box 1, Annual Report 1973–74 Folder. In 1980 Colonel Frank Reeder, PAS at Michigan, advised his colleagues that the best way to assure good relations with civilian faculty was to "demonstrate your worthiness to become an integral part of the academic community in which you are a relative and perhaps unwelcome stranger." *Air University Air Force ROTC Education Bulletin,* Academic Year 1979–80, Air University Library, Maxwell AFB, Montgomery, Alabama, p. 18.

25. "Report by the Committee on Courses," Apr. 6, 1976, Archives, University of Colorado at Boulder Libraries, Central Administration, President's Office, Series I, Box 330, ROTC General Information, 1973–1976 Folder.

26. Committee on Curriculum Special Meeting—Credit for ROTC, Jan. 14, 1975, University of Michigan Navy ROTC Accreditation/Relations File 1973–1974, North Hall.

27. The results of this survey can be found in *History of the Air University,* Jan. 1 to Dec. 31, 1978, Call Number K239.01, vol. 22.

28. A similar pattern emerged at the University of Texas, but without the unanimity. Between 1954 and 1970 only seventeen of the eighty-seven ROTC instructors whose level of education could be determined had a master's degree. Between 1970 and 1980, however, fourteen of the eighteen officers assigned had a master's degree.

29. "Report of the Army Advisory Panel on ROTC Affairs Meeting," Washington, D.C., June 27, 1974, University of Michigan Archives, Bentley Historical Library, President's Papers, Box 45, ROTC Folder.

30. Robben Fleming to William Bowen, Mar. 10, 1975, University of Michigan Archives, Bentley Historical Library, President's Papers, Box 52, ROTC Folder.

31. Charles Witke to Executive Committee on Guidelines That May Generate Credit, Jan. 2, 1974, University of Michigan Navy ROTC Accreditation/Relations File 1973–1974, North Hall.

32. Some issues that proved contentious in liberal arts colleges in the 1950s never developed as serious issues in engineering colleges. Professional qualifications for instructors mattered much less to engineering colleges, where as late as the mid-1950s, instructors with Ph.D.s were rare at many schools. At the University of Texas in 1955, for example, only 27 percent of the eighty-eight faculty members in the College of Engineering had a Ph.D. At the same time, 86 percent of the College of Arts and Sciences faculty had a Ph.D. Most of those who did not were concentrated in one department, Home Economics. Like the military, engineering colleges were willing to substitute job experience for formal educational qualifications. Qualifications derived from *The University of Texas College of Arts and Sciences Catalogue,* 1955–1957, and *The University of Texas College of Engineering Catalogue,* 1954–1956.

33. "A Statement to the Board of Regents' Meeting," University of Colorado, Sept. 26, 1973, Presented by the ROTC Commanders, University of Colorado at Boulder Library, Archives, Central Administration Faculty Council General Files, Series IV, Box 4, Folder 16.

34. J. W. Peltason to Brigadier General James Leslie, Apr. 27. 1976, University of Illinois Archives, President John Corbally Papers, Box 86, ROTC—Military Science. Emphasis in original.

35. Robben Fleming, interview with the author, Ann Arbor, Michigan, Dec. 12, 1995.

36. John Capitman, "CAS Cabinet Denies ROTC Credit Review," *Pitt News,* Oct. 30, 1972, p. 1.

37. Sara Rimer, "LSA Committee Approves Amended ROTC Plan," *Michigan Daily,* Jan. 15, 1975.

38. "Report of the Subcommittee on MOEP to the LSA Committee on Curriculum," Jan. 14, 1975, University of Michigan Navy ROTC Accreditation/Relations File 1973–1974, North Hall.

39. Quoted in Rimer, "LSA Committee Approves Amended ROTC Plan."

40. John Sinkevics, "LSA Faculty reopens ROTC credit issue," *Michigan Daily,* March 28, 1979

41. B. E. Frye, Acting LSA Dean, to Freeman Miller, Feb. 5, 1975, University of Michigan Archives, Bentley Historical Library, President's Papers, Box 52, ROTC Folder. Emphasis in original.

42. Minutes of the LSA Curriculum Committee Meeting, Mar. 27, 1979, University of Michigan Archives, Bentley Historical Library, Vice-President for Academic Affairs Papers, Box 116, ROTC—Military Officer Education Programs Folder.

43. John Knott, Associate Dean, LSA, to Vice President Harold Shapiro, May 7, 1979, ibid., Box 106, Military Officer Education Programs (ROTC) Folder.

44. Department of Naval Science, "Annual Report for the Academic Year 1972–1973, Aug. 2, 1973," University of Illinois Archives, President John Corbally Papers, Box 33, ROTC.

45. [Rasin Tek], "Proposal concerning College of Engineering—Military Officer Ed-

ucation Program Policies," Apr. 5, 1978, University of Michigan Archives, Bentley Historical Library, President's Papers, Box 86, ROTC Folder (1); Minutes of the Faculty Meeting of the College of Engineering, Feb. 27, 1979, ibid., Vice-President for Academic Affairs Papers, Box 106, Military Officer Education Programs (ROTC) Folder. Michigan required its engineering students to take twenty-four hours of social sciences and humanities. Under the 1978 guidelines, then, two-thirds of a Michigan engineering student's social sciences and humanities requirement could be fulfilled through ROTC.

46. It is not clear, however, that ROTC had more vocal supporters in engineering colleges. Because of the intensity that characterized debates in liberal arts colleges, some faculty members became just as strident and unwavering in their support of ROTC as others became in their opposition.

47. Captain William L. Rigot to Ralph Banfield, Assistant to Vice President for Academic Affairs, May 21, 1976, University of Michigan Navy ROTC Accreditation/Relations File 1975–1979, North Hall.

48. John Shy to Unit Heads and Executive Committee of the History Department, Apr. 25, 1974, University of Michigan Navy ROTC Accreditation/Relations File 1973–1974, North Hall.

49. "Report of Recent Senate Action," Apr. 14, 1976, University of Illinois Archives, President John Corbally Papers, Box 86, ROTC—Miscellaneous.

50. Department of Defense, *Report on the Reserve Officers Training Corps* (Washington, D.C.: Government Printing Office, 1980).

51. ROTC scholarship winners were selected nationally. Once selected, students could use their scholarship to attend any school that admitted them.

52. Impossible though it seems today, the University of California did not charge tuition for state residents until 1970.

53. *Fore 'n Aft*, Georgia Tech NROTC Newsletter, 1971, Georgia Institute of Technology Library and Information Center, T171.G46 F6X.

54. Kenneth Irish to Freeman Miller, Apr. 11, 1974, University of Michigan Archives, Bentley Historical Library, Vice-President for Academic Affairs Papers, Box 139, Army Correspondence Folder, 1973–1978.

55. W. L. Rigot to Center for Naval Education and Training (CNET), Feb. 27, 1975, University of Michigan Navy ROTC Accreditation/Relations File 1975–1979, North Hall; K. M. Irish to Robben Fleming, May 30, 1974, University of Michigan Archives, Bentley Historical Library, President's Papers, Box 45, ROTC Folder; Freeman Miller to LSA Associate Dean Jean Carduner.

56. Captain William L. Rigot to Ralph Banfield, Assistant to Vice President for Academic Affairs, May 21, 1976, University of Michigan Navy ROTC Accreditation/Relations File 1975–1979, North Hall.

57. I am grateful to Professor Kenneth Hagan of the Naval Academy, Captain Bob Shaw of CNET, and Commander Greg Young of the Air Force Academy for sharing their thoughts with me on this subject.

58. Juan Cameron, "Admiral Rickover's Final Battle," *Fortune* 94 (Nov. 1976): 198.

59. The best critique of the 80-20 plan from a uniformed officer can be found in Edward Bouffard, "NROTC: Quo Vadis?" *U.S. Naval Institute Proceedings* (July 1977): 33–42.

60. Rear Admiral James Holloway, "The Holloway Plan," *U.S. Naval Institute Proceedings* (Nov. 1947): 1299.

61. Chief of Naval Education and Training and Director of Naval Educational Development, "The NROTC Academic Program," Oct. 1973, University of Michigan Navy ROTC Curriculum File, North Hall.

62. Captain D. V. Murray to Ralph Banfield, July 5, 1978, University of Michigan Archives, Bentley Historical Library, Vice-President for Academic Affairs Papers, Box 141, Assoc. of NROTCCU, 1973–1978 Folder; Bouffard, "NROTC: Quo Vadis?" p. 38.

63. NROTC SITREP, Presented to ANROTCCU Nov. 5–7, 1978, University of Michigan Archives, Bentley Historical Library, University of Michigan Vice-President for Academic Affairs, Box 141, Assoc. of NROTCCU, 1973–1978 Folder.

64. Adam Yarmolinsky, review of *School for Soldiers*, by Joseph Ellis and Robert Moore, and *Ivory Fortress*, by Richard C. U'Ren, *Society* (Sept./Oct. 1975): 92.

65. Dr. Ray Bice, telephone interview, Feb. 20 1996. Dr. Bice was president of the ANROTCCU during the 80/20 debates.

66. Robert Etheridge to Members of ANROTCCU, Mar. 23, 1977, University of Michigan Archives, Bentley Historical Library, Vice-President for Academic Affairs Papers, Box 141, Assoc. of NROTCCU, 1973–1978 Folder.

67. Captain D. V. Murray to Ralph Banfield, Aug. 1, 1977, ibid.

68. C. Peter Magrath to CNET, July 14, 1977, ibid.

69. Marvin Grunzke, "Status Report on Air Force Reserve Officers' Training Corps Program at the University of Michigan," n.d., University of Michigan Navy ROTC Accreditation/Relations File 1973–1974, North Hall. Emphasis added.

70. "ROTC Marches Back," *Princeton Alumni Weekly*, Feb. 1, 1972.

Primary Sources

Duquesne University Archives, Pittsburgh
ROTC Papers

Gerald Ford Presidential Library, Ann Arbor, Michigan
Theodore Marrs Files, Box 6

Historical Society of Western Pennsylvania, Pittsburgh
Robert McConnell Papers

Lyndon Baines Johnson Presidential Library, Austin, Texas
Alfred B. Fitt Oral History

Kansas State University Archives, Manhattan
Chester Peters Papers
James A. McCain Papers
Kansas State University Historical Index
President's Papers

Kent State University Archives, Kent, Ohio
Charles Kegley May 4th Materials, Series Number 34.13.42
President Robert White Papers
Series Numbers 4.25.30, 4.25.31, 33.13.1, 33.13.2, 33.13.3

National Archives, Washington, D.C.
Record Group 319

Rutgers University Archives, New Brunswick, New Jersey
Army ROTC Headquarters Library Materials
President William H. Demarest Papers, 1915–1925
President James M. Thomas Papers, 1925–1932
President Robert C. Clothier Papers, 1932–1951
President Lewis W. Jones Papers, 1951–1958
President Mason Gross Papers, 1959–1971
President Edward J. Bloustein Papers, 1971–1980

William Snyder Papers (in author's possession)
    Army Advisory Panel Reports
    Princeton Army ROTC Papers

Suitland Federal Records Center, Suitland, Maryland
    Chief of Army Reserve General Correspondence, 1948–1954, RG 319
    Secretary of the Army General Correspondence, RG 335

United States Air Force Historical Research Agency, Maxwell AFB, Montgomery, Alabama
    Histories of Air University
    Histories of Air Force ROTC
    Histories of Women in the Air Force
    J. C. Shelburne Papers
    Oral History of Major General Stanley Beck, Dec. 12–14, 1988.

United States Air Force ROTC Office, Maxwell AFB, Montgomery, Alabama
    Histories of AFROTC

United States Army Center of Military History, Washington, D.C.
    ROTC Papers HRC 326.6

United States Army Military History Institute, Carlisle, Pennsylvania
    General Donn Starry Papers

University of Colorado at Boulder Library, Archives
    Central Administration, President's Office, Series I, Boxes 133, 330, 331, 332
    CU History (Departments)
    Faculty Council General Files, Series IV, Box 4
    News Media Relations Office, Student Unrest 1951–1972
    Regents Minutes, volumes 35, 36
    Vice-Chancellor for Academic Affairs Papers

University of Illinois Archives, Urbana
    Army ROTC Subject File, Series Number 27/3/1
    Chancellor's Office Papers, Series Number 24/1/1
    Committee on Educational Policy, Series Number 4/2/14
    Military Affairs Committee, Series Number 4/6/26
    National Association of State Universities and Land-Grant Colleges Papers, Series Number 10/3/57
    President David Henry Papers
    President John Corbally Papers
    Student Life Papers
    Vice-President for Academic Affairs Papers, Series Number 5/1/2
    Voluntary ROTC Program Files, Series Number 27/3/5

University of Illinois Department of Military Science Library, Urbana
    Annual Reports
    Recommendations of the PMS

University of Michigan Archives, Bentley Historical Library, Ann Arbor
  Harlan Hatcher Papers
  President's Papers
  Vice President for Academic Affairs Papers

University of Michigan Military Officer Education Program Papers, North Hall, Ann Arbor
  Air Force ROTC History/Accreditation Files
  Army ROTC History/Accreditation Files
  Navy ROTC History/Accreditation Files
  ROTC Curriculum Files

University of Pittsburgh Archives, Hillman Library, Pittsburgh
  Department of Military Science, 90/6-B
  Military Science Papers, 35-A, 35 2/B, 35 2/1
  Minutes of the Meeting of the University Senate, 3/10/3
  University of Pittsburgh Chancellor's Papers 0/3/1, 2/10, 55/1
  University of Pittsburgh Provost Office Files, 3/1/1

University of Texas Center of American History, Austin
  Department of Military Science Papers
  General and Comparative Studies, AR 85-215
  Liaison Officer for ROTC Papers, AR 80-50
  University of Texas President's Office Records, VF 17/C.a, VF 20/A.b, VF 30/A.b

University of Washington, Allen Library, Seattle
  Classification Numbers 71-34, 72-14, 72-35, 82-29, 95-281, 95-288, 95-289
  W. U. Presidents Papers
  W. U. Reserve Officers' Training Program

Index